Chase, Chance, and Creativity
the lucky art of novelty

Every man depends on
the work of his predecessors.
When you hear of a sudden unexpected
discovery—a bolt from the blue as it were—
you can always be sure that it has grown up by the
influence of one man on another, and it is this mutual influence which makes the enormous possibility of scientific advance.

Lord Rutherford

NEW YORK   COLUMBIA UNIVERSITY PRESS

CHASE
CHANCE
and
CREATIVITY

the lucky art of novelty

JAMES H. AUSTIN

1978

James H. Austin is Professor and Chairman, Department of Neurology,
University of Colorado Medical School.

Portions of chapters 9, 14, 15, and 18 originally appeared,
in somewhat different form, in *Executive Health* 13 (8), May 1977.
Copyright © 1977 by Executive Publications. Used by permission.

Library of Congress Cataloging in Publication Data
Austin, James H 1925–
Chase, chance, and creativity.
Bibliography: p.
Includes index.
1. Neurologists—Biography.   2. Austin, James H., 1925–
3. Creative ability in science.   4. Serendipity in science.
I. Title.
RC339.52.A97A34   616.8'092'4 [B]   77-23011
ISBN 0-231-04294-9

Columbia University Press
New York   Guildford, Surrey
Copyright © 1978 by Columbia University Press
All Rights Reserved
Printed in the United States of America

To my parents and teachers who set the example,
to friends and co-workers who helped at all stages,
and to my wife, Judith, who made the rest possible.

Contents

List of Figures

Preface

What scientists do has never been the subject of a scientific, that is, an ethological* inquiry. It is no use looking to scientific 'papers', for they not merely conceal but actively misrepresent the reasoning that goes into the work they describe.

Peter Medawar

This is a story of the ways persistence, chance, and creativity interact in medical research. My thesis is that novelty in research is like that in any endeavor—it springs from the dynamic interplay among several ingredients: personal life style, people, luck, intuition, and system.

The idea for the book evolved when I was invited to deliver the first Saul Korey Lecture at the Albert Einstein College of Medicine. Thinking over what I might say, it occurred to me that here was a unique opportunity. This time I could depart from the traditional formal scientific lecture and do what I had really wanted to do for years; trace the roots of our medical research back to their very beginnings. Finally, I could "tell it like it really was," stress the interactions with other persons and emphasize the elements of chance, for these two factors often determined not only the direction of our research but also its success or failure.

To write such an "inside" story, the first part of the book had to take the form of a personal narrative. Neurologists in particular, and scientific investigators in general, rarely write this personal a statement of their thoughts and actions. Perhaps the real reason is that there is no survival value in using the pronoun, "I," and even remotely appearing smug, self-seeking, and pretentious. After all, why risk the immodesty of writing about yourself if you're not Alexander Fleming, and if penicillin, DNA, or the Nobel Prize are not involved? Too high a price is exacted by the scientific community for any display of ego.

Several reasons dictated my going ahead this way despite the personal cost. The first is that I have always been deeply interested in the mecha-

---

* The scientific study of behavior in animals, including man.

nisms by which things happen. Experience tells me that research is a series of contingencies, of zigzags, joined by one fragile link after another. You would never realize this from reading the tidy, aseptic research accounts that fill our libraries. For balance, someone should present a different side of the picture—show some contemporary research in all its haphazard, unpredictable complexity. This book aims to do so.

A second reason for going ahead is to help clear up serious recurrent misconceptions about medical research among many laymen and their elected representatives. The illusions: crash programs with "big" money will "buy" big results; all research can be "directed" on a contract basis toward specified "targets"; exploration is justified only insofar as it brings practical results at predictable times. It is crucial to dispel these misunderstandings, because many grants for research have been increasingly slashed since 1967 (the year of the high-water mark in federal support for research). All the more reason then, to encourage benefactors in government agencies and foundations to permit their investigators enough independence so that they may be free to follow their creative instincts most fruitfully.

We are all creative, but often only to the extent that we are lucky. What determines luck is the subject of the second part of this book. It turns out that there are more kinds of chance than we realize, and chance involves more than that poorly understood term, serendipity. All these aspects are developed both in the essays of Part II and in the Appendix.

Why is creativity important? The answer is simple: *novelty* is what creativity, research, and much of the zest in life are all about. It is curious how relatively little we know about the creative process and how it operates. Misunderstandings about creativity by administrators are legendary, but it is also surprising to find how many investigators themselves are unaware of recent evidence that suggests the ways their own brain functions when it creates new ideas. The third part of this book therefore attempts to remedy this situation. It includes a series of essays on those psychological and physiological aspects of the creative process the significance of which transcends creativity in science. Creativity is multifactorial, and some of its factors can be consciously encouraged. It is therefore a practical subject, full of benefits for those who know something about it. To humans, then, creativity is much more important a subject than, say, ornithology is to the birds. Parents, teachers, businessmen—anyone concerned with fostering novelty in themselves or others—may find something of profit here. A prescription for creativity ends this section.

A glossary will help you understand the technical terminology, but some disclaimers are in order, for many other things are *not* in this small book. You will be spared my more planned, rational experiments, and those that failed because they were poorly conceived, stupidly executed, or soundly defeated by circumstances. I will emphasize the strength the creative process gains through its depth and its diversity, rather than attempt to codify it. True, I will pull things together in the summary and in a prescription, but you won't be pressed into a big unified system of thought about scientific investigation. Organized science already has its champions, myself included, who treat it every day in the journals with the profound respect due a great intellectual enterprise. So it is with the idea of restoring some semblance of balance, not to downgrade the intellectual process, that I choose here to present the more capricious side of discovery. To complete the paradox, chance—that seemingly most capricious of topics—will here be given a more systematic examination.

I include a few autobiographical and factual documents of psychoanalytical interest about the writer, agreeing with Jung when he said, "Creative man is a riddle that we may try to answer in various ways, but always in vain, a truth that has not prevented modern psychology from turning now and again to the question of the artist and his art."[1]

Many helped bring this book into being. I am grateful to the following persons for their helpful comments at various stages in the preparation of the manuscript: Paul, Bertha, Judith, Scott, and Lynn Austin, Dr. Stephen Bondy, Dr. John Conger, Mr. Norman Cousins, Mr. Dan Gillmor, Mrs. Helene Jordan, Dr. Robert Katzman, Mr. Joseph Mori, Dr. Gerhard Nellhaus, and Dr. Stuart Schneck.

Special thanks go to Mrs. Kathleen Ogsbury, Mrs. Bea Belmont, and Miss Toni Cervenka, who not only typed but deciphered the manuscript throughout the many steps in its preparation.

Finally, the lecture, and the book, are intended both to honor Saul Korey, who established the first Department of Neurology at Albert Einstein College of Medicine, and to repay part of my scientific debt to him. Saul was a man who in a brief span of only forty-five years achieved with grace the magical union so many of us aspire to: clinical neurologist, investigator, teacher, administrator, and stimulator of creativity in others,[2] a direct man, inviting controversy—a stimulating, vital, and altogether refreshing human being. We need more like him.

Denver, Colorado   James H. Austin, M.D.
April, 1977

By Way of Introduction

The picture is not thought out and determined beforehand, rather while it
is being made it follows the mobility of thought. Finished, it changes
further, according to the condition of him who looks at it.

Pablo Picasso

This is a personal narrative, and the reader is entitled to an autobiographical glimpse or two. Some images readily pass across my mind's
eye.

I start as a hybrid. Take, for instance, my grandfathers, whose names
I bear. I remember one, James Austin, Jr., as a poet, a liberal humanist
lawyer, and later a kindly judge in the court of domestic relations in
Toledo, Ohio. He must have had restless legs as a young man because
he hiked and bicycled a great deal, and he regularly walked a total of six
miles to work and back until he retired. "The Judge" also read volumi-
nously and delighted in problem solving: two crossword puzzles a day
for many years. My other grandfather, Henry Holtkamp, started out as
a school teacher, and later, pursuing his musical hobby as an organist,
went into pipe organ manufacturing in Cleveland, Ohio.

The Judge's wife, Mina, had a brother, Gus, who lived outdoors whenever he could. He loved to hunt with his favorite pointer, Dash, and it
was said that my own father strongly resembled his legendary Uncle
Gus. My mother's mother, Sophia Holtkamp, passed on her love for the
earth itself. From her I learned the good elemental feel of dirt between
the fingers while I tilled, planted, weeded, and harvested vegetables
from her garden. It was she, gentle lady, who gave her young grandson
the old Indian hatchet head made of basalt that launched my Indian
collection and sparked my interest in archaeology.

I recall: the boy of seven questioning his parents, *"What is it exactly
about the chemical make-up of things that causes a color to be a color?"*
. . . the lad of ten dissecting with great curiosity an old (and very dead)
alley cat, noticing that the distended bag in the lower abdomen must be
the urinary bladder . . . and the skinny seventeen-year-old, who per-

sisted for two hours over the spoor of the rabbit in the snow until he finally caught (and then released) the rabbit.

Also far distant in the background, but formative, I can recall the youth fascinated with biological topics of all kinds, animals and wood-lore above all. I grew up reading, and rereading all the wild animal and outdoor stories of Ernest Thompson Seton.

In particular, there were the memorable summers on Uncle Gibby's farm in Ohio, listening to him discourse about a patient in his deep, resonant rumble, having free time to browse among his medical books. Here was the place a boy from the city could fall in love with the earth and the sky, working in hay fields, going fishing at every opportunity, and seeking out unknown paths for exploration in the dark woods. And here, finally, while weeding the vegetable garden, I tingled to the discovery of my first Indian arrowhead! Then, at age fourteen, there came the bout of severe pneumonia, when I could watch my own life being saved by a new sulfa drug. Medicine, not outdoor writing, would thereafter become my goal.

In medical school, I remember being impressed as a second-year student by Raymond Adams' superb clinical neuropathological teachings. A year later, I had a poor course in neurology, and to compensate for this, I felt I had to take extra elective courses in neurology in the fourth year.

But in most other respects my background as a Midwesterner, Unitarian, middle- to upper-middle class, with German-English-Swiss genes, falls well within the boundaries found for the average researcher.[1] Beyond this, I write with some personal bias and out of some eccentricities which should be declared at once. I find medicine and science are meaningless unless they are interwoven with the rest of nature, the arts, and humanities. To me, they are all connected and the links between them have always been fascinating.

I yield any time, anywhere, to a *visual* imperative. I have been a Sunday painter of sorts and paint in watercolors exclusively. Using this medium, colors can be splashed on at first with broad brush strokes instead of being applied precisely; a watercolor is finished quickly and need not be worked over repeatedly; completely unexpected effects occur. I prefer intense, realistic colors, and usually choose landscape scenes with plenty of clouds and a long view sweeping out to a low horizon.

This hobby perfectly complements my other self—the reasonably compulsive physician that a neurologist usually is. When preparing slides to be shown at various scientific meetings, I enjoy coloring the slides or designing them myself. And, from the standpoint of color, the diseases I've been interested in have always been visually rewarding ones to study.

I also enjoy music. In music, too, I have inherited the interests of my father, who played the piano and composed songs in order to support himself through college. The kind of music that really rivets my attention is good Dixieland jazz. What delights me besides the obvious enthusiasm of the performers, are the alternations between free flights of improvisation and exuberant, throbbing reunions of the ensemble as a whole.

My active participation in music now is chiefly through barbershop harmony. But the melody has always had less appeal for me than other notes improvised spontaneously and tucked into the one place in the chord that makes for close resonating harmony. As for symphonic or other classical music, after only a few minutes of listening, my sequences of association are speeded up, and my mind rapidly goes off in many different directions. New combinations of ideas pop quickly into my head, skipping about like summer lightning. The result is that the whole exposure to music turns out to be more stimulating intellectually than musically. Because many new (and some useful) ideas about experiments or methods flash into my thinking anywhere and anytime, I keep a shirt pocketful of file cards to quickly jot down these ideas before they vanish.

By now you are familiar with at least some of the preamble.

ONE

The Meandering Chase

Experimental ideas are very often born by chance
as a result of fortuitous observations. Nothing
is more common, and it is really the
simplest way to begin a piece of
scientific work. We walk, so
to speak, in the realm of
science, and we pursue
what happens to present
itself accidentally
to our eyes.

Claude Bernard

1.

Of Nerves and Neurologists; Boston, 1950

The destinies of man are guided by the most extraordinary accidents.

Hans Zinsser

I am in neurology because it is inherently rational. When the neurologist elicits a clinical history from his patient, then performs his specialized examination, he should be able to reason his way to the correct diagnosis, sometimes literally with pinpoint accuracy. One likes to think that the mental sequences involved in neurological diagnosis are intellectually rigorous, scientific, logical, and predictable. This is the core of my belief.

But let me now share some experiences on the periphery of my beliefs which have shaken the center from time to time. These experiences, both in the clinic and laboratory, are, in essence, happy accidents. They involve events which are *ir*rational, nonscientific, and unpredictable. In the language of today, they are "happenings" of a special sort. That "happenings" do occur has been known for centuries. The experiences of Claude Bernard, the pioneering physiologist, occurred during what he called *walks* in the realm of science; my own have occurred more circuitously, during what I would characterize as *meanderings*.

Let us begin this narrative with an incident in 1950.[1] By then I had already completed college, four years of medical school, and a one-year internship. I was twenty-five years old and starting my first year as a resident physician at the old Boston City Hospital. At that time, my ultimate goal was to be a specialist in internal medicine and enter private practice. First, however, I wanted a year's experience in neurology, because I still didn't know enough about the diagnosis and treatment of diseases of the nervous system. I was drawn to the neurology service at City Hospital both by its fine academic reputation and its wealth of clinical material. Moreover, the chief of service there was an excellent teacher, Harvard Professor Derek Denny-Brown. Born in New Zealand, he had had his training in neurophysiology at Oxford and Yale, and in clinical neurology at the famous National Hospital, Queen Square, London.

Professor Denny-Brown was very familiar with the neurological literature, foreign and domestic. He could therefore inject unusual and stimulating observations into a discussion. His comments were provocative, sometimes to the point of heated controversy. But for present purposes, it doesn't matter whether the data he used and the interesting hypotheses he developed were correct or incorrect. What was important was that a given issue was dramatized and people were set into motion.

So it was, one Saturday morning in the drab conference room at Boston City Hospital when another neurology resident presented the first patient. She was a woman in her forties who over several decades had slowly developed the symptoms of a degenerative disease of the nervous system. The essential findings were those caused by a failure of her peripheral nerves to conduct impulses. As a result, the muscles of her hands and feet were wasted and weak, her reflexes were lost, and her sensation was impaired.

The professor—a tall, distinguished-looking man, formal in manner—stepped forward to check the findings. He felt for the *ulnar nerves at the elbow and the peroneal nerves at the knee.* This was interesting. I had not seen this done before.

The nerves were not enlarged. Perhaps a bit firm, but not enlarged. Dr. Joseph Foley, the attending neurologist in charge of the ward at the time, gave a good discussion of the several diagnostic possibilities and then turned to Dr. Denny-Brown for his final comments. Dr. Denny-Brown thought the patient might have hypertrophic neuritis.*

"Hypertrophic neuritis?" questioned Joe with a startled look. "How can the patient possibly have this when her nerves are not enlarged?"

"In *some* the nerves are not enlarged," said Denny, quite casually.

A certain amount of heat began to displace light. It seemed increasingly evident—almost by definition—that a patient with hypertrophic neuritis deserved to have enlarged nerves, if anything (figure 1).

Joe Foley became eloquent in his perplexity, but Denny sputtered on with some firmness. The issue was left hanging, unresolved. The staff hurried on to the next patient. We were left with the impression that Denny's view of the first case was unique.

---

*The nonspecialist is encouraged to use the glossary for clarification of this and other terms. See also figure 1 and subsequent figures.

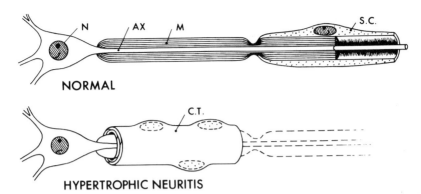

Figure 1. A normal nerve fiber, and the way it is affected in hypertrophic neuritis.

A *normal* nerve fiber is shown at the top. Its cell body at the left has a nucleus (*N*) and an axon (*AX*) which conducts its nerve impulses from left to right. The myelin sheath (*M*) is the fatty layer surrounding the axon. It is synthesized by the sheath cell (*S.C.*) which envelops it.

In *hypertrophic neuritis*, the myelin sheath breaks down (dotted lines), and some axons also degenerate. Sheath cells multiply (note the three oval nuclei instead of one), and they produce an abnormally thick layer of connective tissue (*C.T.*). This forms a large fibrous cylinder around the nerve fiber, causes the nerve trunk as a whole to enlarge, and makes the peripheral nerve palpably enlarged beneath the skin.

It was only some years later that I found an isolated report of a patient whose nerves were *not* enlarged. The article was buried in the French medical literature of 1912. However, to the point of this anecdote, this 1912 case doesn't really matter. What did matter was that opinions were stated forcefully, and that a controversy was aired. Students and residents inhaled a heady atmosphere: there were still facts left unsettled in neurology; there were big gaps in our information; the facts, and their interpretation *mattered*.

It is always very difficult to remember to feel for peripheral nerves. Neurologists often forget to do so, because most patients with neurological diseases will have nerves neither too large nor too small. Hence it is assumed that there is really no point in routinely feeling for nerves. The trouble is that sooner or later the rare patient does come along with the rare disease that causes peripheral nerves to become enlarged. How, then, does one remember to palpate his nerves? What is the special mental set which prompts one to remember to elicit the unusual but crucial sign when it is there? As for me, my mind retrieves best after I have participated, even as an onlooker, in a dramatic issue. Teachers who made an academic issue come alive have stimulated my enduring interests. Thus, to me it is clear that I remember to palpate peripheral nerves because of Professor Derek Denny-Brown. What happened at that Saturday morning conference profoundly influenced me to this day and had an incalculable effect on the rest of this story.

2.

Enlarged Nerves; Oakland, 1951

Concerning all acts of initiative (and creation), there is one elementary truth . . . the moment one definitely commits oneself, then Providence moves too. All sorts of things occur to help one that would never otherwise have occurred. A whole stream of events issues from the decision, raising in one's favour all manner of unforeseen incidents and meetings and material assistance which no man could have dreamt would have come his way. I have learned a deep respect for one of Goethe's couplets:
"Whatever you can do, or dream you can, begin it.
Boldness has genius, power, and magic in it."

W. H. Murray

A year after the Saturday conference I was a naval medical officer stationed at the Oak Knoll Naval Hospital. My wife, Judy, and I lived in a small bungalow nestled in the hills above Oakland overlooking San Francisco Bay. To a native Midwesterner who had spent his summers in the flat farmland of Ohio, the Bay Area was an eye-opener. Its ambient sunshine, mild winters, abundant garden crops, mountains, and salmon fishing made a deep impression, one that would soon convert me into a Westerner.

One day at the hospital I admitted a twenty-two year old seaman by the name of Knox who had noticed a progressive weakness of his hands and feet for the past seven years. The findings on my standard neurological examination were those of a chronic peripheral nerve disorder. So, then what? The next moment was critical. Subliminally, I must have recalled the events at that earlier conference back in Boston. Somehow, I did remember to feel for the size of his peripheral nerves.

The nerves were enlarged. I had encountered my first patient with hypertrophic neuritis (figure 1). But what was this illness? And, more important for the patient, what could be done about it?

The answer was: nothing, until one found out the cause. I still knew almost nothing about hypertrophic neuritis and accordingly set out to inform myself. Textbooks weren't very enlightening, and when I started to search the medical literature, it was clear that much remained to be learned. The disease was something of a puzzle. How much of it I was really going to understand would depend largely on my own efforts. This in itself was provocative. I began to haunt the library and soon became totally involved in the subject. As the project grew, it focused my interests on neurology instead of internal medicine, and within the year I had made the big decision to become a neurologist.

Toward the end of my two years in the Navy, I was accepted for the two final years of training as a resident in neurology at the Neurological Institute of New York, a part of the Columbia-Presbyterian Medical Center. Another important decision then faced me. The job as a resident would not start until six months after I left the Navy. What was the best way to spend these six months? During my earlier training, Dr. Raymond Adams had made a strong impression on me as an outstanding teacher, both of neuropathology and clinical neurology. Given his example, I decided that it would be best to use the intervening months to learn some neuropathology. So it was in this offhand way that I fell into a neuropathology fellowship that, happily, Professors Houston Merritt and Abner Wolf improvised for me at Columbia-Presbyterian in New York. Before I left Oakland, I called up former seaman Knox, who had since been discharged from the Navy, and told him I would keep trying to find out the cause of his disorder. I still am.

Those fortuitous months in neuropathology became a springboard for much of what followed. During this period, I could continue the studies on hypertrophic neuritis.[1] Later, this interest would branch out and lead to a treatment for still another disorder of peripheral nerves. And, during these months, the rest of my research career would take form.

What factors shape a career? Are they readily definable? Are they the product of a free choice, decision, or logic alone? Not in my case. For thus far, the pivotal influences have been more subtle or unplanned things: the resonance of an uncle's voice, impromptu drama in a Saturday conference, the happenstance of military assignment and of job scheduling. And from now on, the turning points in the story will hinge on other fragile events: the words of a friend, a mother's resolve against a fatal disease, and the vigor of a dog running wild and free on a chase in the field.

3.

Metachromasia; New York City, 1953

I find that a great part of the information I have was acquired by looking up something and finding something else on the way.

Franklin P. Adams

New York City was a far cry from the splendor of the Sierra mountains, but we escaped by living in semirural New Jersey. Still, the big city must have impressed me. It was from the Palisades overlooking the Hudson River that I would paint its details into my first watercolor landscape: the soaring bridge in the foreground, then the Neurological Institute of New York, and finally the long, hazy view south down Manhattan Island to the skyscrapers in the distance.

As I rode in to the medical center on the bus each day, I was still reading articles about hypertrophic neuritis. Even to the unaided eye, the peripheral nerves in typical hypertrophic neuritis are large, firm, and elevate the skin as might an underlying pencil. Under the microscope, the nerve is a sea of connective tissue surrounding the few islands of remaining nerve fibers (figure 1). It is this loose connective tissue which causes the nerve to enlarge. Some investigators had even described areas of metachromasia in the loose connective tissue.

Metachromasia? What did that mean? I had to look up the term in a medical dictionary. I found that metachromasia refers to a color change from blue to red, something similar to the way blue litmus paper changes when it is placed in an acid solution. The differences are that metachromasia is a staining reaction, and the blue indicator dye used to detect it is in solution, not on paper. What causes the dye to turn red is intimate contact with a large acid molecule. The prefix *meta* (change) is used because the blue dye turns a color other than that of the original dye, and *chromasia* refers to color.

I became excited about the neurological implications of meta-chromasia. For when metachromasia was seen under the microscope, it meant that an acid molecule was there carrying a net negative charge. It seemed an important concept that molecules that were charged negatively could exist within the nervous system. We know that the nerve impulse itself and excitability in general are intimately associated with fast changes in the position of positively charged ions (sodium, calcium, etc.). Opposites attract. Therefore, it was plausible to think that negatively charged molecules in the nervous system might sometimes, like a powerful magnet, attract these crucial positively charged ions.

With the concept of opposite charges strongly in mind, I decided to look further into what was known about metachromasia. I had a vague feeling of being drawn to the word as though it were the pole star. Fortunately, a key feature of the neuropathology fellowship at Columbia was that I was largely left on my own to repair my ignorance. This gave me considerable time to browse in the library. There, one day, meandering, and looking up the term in the Cumulated Index Medicus, I chanced across the pivotal cross-reference. The prime article was written by two eminent English physicians, W. Russell Brain, a neurologist, and J. G. Greenfield, a neuropathologist. It had been published three years earlier and was entitled "Late infantile metachromatic leukoencephalopathy." [1] I was frustrated because, as is so often the case, the whole volume containing this one article was out of the library. It would have been quite easy to have let the matter drop right there. But I was mildly curious to know what this new disease was, and persistent enough to put the volume on reserve.

Weeks later, when I first saw the article itself, its contents had an almost physical impact. I still remember vividly the entire flash of discovery at the library table. During the moment itself, I was all a participant, suffused not only with a compellingly fresh intellectual idea but with the feeling that all my perceptions were on edge. As it was then, so I can easily visualize it now, but with one curious difference. Now, I am the onlooker; my vantage point is always about fifteen feet up and about five feet over to the left. There is the large library, the big library table, and at its center is the lone figure of a young doctor in white, sitting and peering into a large book.

The sequences of illumination at the library table that day went somewhat as follows. First, I found myself reading with increasing fascination about this other intriguing disorder, also characterized by metachromasia. Indeed, I was impressed by the special feature of the new disease: massive amounts of metachromatic material were scattered throughout the nervous system. Next, I was struck by the black and white photograph. It showed that other deposits (said to be metachromatic) also lay in and near the *kidney* tubules. Suddenly, my mind raced and turned inward, a burst of blurred images flashing in quick succession: kidney deposits entering the urine; a centrifuge; a metachromatic stain; a microscope. The complete working hypothesis leaped forth in sharply visual form: the material present in the kidney has entered the urine; being heavier, it will be centrifuged down into the urine sediment; there, the deposits turn a metachromatic color when stained with toluidine blue; this disease of the central nervous system can be diagnosed during life by looking at the urine sediment under the microscope.

All the mental steps in this process unfolded in perhaps two seconds. Proving the hypothesis took three years.

4.

Microscopic Studies; New York City, 1953

A favorable condition for productivity in research is variety of experience, both one's own experience and that which may be derived through observation of others who are at work on different problems. Especially is this important during the early years of education and discipline. Thus insight into diverse methods is acquired, as well as acquaintance with ways in which they are applied. As an investigator continues in his career, accident will present him with unpredicted opportunities for research, perhaps in quite new directions. The early knowledge of various ways of solving problems provides him promptly with readiness and versatility of attack.

Walter Cannon

Every specialist, whatever his profession, skill or business may be, can improve his performance by broadening his base."

Wilder Penfield

If I never had examined urine before, the hypothesis and the subsequent experiments would never have occurred. But I could proceed straightaway for two reasons. Back in the summer of 1946, while I was a second-year medical student, I had routinely examined urine sediments. Always drawn to the out-of-doors, I had taken a job as a "camp doctor" in New Hampshire during summer vacation. The job proved more than I bargained for. The camp was soon overcome by a major epidemic of virus peneumonia, and many were very sick for one or two weeks. Some had a second recurrence of fever, and I placed them on sulfadiazine, following a fashion of the time, in order to avoid secondary bacterial infections. The problem was that excessive concentrations of the sulfa drug could form harmful crystals in the kidney. Therefore, I had to search the urine sediment for sulfa crystals with the microscope.

I worried over my patients as only a second-year medical student can—like a mother hen over chicks. Would they get a bacterial pneumonia? I already knew what that meant in personal terms. Would the sulfa drug I was giving them plug up their kidneys? Kindled by my worries that summer, the memory traces that would lead to my using a microscope were glowing and ready for use whenever the appropriate occasion arose.

The second reason it was easy to look at urine sediment had to do with the nature of my internship. I was fortunate to intern at the Boston City Hospital at a time when interns themselves performed all basic urine and blood studies. I was already doubly primed, as it were, to regard body fluids as a source of medical information, and I turned to this approach quite naturally. If I had been limited to the microscopic experience that students and interns receive today, I probably would never had started, let alone continued, this line of research.

In March of 1953 two brothers whom I will call Clausen were admitted as patients to our child neurology ward at Columbia. Dr. Charles Poser, then a neurology resident, presented them at a conference. They were normal at birth but at the age of a year and a half had each developed a progressive neurological disorder. Their parents first noticed a clumsiness in walking. Gradually they became blind, and their arms and legs became paralyzed. Eventually, they lost the ability to talk, think, and feed themselves. The disease seemed to be genetically determined because their older brother had died earlier in Cleveland of exactly the same illness. Autopsy reports from the Cleveland hospital showed that this first brother had died of metachromatic leukodystrophy (MLD).*

The stage was now set to test the hypothesis developed at the library table ten months before. I centrifuged a urine sample from each brother, poured off all the lighter liquid at the top, and transferred the heavier sediment to a glass slide. With mounting excitement, I next added a few drops of dilute toluidine blue dye, stirred the mixture with a wooden stick, and then covered it with a glass cover slip. Under the microscope, the slide from each brother did show clumps of metachromatic material scattered throughout the urine sediment. It was *red* to *reddish-purple* in color. Large strands of this metachromatic material were quite obvious, even when I looked at the slide with the unaided eye.

Sometime during my intellectual development I acquired a passion to do carefully controlled studies. So, at the same time that I prepared sediments from the two brothers, I also made similar slides from several other (control) persons. I included my own urine sediment and also sediments from patients with various neurological illness. A search soon revealed that *all* of these subjects had variable amounts of reddish-purple metachromatic material in the urine sediment. The material from the control patients looked essentially the same as did that from the two Clausen children. Clearly, this metachromatic material was of no diagnostic use. The hypothesis appeared to be of no value.

Still, I looked again at fresh urine sediments the next day. I searched the slides and drew pictures of what I encountered. Gradually, my attention focused on something first casually interesting, soon arresting.

Material of another color was present. This special material occurred only in sediments from the two brothers. I had been expecting something which was reddish or reddish-purple. What I saw, instead, were shades of *golden-brown*. Furthermore, there was a distinctive structure to this material: it was globular or granular (figure 3). Sometimes several globules were stuck together, resembling a cluster of grapes. In some instances, golden-brown granular material could be seen inside the cytoplasm of a cell. The appearance of the cell indicated that it had become detached from the kidney and had then found its way into the

---

* The term leukodystrophy has replaced leukoencephalopathy. Because "metachromatic leukodystrophy" is cumbersome, it is simply shortened to MLD.

urine. In other instances, the material formed a large cylindrical cast conforming to the rounded shape of the inside of the kidney tuble.

Trial and error soon showed that the urine had to be fresh for best results. Even then, the amount of material fluctuated from day to day. But the older brother, whose disease was more advanced, almost always excreted much more material. As the size of the control series grew from ten to fifty and included more patients with other disorders, it became evident that abundant material like this, especially that in kidney cells, was not to be found in patients with other diseases. The urine findings seemed specific for metachromatic leukodystrophy.[1] This gave us the first medical laboratory technique for diagnosing MLD during life.

Research proliferates,[2] and for a simple reason: as one question is answered, at least two new ones arise. The new questions soon arose. Unstained sediment showed nothing; the material itself was colorless and only took on the golden-brown shade when stained with the toluidine blue dye. Only then did it become metachromatic. But why did the material have this curious golden-brown color, particularly when the deposits described in the earlier article by Brain and Greenfield were shades of reddish-purple? These unanswered questions nagged me for almost two more years. The questions prompted other experiments, most of which yielded answers different from those sought.

A peripheral issue also remained to be settled. Both brothers had a yellow-orange color to their skin. Their blood plasma also had a yellowish-brown color. Why? It turned out that at home they had been fed large amounts of vegetables and other strained foods. Having ingested large quantities of yellow vegetable pigments (carotene) they had developed carotenemia. Concentrated carotene has a golden-brown color. Could the carotene in the blood somehow have been deposited in the kidney, then become decolorized and finally recolorized by toluidine blue? This all seemed unlikely. Still, I had to eliminate it as a possibility.

No human patients with carotenemia showed up to test this point. So I became a rat doctor for the first time. I fed rats huge amounts of carotene daily. They failed to show any golden-brown deposits in the kidney or in the urine resembling those found in MLD urine. Therefore, there was no reason to think the urine findings in human MLD were caused by the carotenemia.

The simpleminded rat studies seemed a diversion at the time. However, they were my first really personal demonstration of how animal experiments might help clarify the mechanisms involved in a human disease. The rat experiments also introduced me to the useful technique of making thin sections of frozen tissues that could be looked at under the microscope. To do this, I found I had to purchase a tank of carbon dioxide and scrounge old frozen section equipment from the anatomy department. I had no technician to do these things for me. As a result, I had the opportunity to learn the basic histological skills which were to become essential for work with lipids later on.

The six months' fellowship in neuropathology was soon over. My primary responsibility now was to care for patients on the wards and in the out-patient clinics. If I was going to continue my research, I had to add it on to an already hectic neurology residency. I had an even more practical problem. I badly needed a refrigerator, both to delay the fading of the golden-brown color on the slides and to keep the urine from spoiling. The refrigerator space in neuropathology was already spoken for. Besides, one could anticipate no great enthusiasm in neuropathology for a neurology resident who was working on his own. So I did most of my research after hours or during the evenings when I was on duty that night. I did the rest of the work during daylight hours in whatever inches of space I could beg away from the technicians in the crowded clinical laboratory. Naturally, these good women protested mildly when increasing volumes of urine started to flood the laboratory and clutter up their refrigerator. However, they seemed mollified by three things: I was enthusiastic about what I was doing and took the time to demonstrate the abnormal urine material to them; I also enclosed these urine bottles in brown paper bags to mask their prosaic contents; and finally, I demonstrated my own high regard for the aesthetic aspects of their refrigerator by choosing to keep my own luncheon sandwiches in it. Nevertheless, my status as a persona grata in the laboratory remained precarious for the next two years.

It is not easy to persuade harried nurses on busy wards to collect urine samples for research. Then, too, there was the matter of wishing to study children who appeared to have a hopeless disease. What practical good could come out of all the bother? Gradually, to my surprise, I found that it was really difficult to conduct clinical research in a busy hospital. Medically oriented people, even in university teaching centers, are not automatically receptive to new ideas in research. The investigator must endure subtle harassments, both major and minor, in order to prevail. But all of this became relatively easy because of my own growing enthusiasm for the project. Directly ahead lay the big intriguing question: What was the chemical nature of the metachromatic material?

A neurology resident acting in a vacuum could never have approached a problem of this dimension. What made the difference were the friends, collaborators, and colleagues who publish in the scientific literature. They helped generate ideas about how to pursue this research and provided all kinds of other assistance.

For example, I had one other important chance encounter in the library at the Neurological Institute of New York. While browsing there one day, I happened to meet Dr. Robert Katzman, a fellow resident. Bob had had some earlier training in neurochemistry before he started to specialize in neurology. I told him that my solubility studies showed the unknown material was some kind of a lipid, a fatty substance. In fact, I had just found that the material dissolved slightly in alcohol but not in ether. Bob made the helpful suggestion that I look up the writings of Dr. Jordi Folch-pi and his group of chemists at Harvard. These workers had recently been concentrating on lipids in the nervous system. Lipids, I recalled, were the distinctive constituents of the brain, making up half its total dry weight. There were more lipids in the nervous system than in any other tissue. In my reading, I found that the Harvard investigators could readily dissolve these lipids in a mixture of two parts of chloroform to one part of methanol (wood alcohol). Perhaps this solvent mixture would help free the metachromatic material from MLD tissues so that I could then identify it.

But, by then, my neurology residency in New York was almost over. Judy and I now had two young children to think about. I had to interrupt my studies. Where to go? What was the best way to combine teaching, research, and patient care responsibilities, yet still be able to feed, clothe, and house a family of four? I had seen California while in the Navy, and the vision of the West Coast was still a very attractive one. A new opportunity at Portland, Oregon, was particularly appealing. There, at the University of Oregon Medical School, Dr. Roy Swank had just opened up a new Division of Neurology. Roy was an energetic, friendly, open, and generous man who approached neurological diseases through biochemistry, and I was increasingly sympathetic to this point of view. After visits to, and correspondence with, various medical centers, I happily accepted a position at Oregon.

July, 1955, found us on the road, heading West, immensely excited and full of wonder and curiosity about what the future would bring. My starting salary as a full-time faculty member, seven years after graduating from medical school, would amount to the heady figure of $8,000.

5.

Sulfated Lipids; Portland, Oregon, 1955

New medical observations are generally made by chance; if a patient with a hitherto unknown illness enters a hospital where a physician comes for consultation, it is surely by luck that the doctor encounters this patient.

Claude Bernard

The new job posed some stimulating challenges. When I arrived in Oregon, no MLD patients were known to live there. I had no fresh-frozen or formalin-fixed autopsy material to study, and knew essentially nothing about the practical aspects of neurochemistry. I started with no laboratory space as such. My work bench was a cluttered corner of a borrowed laboratory space still used for demonstrations in physiology. Furthermore, to practice clinical medicine in Oregon, I first had to pass a certifying examination in the preclinical sciences. My knowledge of biochemistry was fragmentary, and I had to study a great deal of basic chemistry to pass the exam. This was painful but very important. I found that I could learn, and this gave me the minimal confidence I needed to approach a neurochemical problem that was really way beyond me.

On the positive side, the academic setting at the medical school was favorable. The biochemical approach to neurological disorders was exemplified both in Dr. Swank's work and in that of Dr. Jack Fellman, a helpful young neurochemist who had also joined us. Then, too, there was the intervention of chance.

Two months after we arrived in Portland, a boy was admitted to the medical school hospital. I will call him Warren Thompson. His symptoms were ominous. When he was five years old his parents noted a slight limp affecting his right leg. By age seven, walking was much impaired and climbing stairs was impossible. He became clumsy and developed thick speech. In brief, the pattern of his reflex changes (some were increased, some were decreased) was consistent with a disorder causing widespread breakdown of the myelin sheath (figures 1 and 2). The sheath is an insulating layer of lipid that normally surrounds each nerve fiber in the brain, the spinal cord, and the peripheral nerves. When it breaks down, the fiber stops transmitting its impulses. All neurological functions (motor, speech, vision, etc.) then gradually shut down. Because the Thompson child was older when his symptoms began, his history and examination differed somewhat from the Clausen brothers in New York. Still, it seemed possible that he might have the kind of MLD that starts later in childhood.

I stained his urine sediment. Again, I saw the distinctive golden-brown material. Here was a new case of MLD and fresh lipid material with which to work. The trouble was that urine sediment is a potpourri. Knowing that this small amount of material existed was only the first step toward understanding the disease. If I ever wanted to identify this unknown lipid, my first job was to separate the minute amounts of it from the vast quantity of other material in the urine sediment.

After much trial and error, I discovered three things: 1) The mixture of chloroform and methanol I had read about in New York did indeed dissolve the metachromatic lipid. 2) When this mixture was exposed to water, it separated into three layers as had been described by Folch-pi. Lipids (fats) in the middle layer could be suctioned up with a pipette, placed on filter paper and then stained with toluidine blue. 3) In normal patients the lipids did not show a strong red metachromasia. However, lipids from the Thompson child with MLD always gave a strong red color.

Now the unknown lipids could be extracted out of MLD urine and concentrated. But what were they? On a trip back to Columbia-Presbyterian Medical Center in New York, I looked up an old medical school classmate, Dr. Jerry Phillips. Bright and hard-working, Jerry had become a serious investigator in the lipid field. I mentioned to him that the unknown lipid was highly metachromatic, and that for this reason part

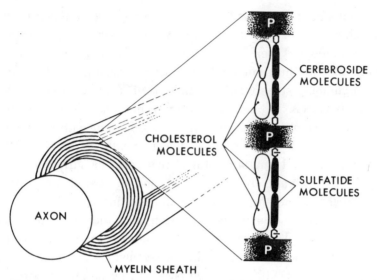

Figure 2. The normal myelin sheath and three of its molecules, magnified 57 million times.

The nerve fiber (axon) normally conducts nerve impulses down to innervate muscles or other nerve cells. Surrounding it is an insulating fatty coat, the myelin sheath.

The myelin sheath, like a jelly roll, is made up of many individual layers. Each layer is composed of molecules of lipids, protein and water. In this diagram, part of the molecular architecture of one layer is expanded and shown schematically.

The layer resembles a double-decker sandwich: the two lipid "fillings" are contained within three protein (*P*) layers. If you look carefully at each lipid filling, you will see that it contains two cholesterol molecules. (The gourd-like structures approximate the actual shape of a cholesterol molecule.) The two other molecules shown are either two sulfatide or two cerebroside molecules. Sulfatide molecules (also termed cerebroside sulfate) differ from cerebroside only in that they possess a sulfate group. This group is a locus of negative charge, indicated by a minus sign.

Cerebrosides and sulfatides are the two most distinctive molecules of the myelin sheath. Normally, there are perhaps four cerebroside molecules for each sulfatide molecule. The sheath breaks down if it contains too many cerebrosides or too many sulfatide molecules. It crumbles as would a brick wall with too much sand and too little cement in the mortar. This degenerative process is termed a leukodystrophy.

of the molecule should carry a strong negative charge. Going by the analogy with other known molecules in biology, I favored a negatively charged sulfate group over a phosphate group. What did he know about sulfated lipids? This wasn't Jerry's métier, but he did recall a report in the Federation Proceedings some months back. I finally located the reference, a brief paper by Marjorie Lees[1] in Folch-pi's group at Harvard Medical School.

At this point, the good will of four other people played a crucial role in the story. First, there was another medical school classmate, Lowell Lapham. Lowell dug into his old pathology files and sent me a small portion of MLD kidney material to work with. This fragment, fixed in formaldehyde solution, had remained in Cleveland, left over from the autopsy of the first child in the Clausen family. The second person was Frank Witmer, who, as we shall soon see, added his invaluable expertise in infrared spectrophotometry. A third was Sigfried Thannhauser, who donated an authentic sample of a sulfated lipid in early 1957. Thereafter, his prototype compound served as our reference standard for the sulfatide molecule. The fourth person was Mrs. Thompson. It was she who firmly persuaded the rest of the family to consent to the postmortem examination when her son finally died of MLD.

I made thin frozen sections of the MLD kidney material sent by Lowell Lapham and stained them with toluidine blue. This was to be my first real glimpse of the disease I had worked on for so long. I awaited the result with mounting excitement. Looking into the microscope, I finally saw the MLD kidney tubules—packed with vast amounts of the abnormal lipids. The deposits stained a sensational mixture of red, red-purple and golden-brown colors, and I immediately recalled the stained glass windows of the Saint-Chapelle in Paris, which until that moment had been my ultimate visual experience. I have never forgotten the way this slide looked; I can still see it vividly in my mind's eye—an aesthetic delight!

If some symbolism is involved in this earlier work in MLD, surely it lies close to a profound appreciation of these colors. They are among my favorites, and working with them has always been deeply satisfying.

I've had favorite colors before, and the first I can clearly remember as a small child is the rich olive green color of a crayon. There is nothing subtle about how it became my favorite; it was the color of Palmolive shaving cream with which I watched my father lather up his beard each morning. Later on, reds and blues would echo throughout a series of other experiences. When I was about nine years old I received a chemistry set from my parents. The experiment I had the most fun with was the one in which a water clear solution of a base (like sodium hydroxide) is added to a clear alcoholic solution of phenolpthalein. The mixture—magically—turns a deep rich red (like "wine," the directions hinted). Then, in later years, I remember how impressed I was by the stained-glass windows in the churches in which I sang in the choir for many years.

Now, I was looking at the microscopic sections from MLD kidney, and they provided another satisfaction. I had long been puzzled by the fact that the material in the urine stained a golden-brown color. This was a new metachromatic color that hadn't been reported before. Why didn't the granular material in the urine stain the conventional red, or purple metachromatic colors? Now I could guess part of the answer from the kidney sections. They showed that the original material upstream in the tubules was indeed more reddish colored. But later on, and lower down in the tubules, when the material was poised to enter the urine, it turned golden-brown. Clearly, the lipids upstream had changed their staining characteristics toward golden-brown before they entered the urine. Extracted and spotted on filter paper, they turned red again.

By now, I was enthusiastic about my research, but it was difficult at first to persuade others that it was worth supporting. At the time, there was no clear precedent for looking at urine under the microscope to diagnose a disease of the nervous system. When my application for funds went in, it faced considerable resistance, and the validity of the urine sediment findings themselves was open to question. To document the request, I was asked to send a slide off to New York City showing the metachromatic granules. This I could not do at the time, because the metachromatic color was fugitive—it usually faded within a few hours after it was first developed. The application was accordingly turned down.

The portion of MLD kidney sent by Lowell Lapham was useful for another reason. It finally afforded me enough tissue for some vital chemical experiments. I had to find out whether the sulfatide isolation procedure (designed for brain) could also work when applied to kidney.

How could a neurologist be more interested in kidney than brain? Strategy dictated the priority I gave to kidney. I chose kidney because it showed the most striking visual contrast. A normal patient had no metachromatic material in kidney; an MLD kidney was loaded with deposits. I reasoned that it would be simpler to isolate and identify the MLD lipid from kidney. Once the lipid was known, we should be closer to the cause of the disease.

I then isolated sulfatide fractions from kidneys from the MLD patient and controls. It was exciting to find that only the MLD sample yielded a large amount of metachromatic lipid. It was soluble in various solvents like sulfatide; it stained metachromatically like sulfatide. But was it really sulfatide? Couldn't it also be some other lipid, which only resembled sulfatide in its solubilities and staining reactions? I tried for weeks to resolve this question with a technique called paper chromatography, for which A. J. P. Martin and R. L. Synge received the Nobel Prize in chemistry in 1952. This is a method of identifying an unknown compound, based on the fact that each molecule in a solution of appropriate liquids moves at a characteristic rate on a strip of filter paper. In my hands the method didn't work with sulfatide and the literature on chromatography didn't help either. I failed in every attempt.

By now, only a few precious milligrams remained of the unidentified lipid. Under these circumstances there remained only one good technique to identify the whole molecule. This method was infrared spectrophotometry.

Enter Frank Witmer. I still recall the moment he came through the door and ambled to the left into the laboratory. Some years before, he had been enrolled as a medical student, then switched to go into chemistry and business. His wife then developed multiple sclerosis and became a patient of Roy Swank. Roy told him of my work. Now, Frank wanted a sense of personal involvement in neurological research. In particular he wanted to help out in diseases which, like multiple sclerosis, also destroy the myelin sheath. Furthermore, he wished to donate his services. This was helpful, because, lacking funds, I was operating on a research budget of a few hundred dollars. I explained that I was studying such a disease, that I had isolated some material which seemed likely to be a sulfated lipid, but which had not yet been identified. He readily accepted the challenge.

When chemical substances are exposed to a beam of infrared light they let certain wave lengths pass and block others. Each chemical compound has a characteristic identity in its pattern of transmission and absorption—something like a chemical "fingerprint." This method, infrared spectrophotometry, was Frank's area of expertise.

To start to measure small amounts of the unknown lipid, I now had to learn a sensitive new technique of weighing less than a milligram of material. I could do so only because Monte Greer, in a neighboring laboratory, had (as an act of faith) let me use his delicate microbalance.

Within weeks our infrared studies were completed. They told us that

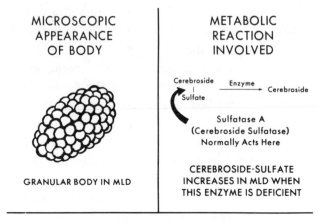

MICROSCOPIC APPEARANCE OF BODY	METABOLIC REACTION INVOLVED

GRANULAR BODY IN MLD

Sulfatase A
(Cerebroside Sulfatase)
Normally Acts Here

CEREBROSIDE-SULFATE
INCREASES IN MLD WHEN
THIS ENZYME IS DEFICIENT

MOLECULE
DEPOSITED IN THE BODY

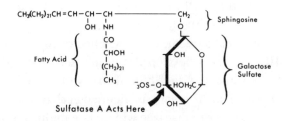

CEREBROSIDE SULFATE (SULFATIDE)

Figure 3. The granular body and its chemical background.

Under the microscope, the granular body of MLD looks something like a raspberry or cluster of grapes. It is composed of many molecules of sulfatide (cerebroside-sulfate). Normally, an enzyme (sulfatase A: cerebroside sulfatase) splits the sulfate group from the sulfatide molecule. If the enzyme is deficient, as in MLD, deposits of cerebroside-sulfate build up. The raised negative sign ($^-$) in ^-_3OS-O- indicates that the sulfate group is a locus of negative charge. The sulfate group is hooked to galactose; this sugar is linked to sphingosine, which in turn is attached to a fatty acid.

the metachromatic lipid isolated in MLD was identical with the sulfatide of Thannhauser. It was basically a lipid which contained sugar (figure 3). To the sugar there was attached a sulfate group. Luckily, this sulfate group caused a major distortion of infrared light at a certain wave length. The more deflection there was at this wave length, the more lipid was present. We could now identify and measure how much sulfatide we had.

Our analyses showed a major increase of sulfatide in MLD. MLD kidney had up to nine times more sulfatide than did normal kidneys, and

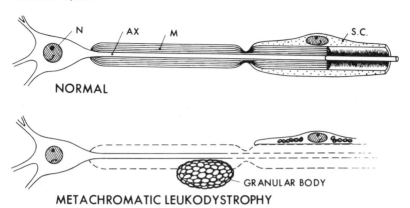

Figure 4. *A normal nerve fiber and the way it is affected in metachromatic leukodystrophy.*

The *normal* nerve fiber shown at the top has a layer of fatty insulation, myelin (*M*), surrounding its axon. This layer is formed by a sheath cell (*S.C.*) which envelops it.

In *metachromatic leukodystrophy,* sheath cells and myelin itself develop abnormally high levels of sulfatide. The myelin sheaths and some of their axons then break down. The nerve fiber no longer conducts impulses. The sulfated lipid (sulfatide) accumulates in granular deposits, termed granular bodies, inside large scavenger cells (phagocytes). Granular deposits of the lipid also build up in sheath cells.

even the devastated white matter from MLD brain had twice as much sulfatide as normal. We studied other diseases which destroy the myelin sheaths of white matter (multiple sclerosis, for example). Here, in contrast to MLD, sulfatide values were decreased much below normal. The fact that sulfatides were increased in MLD white matter was unique.

Because sulfatides were increased not only in MLD brain and kidney, but also in other tissues, we could conclude that MLD was a generalized sulfatide deposition disease. Another term for this is sulfatide lipidosis (figure 5). Somehow, the excess of this lipid caused the nervous system to break down (figure 4).

In this respect, MLD resembled other disorders which had been described for years—the so-called lipid storage diseases. One useful feature of these deposition diseases is that the stored molecules clump together; under the microscope the chemical quarry is in full sight when the tissue section is properly stained. I had heard about these illnesses in medical school, but, like all medical students, I found it hard to remember which molecule was increased in which disease. It would have been completely impossible for me to believe, while still a medical student, that ten years later I would help identify the lipid in another

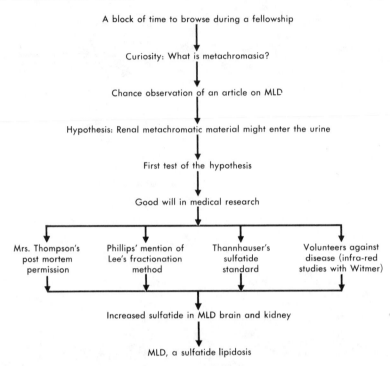

Figure 5. Sequences in the Metachromatic Leukodystrophy Story

storage disease, and my teachers would have been equally incredulous.

Up to this point, the search itself had provided a steadily accelerating excitement. But, now that the sulfatide proof was in, I reached a stage of intellectual exhilaration. I remember vividly the hours when the sulfatide discovery made its full impact on me. I lay awake that night. Images raced and tumbled through my mind—colors, people, places, contingencies. Foremost among my thoughts were two I can recall even now. To a biologist, one of these thoughts was deeply gratifying. It seemed as though I would probably be worth my grain of salt on some eternal time scale. Our work had added one fact to the mass of information in the universe. The other thought served to counterbalance any possible sense of smugness. It was the nagging awareness that the hard central question still lay ahead: what kind of metabolic error caused the increase in sulfated lipids in MLD?

6.

Molecules and Meanderings, 1957

Anybody who looks back over an experimental development which . . . .
has continued for many years, can hardly fail to notice that it has pursued
an exceedingly wobbly course. If the surveyer is himself an experimenter,
he will know that the recorded wanderings are fewer and less extensive
than those which actually occurred.

Frederick Bartlett

My report that sulfatides were increased in MLD created little stir when
it was first submitted in 1957. At the time, there was no good precedent
for thinking that a primary disease of the myelin sheath was caused by
an increase in one of its molecules, and the program committee of the
American Neurological Association did not accept the paper for presen-
tation. But even in 1957, it was reasonable to postulate that an enzyme
deficiency caused the increase in sulfatides. By then, separate enzyme
deficiencies were increasingly being pinpointed as the cause of genetically determined diseases.*

Let us briefly review what an enzyme is in order to appreciate what
happens when an enzyme is deficient. We may think of an enzyme as a
protein molecule which greatly speeds up a chemical reaction. Were it
not for the hustling, catalytic action of many enzymes, each orchestrated beautifully with the others, our body's vital metabolic reactions
would come to an abrupt halt. The reason is that some toxic compounds
would reach damagingly high levels, while the supply of other essential
molecules would dwindle to harmfully low levels.

What kind of an enzyme might be deficient in MLD? There were two
clues. One was the presence of the sulfate group itself—the distinctive
feature of the sulfatide molecule (figure 3). The other was a report I

---

* For example, in 1953, Dr. George Jervis showed that an inherited form of mental deficiency (PKU; phenylketonuria) was the result of a deficiency of an enzyme that normally
catalyzes the conversion of one amino acid, phenylalanine, to tyrosine. The enzyme block
creates a bottleneck, and phenylalanine builds up behind it to toxic levels.

had read indicating that a *phosphatase* enzyme deficiency existed in quite a different disease. I wondered, therefore, if MLD might be an analogous situation—a disorder caused, in this instance, by a *sulfatase* enzyme deficiency.

I knew nothing about sulfatases. However, I soon read everything available in the library. A sufatase, I found, was an enzyme that helped split off sulfate (SO_4) groups (figure 3). The function of the enzyme, therefore, was to keep the number of sulfated molecules down to an appropriate biological level. Different sulfatases were measured by using special chemical reagents. Each reagent had a sulfate group linked to it, and the point of attachment served in a sense as the "target" on which the enzyme acted. When the sulfatase split off the sulfate group, the reagent turned a new color. By measuring the amount of this new color, one knew how much sulfatase activity was present.

Formidable technical problems remained. What sulfatase method should I use, and which tissue should be studied? The answers are simple now, but getting them at that time took almost four years. In the interim, there was considerable meandering around. To illustrate, one day I was browsing in the library looking for information about metachromatic compounds and various storage diseases. I happened across a report by Lahut Uzman and took it back to my desk in the laboratory. Uzman had been studying Hurler's disease, a separate disorder in which the patients had both mental and bony abnormalities.[1] His report happened to mention that the white blood cells of these patients contained abnormal deposits of stored material. This was new to me. The article alerted me to the possibility that storage products might accumulate in readily accessible cells, such as circulating white blood cells. Accessibility is an important consideration for the researcher. A surgical operation to sample a piece of the human central or peripheral nervous system is troublesome for the patient and the physician. It is always preferable to diagnose a disease by studying cells that are easily obtained, as are white cells in a drop of blood.

While reading about white cells in Uzman's article, the idea struck me to study white blood cells in MLD. Perhaps they too contained metachromatic deposits. If they did, then it might be practical to test these cells for sulfatase activity. It took perhaps four seconds for all the visual steps in this hypothesis to unfold together with the methods for testing it out. I remember being swept up in a moment of intense heightened awareness. The effect was something like having the volume turned up on your television set—yet with a corresponding reduction in static— while at the same time perceiving the sounds of a deeper bass, a higher treble, and an image with enhanced colors in sharper focus. Even now, writing these lines, I retain a clear visual image of the scene at the desk where these ideas burst forth. This time, in a kind of mental double vision, I am both a participant in the process and a spectator hovering over a point about five feet up and ten feet directly to the rear.

There was a precedent for my looking at white blood cells (just as there had been earlier for examining urine sediment). Eleven years before, in medical school, I first became interested in blood cells and collected boxes full of slides showing the typical changes in white blood cells in different diseases. I had long viewed the making, staining, and examining of a blood smear as a natural extension of the clinical method of diagnosis.

By this time we had discovered two more Oregon patients with MLD—a brother and sister in the McLean family. Their symptoms began when they were about a year old. I promptly made a blood smear on each and stained it myself with a standard technique. The results were startling; their white blood cells were stuffed with many abnormal granules!

I worry whenever a hypothesis is too quickly confirmed, and immediately suspect that something must be amiss. This lingering anxiety helped spark the usual long period that followed of examining control blood smears from many other sick children the same age. Only after looking at these controls could I conclude that the abnormal white cell granules were confined to just these two children with MLD. In fact, even the other MLD patients did not have the abnormalities. This ambiguity was puzzling, but at least now I had some accessible cells that could be tested for a sulfatase deficiency. The question was, how to do so?

At this point, another lively collaborator appeared on the scene: Margaret (Margo) DeMerritt. Margo not only knew about blood cells but also had the enthusiasm and sparkle that are important in any research activity, particularly on the many routine days when everything else in the laboratory either plods along or turns out wrong. In the course of these blood studies, and particularly when it came to interpreting the kinds of cells in bone marrow, I became increasingly dependent on Margo's skill and enthusiasm. She started in the lab as a part-time technician, then became more and more a full-time collaborator. Finally, growing all the while in scientific stature, she entered our medical school at Oregon and graduated with distinction.

Our research problem was this: we could see abnormal deposits in white blood cells of the two MLD children, and some of these deposits were metachromatic with toluidine blue. But no good histochemical method existed which could clearly tell us whether sulfatase activity was deficient in white cells. We had to devise our own.

There are three different groups of sulfatases: A, B, and C. Our original method measured all at once and did not distinguish among them. Therefore, if any single sulfatase were absent (A, for example), the evidence might be obscured because the two other sulfatases were still active in the cell. For this reason, even though MLD white blood cells showed no consistent decrease in sulfatase activity, we could still not conclude they were not deficient in a single sulfatase. It was discouraging to have invested a great deal of time perfecting the histochemical method only to have ended with nothing conclusive.

Let me now move ahead in the story briefly to emphasize a point. Years later, despite the initial setback, the histochemical method did help us after all. All we finally had to do was make a minor change—run the test in an alkaline solution instead of an acid one. In doing so, we finally had a test for the one sulfatase (sulfatase C) which is active under more alkaline conditions. This modified test finally showed us that sulfatase C was deficient in tissues from the MLD patients in the McLean family who had abnormal granules in their white blood cells. The vignette illustrates how unpredictable research can be: first, the hypothesis is formulated, then a method is developed to test the hypothesis. The method fails at first, but later on, it turns out to be most helpful if carried out in just a slightly different way.

Back in 1957, our research in one area spun off into another. For example, I was still curious to learn more about metachromasia and wondered whether sulfated metachromatic molecules like sulfatides could be harmful in high concentration. Two questions arose: 1) Could one create an experimental metachromatic disorder by injecting animals with an excess of sulfated molecules? 2) Would the response of the tissue to an excess of these metachromatic molecules help us understand any of the changes seen in hypertrophic neuritis? Here, of course, my thoughts were looping back to the starting point—to my old interest in hypertrophic neuritis. I was still trying to understand why metachromatic areas occurred inside the peripheral nerves in that disease. Writing this years later, I still am not certain.

From John Harris, an ophthalmologist, I learned that a new sulfated molecule had been produced by a drug company. It was a complex sugar (polysaccharide) called hyaluronic acid sulfate. I decided to use this soluble metachromatic molecule in an experiment that was designed to answer several questions. The questions could all be formulated quite consciously.

Too consciously. The plan was to inject large amounts of the compound into experimental animals. I would then look at the white blood cells under the microscope to see if some of the material had entered them and at the kidney to find out if it had entered the tubule cells. Moreover, by injecting the compound near the sciatic nerve, there was the remote possibility that some of it might penetrate inside the nerve. This might create a local excess of metachromatic material as occurs in hypertrophic neuritis.

I chose young rabbits in order to create a research situation analogous to that of the MLD children we were studying, reasoning that when a young animal is growing rapidly, it might be most vulnerable to a metabolic error. In approach, the new experiment was rather simpleminded, but from it there evolved an astonishing variety of unexpected observations.

We started by injecting hyaluronic acid sulfate under the skin of the back of young rabbits. A few days later, the rabbits dragged both hind legs. Our first thought was that their peripheral nerves or spinal cord might have been damaged. I discovered, however, that being a rabbit doctor required more diagnostic skill than I had anticipated. In fact, the physical examination showed that the rabbits had fractured both thigh bones. X rays and subsequent microscopic examinations showed that the bones had broken because they were abnormally thinned and softened. Then, a few days later, each rabbit began to develop a large lower abdominal hernia. Microscopic examination later showed that these hernias were caused by weak abdominal muscles and weak connective tissue. The hernias were filled with intestines which had spilled out from the abdominal cavity and entered the hernial sac. Not only were bones, muscles, and connective tissues weakened, but the skin and subcutaneous tissues were easily torn.

These major results were far removed from MLD and from hypertrophic neuritis. However, they were reminiscent of some abnormalities found in other diseases affecting connective tissue. We had stumbled onto a new kind of experimental model. The animal model was of considerable interest, because genetic diseases of connective tissue do exist in man in which bones fracture, hernias develop, and skin becomes thin and weak.

But what was the real explanation for these disorders? What was going on down at the submicroscopic level—at the level of the molecules themselves? We decided to explore the situation. Briefly, what we found was that hyaluronic acid alone (which lacks sulfate groups) did not produce the abnormalities in our rabbits, nor did other similar polysaccharide molecules which had only a few sulfate groups. Essentially, two things were required to produce the experimental lesions: 1) The molecule had to be a special kind containing many negatively charged sulfate groups. 2) This sulfated compound had to be concentrated in the tissues.

To the world at large, the hyaluronic acid sulfate experiments could only be judged a failure. They produced nothing resembling hypertrophic neuritis, nothing like the white cell changes in MLD, and led to no published results. The editorial boards of three different journals rejected the manuscripts. Yet, on the other hand, the experiments were not merely a diversion, nor were they a waste of time. They reinforced my keen interest in determining exactly what it was about the configuration of a molecule that caused tissues to undergo a pathological change. The studies also showed us that an excess of sulfated molecules could cause a tissue to break down slowly. This might be one of several potential mechanisms by which myelin sheaths could break down in metachromatic leukodystrophy. During these studies we also learned how properly to control an animal experiment, and how to think of disease in terms of the disintegration of large molecules in a tissue. I also got into the habit of injecting a certain molecule and then looking at the injection site under the microscope. Each hard-won lesson turned out to be prerequisite for the next experiments.

7.
Controls and the Experimental Globoid Response, 1960

Scientific investigations and experimental ideas may be born as a result of fortuitous and almost involuntary chance observations which present themselves either spontaneously or in an experiment designed with quite a different purpose.

Claude Bernard

In 1890, the German bacteriologist Robert Koch formulated the scientific rules for proving that a certain microorganism was, in fact, the cause of a given disease. The microbe must first be isolated from the infected patient. Then, after being cultured, it must cause the same disease in a normal experimental animal. And finally, the organism isolated from the diseased animal and grown in culture should be the same as the one cultured earlier from the sick patient. These rules, termed Koch's postulates, still form the foundation for our contemporary research in infectious diseases.

While in Oregon, I decided to use a somewhat similar approach in my chemical and histochemical research. I chose the sulfatide molecule instead of a microorganism, and a metabolic disease, MLD, rather than an infectious one. In these experiments, I teamed up with Darwin Lehfeldt, a hard-working, tenacious medical student from Montana, who has since gone on to specialize in pathology. First, we devised a system for injecting human sulfatide (obtained from the brain of a patient with MLD) into the white matter of rat brain. We next waited two weeks or more for the tissue reaction to evolve, then made frozen sections of the injection site and stained them with toluidine blue. The results were striking. Within a few days the sulfated molecules were engulfed by phagocytes, scavenger cells that engulf debris, digest it, and thus serve a cleanup function.

The phagocytes in the rat brain became enlarged and gave a strong red-purple metachromatic stain. Moreover, after working over the sulfatide molecules for a few more days, some scavenger cells turned the deposits into the golden-brown color associated with human MLD. It seemed to take at least three weeks before the cell could reorganize the sulfatide molecules it had ingested. These experiments in rats finally suggested an explanation for the old mystery of why some sulfatide deposits in humans stained a golden-brown color: it took time for the appropriate arrangement of sulfatide molecules to evolve in the human deposits. The important finding, in any event, was that sulfatides caused the metachromatic phagocytes of MLD. This was now clear.

But once again, the most striking finding was completely unexpected. The surprise awaited me when I examined sections of brain from a rat injected with one of the appropriate control molecules. The following narrative illustrates an important principle—that the unexpected yield from a control experiment may be more fruitful than that from the main experiment.

First, an explanation about what the word "control" means when used in this context. Suppose you wish to test the theory that molecule X, and it alone, will cause a given abnormality in tissue. A basic philosophical principle governs the way you set up the experiment: you design the experiment as if to prove yourself wrong. Indeed, the principle is so fundamental that you become operationally defined as an investigator only to the degree that you adhere to it. This means doing more than injecting molecule X. It means you must test out at least three other groups of animals to cover (and thus to control) the unforseen pitfalls in the experiment. For example, your control groups will include: 1) no injection—this to make certain that your animals are free from a disease that might itself cause the abnormality; 2) sham injection—this to find out what changes the stress and the needle alone make; 3) injections of closely related molecules (K, Y, and Z, for instance, which resemble X)—these injections will determine whether molecule X is really unique in its effects.

In our experiment, I included cerebroside into the design of the experiment as one of the control molecules. The idea was simply to see how cells in the brain would react to injections of a relevant molecule closely resembling sulfatide but lacking a sulfate group. In fact, the only difference between the two molecules is that sulfatide has a sulfate group and cerebroside doesn't (figures 2 and 6).

The results were startling in their implications. Around the edge of the cerebroside injections, the rats had developed a most unusual tissue response. Indeed, at the injection site, sections of the rat brains resembled the tissue reaction found in yet another human disease! The human illness was called globoid leukodystrophy (GLD) (figure 6). Quite by accident, we had produced one of its manifestations in rats. At the moment this dawned on me, I felt a sober, puzzled amazement, a feeling unlike anything I had experienced during the MLD research and which remains with me to this day.

Let us observe, parenthetically, how little I knew about this other myelin disease. The few fragments of information I possessed formed no coherent picture. They were like a small handful of jigsaw puzzle pieces scattered widely about on the floor. I did recall that the disease was also termed Krabbe's disease, after the late Danish neuropathologist who described it. I reflected back to nine years before, in New York City, where I had seen my only living patient with GLD. As I examined this affected child, D.W., his clinical abnormalities did resemble those of the MLD children, but his symptoms began much earlier, when he was only four months of age. First he became abnormally fretful and cried seemingly without cause. Gradually, he developed stiffness of the neck, back, arms, and legs, accompanied by blindness and loss of mental function. Finally, he died from an extensive paralysis only ten months after his symptoms began. I obtained permission for the autopsy, looked under the microscope at the havoc the disease had caused in his brain, and saw that GLD had damaged his white matter in a very distinctive way.

Now, after a gap of many years, I was astonished to see that our rat brains had developed a replica of some of the same microscopic features of this dread human disease. Peering though the microscope, I saw many similar distended cells (figure 6). Several of these large globular cells in rat brain had more than one nucleus, and they stained the very same way as did cells in human GLD when special chemical methods were used.

Could cerebrosides also cause the globoid response in human GLD?

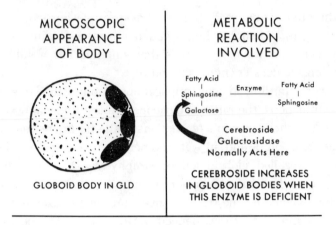

MICROSCOPIC
APPEARANCE
OF BODY

GLOBOID BODY IN GLD

METABOLIC
REACTION
INVOLVED

CEREBROSIDE INCREASES
IN GLOBOID BODIES WHEN
THIS ENZYME IS DEFICIENT

MOLECULE
DEPOSITED IN THE BODY

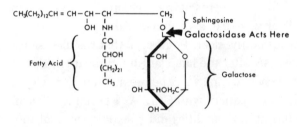

CEREBROSIDE

Figure 6. GLD; The globoid body and its chemical background.

Under the microscope, the globoid body is a distended phagocytic cell that has more than one nucleus. It contains an excess of cerebroside molecules because the cell is deficient in the enzyme cerebroside galactosidase. Normally, this enzyme splits galactose from cerebroside. By this means, the enzyme normally keeps down the level of this lipid molecule. The phagocytic cell reacts to this particular undigested molecule in a very distinctive way. It becomes globular ("globoid") and develops more than one nucleus.

Naturally, we went on to test many other control compounds. After many such rat experiments, it finally seemed clear that, yes, cerebroside molecules in particular could cause the special globoidlike response of globoid leukodystrophy.[1] What made cerebroside molecules so distinctive? Perhaps it was that they were just soluble enough to get into the cell, yet insoluble enough so that even the normal cell could only digest them and dispose of them slowly.

But the findings in rats explained only part of the problem. For the next question was: did *human* globoid bodies, in fact, also contain cerebroside? Soon I encountered more children with GLD in our medical school hospital, and all too soon they succumbed to the harsh momentum of their disease. I also wrote to other physicians who kindly sent autopsy material from their cases for us to analyze. Looking through the microscope at the broken-down human white matter, I could see many scattered clusters of the now familiar globular cells and bodies. What remained, therefore, was to take this devastated white matter, analyze it for various lipids, and see whether cerebrosides were increased. This we did.

The cerebroside results, looked at alone, were disappointing. The data did not support the hypothesis. In fact, our chemical studies soon showed that cerebrosides and *all* other lipids were *reduced* in GLD. Still, we could rationalize away this unexpected result, because the myelin sheaths of white matter that normally contain the lipids were themselves destroyed in the course of the disease (figure 7). Such a process would, of itself, reduce all the lipids. Perhaps, then, there was no absolute increase in cerebrosides, but only a *relative* one that was largely confined to globoid bodies. This turned out to be the case: cerebrosides were relatively elevated when compared with the low levels of all the other myelin lipids. The analyses of human tissue were therefore consistent with our experimental results in rats, for the human data too suggested that a local increase in cerebrosides could be the critical factor in GLD. Still, the evidence was not conclusive.

At this time, Saul Korey himself played a stimulating role in our studies. He visited our Oregon laboratory one day, and I brought him up to date with the findings in our GLD research. Saul's supple mind probed to the root of the problem, and his question was characteristically cogent: "Why analyze all that white matter; why don't you just get out the globoid bodies and look at *them?*" I protested: it would be too formidable a task to get globoid bodies out of the potpourri of other material in the diseased white matter. He agreed; it would be difficult. He also observed that progress wouldn't be made otherwise. That seemed to settle the topic; we then moved on to the next one.

Saul's challenge mobilized my efforts. I had known all along that if I wanted to understand what was inside human globoid bodies I first had to isolate them in reasonably pure form. But that seemed incredibly difficult, and I had not faced up to the issue. Furthermore, I knew I would have to learn the techniques of thin-layer chromatography. This new method of separating and identifying lipids was not simple, but it seemed much superior to the older methods we had used.

Soon, we were launched on two new fronts: isolating human globoid bodies and studying them by thin-layer chromatography. In terms of personal enjoyment, I remember the whole globoid body isolation project as one of the most fun-filled and adventurous. It involved problem-solving all the way. The techniques needed had to be more sophisticated than those used for detecting metachromatic granular bodies in MLD urine. Other requirements were also more rigorous. First, I had to find places in white matter where globoid elements were concentrated and dissect these pieces out. Next I had to free the bodies from surrounding brain tissue without destroying them in the process. This meant grinding the tissue in a loosely fitting homogenizer. Then it was essential to filter out contaminating bits of blood vessels by using a sieve. The next step was to separate out the heavier globoid bodies by centrifuging them down to the bottom of a tube filled with concentrated solutions of sucrose. Because I had very little GLD tissue, I had to make a special, small test tube for this purpose. Finally, I had to devise a new method for taking globoid bodies out from the bottom of this test tube.

It took months to work out all the "bugs" in the method. By this time, our chemical techniques were accurate enough to analyze even minute amounts of globoid-body material by chromatography. Analyses showed that the bodies contained more cerebrosides and fewer sulfatides than normal brain tissue.

How was this to be interpreted? Were cerebrosides increased locally because the enzyme that breaks them down was deficient? Or, were sulfatides decreased locally because the enzyme which builds them up was deficient?

These questions set us off on a new series of experiments.[2] Our first hypothesis was that the deficient enzyme was cerebroside galactosidase—the specific enzyme which splits galactose from cerebroside (figure 6). Unfortunately, at the time, there was no adequate way to measure just this one enzyme. Assays of other related galactosidases were normal. Tests of our second hypothesis showed that the enzyme activity which forms sulfatides was low, but not really low enough in all tissues to satisfactorily explain the disease. Clearly, GLD research had to wait for a new method to resolve the nature of the primary enzyme deficiency.

It finally arrived. Kunihiko Suzuki at Pennsylvania used an accurate new method for measuring the specific galactosidase that splits off galactose from cerebroside. This was the pertinent enzyme. Indeed, he and his group showed beyond question that in GLD this was the enzyme that was chiefly deficient.[3] Collaborating with him and with Roscoe Brady[4] at the National Institutes of Health, we could jointly confirm his finding in our own case material. The deficiency of this galactosidase readily explained why cerebroside was locally increased in the globoid bodies.

A form of GLD also occurs in dogs—in certain inbred strains of West Highland terriers. I knew I had seen this dog somewhere before: it is the white dog on the label of the bottle of "Black and White" scotch! Soon we followed up the studies in human GLD with a collaborative study of the same enzyme in terriers who inherited GLD. We found that GLD dogs had the same galactosidase deficiency as did humans.[5] As we shall see, this would not be the only time dogs would play a vital role in our research.

Two things counted in the GLD studies (figure 8). One was the unexpected finding in *control* experiments that a globoidlike response occurred in rats injected with cerebroside. The other was Saul Korey's prodding to develop a new method. Once we had this basic method, we could then modify it. Later, it would be these modified techniques that would enable us to go on to isolate a whole series of different abnormal structures from human brains in several other diseases (figure 13). But these studies would not unfold for years, and in the interim, some hard international realities, confronting everyone, would have tangible unforseen effects on my personal and professional life.

8.

Enzymes and India, 1961, 1962–1963

There can be no more important education today than education for
personal effectiveness and a sense of connection with big events. However
impressive a man's acquisition of worldly knowledge, however proficient
his ability to marry theory to technique, if he cannot use his thinking
ability and his skills to work for a safer and better world, his education is
incomplete and he is in trouble.

Norman Cousins

My own research has been indelibly influenced by my personal beliefs
and style of living. Nonscientific interests have repeatedly come back to
enrich and invigorate my scientific career.

Take my interests in the outdoors as one example, and those in a rational world order as another. Judy and I enjoyed hiking around Mount
Monadnock in New Hampshire before we were married. Later on, we
were drawn to the American West by its splendid opportunities for
camping, hiking, and fishing. At a faculty party in Oregon, we happened to meet George Dana and his wife, Betsey, and soon found out
that they too had lived earlier near Mount Monadnock. It then turned
out that the Danas were local pillars of an organization called the
United World Federalists. Through the Danas we then became friends
with Phil and Rhita Feingold. Phil, a personable insurance executive,
had been working actively in the World Federalist movement since
college. Through Phil we then met Norman Cousins, President of the
World Association, and were immensely impressed, both by the man
and by his writing. We learned from all these new friends about the goal
of the World Federalists: gradually to strengthen the United Nations
into a really effective body for world government. Judy, and then I, became very much interested in this movement.

Those who remember the start of the cold war, the nuclear overtones
of the 1950s, the fears of an atomic holocaust, and the ominous talk of
bomb shelters throughout the United States, will understand why we

preferred the ultimate alternative of a federal system of law and order transposed onto the international level.

By then, I had a firsthand familiarity with the consequences of war, because I had dressed wounded flesh both in World War II and during the Korean episode. I came to an intense personal realization that my puny efforts to save a few neurological patients would be futile if we were all wiped out by atomic warfare. Moreover, there seemed to be little point in expressing myself creatively as a father of three and as an investigator if everything were soon to be expunged. Thus, like many other citizens, I grew increasingly alert to political issues. Passive acceptance of the situation was not for me. If I were to have any relevance to society, and it to me, I must become involved in political activity—and not work solely in the hospital or in the laboratory.

What was the best course of action under these circumstances? What concrete action should I take—something more than a token demonstration—that might have some remote chance of altering political events in the future?

India. We were drawn toward India for several reasons. It was a country that did not yet have a centralized World Federalist movement, and we thought we could help organize this effort there. Under Prime Minister Nehru, Indian was then one of the leaders of the nonaligned nations. Citizens of these neutral nations were increasingly called upon to be "honest brokers" between the Communist and non-Communist world (a role exemplified by UN Secretaries General Dag Hammarskjold and U Thant). India was also a pivotal country: the largest democratic country, racked by unrest, it could readily fall into a dictatorship. We were under no illusions about how much we could really accomplish in a subcontinent this vast. But however small the result, we knew that making the constructive effort was the only way to live and to respond to the situation in the world at that time.

In medicine, it turned out that New Delhi offered an interesting opportunity. The new medical school at the All-India Institute lacked both a neurology department and a head of neurology. If I could make even a small personal contribution in a school this young, it might lead to a relatively more lasting impression on the subsequent development of neurology.

My first big conflict was whether to spend one-half of my year's sabbatical from Oregon at the Karolinska Institute in Stockholm. Some months before I had completed plans to learn electron microscopy in Sweden, but I soon decided that the experience in India was more in tune with the realities of the times. So, India, it would be.

In 1961, I made a trip to India to see which of several positions would be most fruitful. At that time, the international situation was not merely grim, it was downright ominous. Neighbors in Portland were building bomb shelters in their basements. During my trip, the USSR resumed atomic testing in the atmosphere, and the Berlin Wall was erected. Democracy seemed imperiled. It was difficult to keep a sense of perspective in the downhill spiraling thrust of world events. What influence could one man have?

I stopped over in Athens and attended the "Sound and Light" performance, a superb outdoor dramatization of the ancient history of Greece. I was oddly reassured by what I saw. For that night, the performance vividly reminded me that once before, in 499 B.C., the whole future of Western civilization also had hung in the balance. The issue was decided then by the narrow margin of the efforts of a bare handful of men who managed to eke out a victory over the Persians.

From a scientific standpoint, the key portion of my first two-week visit to India was the trip to the Christian Medical College in Vellore. There, in the south of India, I first met Professor Bimal Bachhawat and visited his laboratory. I had followed his research reports in the journals for some years, and knew we had interests in common. Since receiving his Ph.D. in biochemistry at Illinois, he had been studying many different enzymes. He and I were in our mid-thirties and soon became close friends. I mentioned our histochemical studies on sulfatases and our ideas about a sulfatase deficiency as the enzymic cause of metachromatic leukodystrophy. We decided to pool our resources.

Our meeting in India produced a true cross-fertilization of ideas. Thereafter, our Oregon laboratory would become more oriented toward the assay of enzymes in the test tube and Bimal's would become more oriented toward sulfatides.

When I returned to Oregon from this brief visit to India, I set about creating a shipping box. We needed a special container to carry our frozen MLD specimens and pertinent control tissues of other diseases all the way to India. The logistics of this effort were complicated, but with the help of much insulation and repeated packings of dry ice en route, the shipment finally reached Bimal by air express still safely frozen.

Fortunately, Bimal and I had chosen to start our analyses on that special variety of MLD found in the McLean family (p. 27). We didn't know it then, but in most tissues these patients were deficient in all three sulfatases (sulfatase A, sulfatase B, and sulfatase C).* We couldn't miss finding a sulfatase deficiency, regardless of which sulfatase method we used. Studying any of the three enzymes would still have shown the deficiency. The chemical method used would give a low result if either sulfatase A, or sulfatase B, or both were deficient. And, when we tested histochemically with our modified method for sulfatase C, the deficiency was so marked that my first thought was we must have made some mistake. In contrast, we were delighted to find normal values for all the other nonsulfatase enzymes in the MLD tissue. We controlled and repeated all the observations several times to be certain they were valid. They held up. Clearly, the sulfatase deficiency was specific for MLD.

But which sulfatase deficiency caused the usual form of MLD—the form in which there was a sulfatide excess only? By this time I was in the midst of my sabbatical year, 1962–63, in New Delhi, but fortunately, I had kept our laboratory running in Oregon. In Portland, we still had living MLD patients and could analyze their urine for sulfatase activity. This was possible because some of the enzyme normally made in the kidney escapes into the urine. After studying several MLD patients and many controls, it was clear that all our living patients with the usual form of MLD were deficient in sulfatase A only. Sulfatase B (and C) were normal (figure 7).

Had we not chosen to go to India for largely nonscientific reasons, I would not have met Bimal Bachhawat and started our fruitful scientific venture. The sabbatical was personally rewarding for other reasons. Judy and I worked with a number of enthusiastic Indian men and women of Federalist persuasion. We were able to help start in motion the union of these World Federalist groups that was finally centered in New Delhi. Something else got started: four young Indian doctors who

---

* Liver was a curious exception.

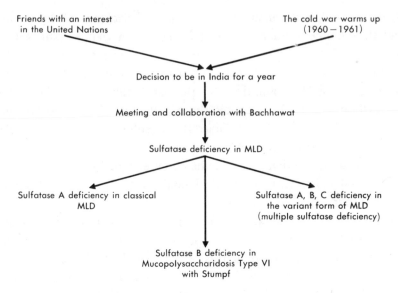

Figure 7. Evolution of Sulfatase Research

studied neurology with me elected to go on and specialize in neurology. Men and women whose training one influences are among the deepest satisfactions that come in academic medicine.

The sabbatical year in India was packed full of colorful cultural surprises. There was, for example, a matter of adjusting to cultural differences in communication and to the sanitary realities of food and drink. We got our first taste of this when a fellow American told us about an enlightening experience she had with her cook. To avoid food infections, she had gone to great pains carefully to instruct her cook to first soak all vegetables from the market in a solution of potassium permanganate. This burgundy colored, penetrating liquid has the useful property of killing microscopic cysts that are an ever-present cause of amebic dysentery. For weeks all went well in the kitchen with the carrots, lettuce, spinach, and other vegetables. But one day, while checking periodically (as one does), she discovered to her amazement that the beets had gone unsoaked. "Why?" she asked. The cook's explanation was simple. "I didn't think I had to soak beets, because they were already red to begin with!"

And then there was the festival of Holi. On this day of celebration, everyone dresses in old apparel appropriate for the rigors of the occasion, and then ventures out of the house laden with powdered pigments of many bright colors—reds, blues, greens, oranges, and yellows. The object is, quite literally, to transform one's friends and neighbors—turning them into a kaleidoscope of colors and dousing them with water too—until everyone, in a frenzy of sputtering, gasping and giggling, turns into a walking Jackson Pollock painting. On Holi day, no one is spared the creative mayhem of his fellows, and if anything, the medical school faculty catches more than its share from the emancipated medical students, residents, and interns. The festival takes its legendary roots in the playful behavior of the milkmaid, Radha, toward her lover, Krishna, but nowadays it assumes the proportions of a gigantic Halloween prank in which people of all ages and stations, friend and stranger alike, share in the mass excitement of giving and receiving. No Westerner will ever forget the unique experience of this riot of color, of being painted on, and painting in return.

Looking back, it is clear that this sabbatical year in India involved some political meddling. This kind of extracurricular activity is not automatically bad, but it is next to impossible to justify to some of your scientific colleagues. I can still see the arched eyebrows with which Professors Adams, Swank, and Korey greeted the announcement that I was going to India for a year. Still, as James Newman has put it: "The responsible scientist must be a meddler. The tendency to regard the scientist as defiled if he mixes in social and political activities arises from the widespread failure to understand that science lies at the center of the network of human affairs."[1]

In this chapter we have observed how intimately one's personal and professional life can be interwoven in the course of an ongoing scientific quest. But there are other elements of the search taking shape long before the investigator comes to maturity. It is from the chase that, years later, the quest evolves. Even now, it is still possible to perceive the earlier behavior patterns, but you have to know where and how to look. Let us, then, climb up the stairs into the attic, open a dusty trunk, and peer into a musty old family album. As our eyes accommodate to the dim light, we begin to perceive in outline an earlier version of the search and see why it sometimes takes on the flavor, persistence, and curious impracticality of the chase.

9.

Flashback; The Chase, 1942

In the album are old clippings from the local newspaper, faded and yellow with age. The print remains clear, however, and the reporter's words, given verbatim below, are still revealing. We move back in time to February 12, 1942. It is mid-winter; the sun is low; snow is on the ground.

WEARIED RABBIT ADMITS DEFEAT AFTER TWO HOUR CHASE
(From *The News*, Robert Edgar, editor)

It was a toss-up, which was more winded, the boy or the rabbit, last Saturday afternoon when Jim Austin stood sweating and dirty in the Police Station, clutching in his arms the weary but squirming body of a wild rabbit.

Jim, age seventeen, was brought into the station after police answered the calls which began to pour into the station from frantic housewives along Bedford Road who reported that a "mad man" and a "lunatic" was seen dashing through the grounds, diving under fences, leaping hedges, and in general cavorting in a "highly suspicious" fashion all around the neighborhood.

The capture came at the conclusion of what Jim later told police had been a two hour chase, all around that section down as far as Three Mile Drive during which he had kept on the trail of the rabbit by its footprints in the snow. "I thought I had lost him one time," Jim confessed, "but I got my second wind."

After the first hour, Jim was on his trail, which by this time was becoming more and more difficult to follow, for Peter was using the same route over and over again. Once Peter ran down the middle of Bedford Road for almost a block and Jim was dismayed; there were no tracks left. He started to walk up the road when he saw Peter, who had paused for a breathing spell, resting near the sign on the corner. The chase was on again.

The rabbit ran into a hole one time, and Jim about gave the chase up, but luck was with him. Another rabbit was already in the hole, an inhospitable rabbit who chased the visitor out. When Jim finally picked up the wild bunny, he instantly recognized him as a former victim whom he had previously caught and let go.

Jim's wind and his ambition may have been proven beyond contradiction last Saturday. But it was a wearied and disarrayed boy who took his way home. His face was muddy with combined dust and sweat. The scarf, tied around his throat, was wet to the saturation point, and his trousers and sweater were completely covered with brambles and burrs.

Assured that, since he was planning to turn the animal loose, there was no criminal or civil charge, Jim was pretty relieved. After all, it would be pretty hard to face the kids as an ex-con.

10.

Tom and Lafora Bodies, 1965

Because new elements, variable and unforeseen can introduce themselves into the conditions of a phenomenon, it follows that logic alone will never suffice in the experimental sciences.

Claude Bernard

Among chosen combinations the most fertile will often be those formed of elements drawn from domains which are far apart.

Henri Poincaré

His name was Tom. He was a handsome, intense, vigorous Brittany spaniel. As the name suggests, spaniels are a hunting breed originating in Spain. Almost 2,000 years ago, Sallust and Pliny described how their Roman compatriots brought pointing spaniels back from Spain and introduced them into France and Italy.[1] Down through the ages, pointing spaniels have always been dogs who show you where the game is.

My longing for a dog of my own to accompany me in the field and forest dates back to early childhood. I waited until I was thirty-eight to own one. Were it not for my passion for running around in the out-of-doors, we should never have acquired this dog. And without Tom, the following events would never have occurred.

The sabbatical year on the dry plains of India was now over, and I was once again back among the green rolling hills of Oregon. We had meandered on from an interest in MLD into the field of other metachromatic molecules. These included hyaluronic acid (chapter 6) and other related sulfated mucopolysaccharides. These molecules are important constituents of the connective tissues which normally hold the body together. Now we needed techniques to identify, and then measure, these different sulfated molecules. The chemical journals described innumerable methods. (This invariably means that no one method is satisfactory.) Margo and I decided to devise some of our own methods. The thin-layer chromatographic methods we finally came up with could detect as little as five micrograms (five millionths of a gram) of sulfated polysaccharides. We originally used these methods to characterize the excess of sulfated polysaccharides in the two MLD children of the McLean family.[2] Would these same methods help us understand any other disease?

I thought back to an illness called Lafora's disease. I had seen one patient with this disease during my training in New York. The disorder affects teenagers, causing epileptic seizures, abrupt muscular jerks (myoclonus), and a progressive deterioration of their mental abilities. Like MLD and globoid leukodystrophy, Lafora's myoclonus epilepsy is inherited as a recessive trait. In families with the disease it affects one out of four adolescents on an average. It is recognized microscopically by the presence of small round red-staining bodies inside the cytoplasm of nerve cells (figure 8). They look like tiny marbles and are called Lafora bodies after the Portuguese neuropathologist who first described them. I had seen them in books but never under the microscope.

We started to study the disease on the wrong assumption. Our mistake was to think that Lafora bodies might contain acid mucopolysaccharides. We thought we could find these complex sugar molecules using our newer method, and were led into this false line of reasoning because existing histochemical techniques were not specific enough.

Soon we were joined in this research by Susumu Yokoi. "Sum" was a neuropsychiatrist and the first of several outstanding Japanese co-workers who came to our laboratory. We had first met in Tokyo in 1962 and were drawn together by our mutual interest in leukodystrophies. I was delighted to find that he and his family wished to come to our laboratory.

I was already partial to the Japanese. When I was stationed there in 1950–51, during the Korean War, I was struck by the beauty of the land, the ancient culture, the industry and friendliness of the people. I felt a deep kinship with their perception that the simplest elements of Nature—the drop of dew, the fallen blossom—were among the most sacred. I envied the way their gardens and homes created a tranquil atmosphere amid the hustle and bustle of their crowded islands. Traditional Japanese qualities of persistence and manual dexterity would soon also impress me in the laboratory.

When Sum arrived, the obvious plan was to isolate Lafora bodies by the same general techniques we had used earlier to isolate globoid bodies. But Lafora's disease is rare. We had no autopsy material to start with. Then, I happened to encounter Dr. Richard Berry when we were both waiting for an elevator at a medical meeting. The elevator took longer than usual to arrive, and we struck up a conversation that continued for about ten minutes. I indicated that we had some new analytical methods to study Lafora's disease, and thereafter he obligingly sent us the material we needed. His kindness at this point was crucial.

We then went on to modify our previous isolation method, first used in globoid leukodystrophy. Sum centrifuged out the Lafora bodies in modest yield, extracted them in a way which should yield mucopolysaccharides, and applied the extract for chromatography. No spot appeared. There were *no* acid mucopolysaccharides. We were up a blind alley. I was not only chagrined; I felt very stupid.

Tom, the spaniel, now came to the rescue. Always a spirited animal, Tom frequently coursed far afield. His white and rich rust-brown colored coat usually showed up well at a distance, but one day we were both going into thick cover. In order to know where he was, I took the precaution of tying a small bell to the front of his collar. The bell is worth noting.

A few days later I noticed a rapidly growing mass on the front of Tom's neck. The growth was hard, slightly tender, not obviously warm, and seemed to be malignant, both in my judgment and in that of Thomas Fletcher, a surgical colleague who was doing research on malignant tumors in dogs. Dr. Fletcher suggested that the mass be removed at once. Unfortunately, I had to leave town to present a paper at a medical meeting and would have to miss the operation. I had a very empty feeling during this trip away from home, because a friend and companion in the field soon becomes one of the family. The thought that this vigorously active dog would be slowed by a cancer moved me to despair.

On my return, Tom bounded up to greet me in his usual frisky manner. The microscopic diagnosis, to everyone's surprise, was not that of a malignant tumor after all. Instead, the slides showed a subacute inflammatory response involving some of the lymph glands in Tom's neck. We were baffled as to what might be the cause of this inflammation. Tuberculosis? Yeast? Fungi? I asked the technicians to make more sections of the tissue and stain them especially for these organisms. A few days later, I heard that the new sections from the mass showed an unusual round "fungus." I hurried over to surgical pathology to look. Round structures were indeed there, and they were *red*. Curiously, they lay around the outside of the mass. None lay inside. All the infectious disease specialists duly called in for sober-minded consultation solemnly shook their heads, for they had never seen a fungus quite like this before. Finally, someone on the surgical service brightened with a happy thought. Perhaps these were not fungi, but round spherules of starch!

Starch? Starch, we all now recalled, is used to dust surgical gloves. Some of it could have remained on the gloves during Tom's operation and could have been transferred to the outside of the mass when it was resected.

When I checked out this possibility and looked at starch dust under the microscope, I finally realized that starch is made up of round spherules. Moreover, because starch is composed of many sugar (glucose) molecules, the starch in Tom's biopsy turned red when stained with a special histochemical stain for sugars. When these elementary facts entered my awareness, they completely transformed our approach to Lafora's disease. Could Lafora bodies in humans be some kind of starch?

To answer this question, I set out with dogged (so to speak) determination to obtain many different kinds of starch. I then studied their size, shape, and histochemical staining characteristics. Soon I could prove that starch spherules and Lafora body spherules shared several things in common: strong red staining for carbohydrate, dense staining with iodine and silver. In addition, both structures sometimes had a Y-shaped crack in the center. Collectively, these findings suggested a new hypothesis: Lafora bodies were not an acid mucopolysaccharide; instead, they were quite a different kind of molecule—one made up of many sugar units linked together in a long chain to form a polymer. Based on this line of reasoning, we abruptly shifted the focus of our research. We turned toward the requisite techniques of chromatography and infrared spectrophotometry. These permitted us to confirm our hypothesis. Within a few weeks we finally knew that Lafora bodies, like starch, were essentially a glucose polymer (figure 8).[3]

By hindsight, it seemed reasonable to postulate that Tom's original inflammation came when the lymph glands in his neck were irritated by repeated contact with his new bell. Next came the operation, and finally, the starch from the surgeon's glove. Without doubt, the pace of our study was accelerated enormously by the chance placement and chance finding of starch in his biopsy specimen. To me, the fragile web of circumstances involved in this whole episode will always remain fantastic, yet one can perceive some of the sequences by looking at them longitudinally and analyzing them from some different perspectives (figure 9).

The crucial point in the story is the intersection between the personal hobby (involving the dog) and the scientific problem (the Lafora body). The two lines meet by chance. A moment of closure occurred where the two joined. Thereafter, the solution almost suggested itself.

If you've ever had an experience like this, you may also have emerged from it sobered and awed, and, one would hope, not left with a fatalistic attitude. Nothing in this story is intended to mean that you can blunder along to a fruitful conclusion, pushed there solely by external events and lacking any sense of your own mental or physical participation. No, the hard core of work involved in research is too much a reality to ignore. Rather, what seems to be superimposed on the conscious work are some personalized drives and sensibilities interacting with chance. Later, we will say more about the qualities of mind, temperament and instinct that underlie this kind of experience. For the moment, let me

MICROSCOPIC APPEARANCE OF BODY	METABOLIC REACTION INVOLVED
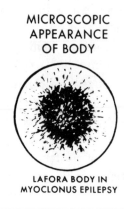 LAFORA BODY IN MYOCLONUS EPILEPSY	Not Yet Known

MOLECULE
DEPOSITED IN THE BODY

CH₂OH   CH₂OH

POLYGLUCOSAN

Figure 8. The Lafora body and its chemical background.
Under the microscope, the Lafora body is spherical and is found inside nerve cells. Chemically, it contains many sugar molecules linked together. In the chemical formula, each hexagonal-shaped link in the chain represents a molecule of glucose.

note that the episode with Tom the dog can be used as an example of the "barking up the right tree" phenomenon. It means that if you happen to be the kind of person who hunts afield, it may be, in fact, your dog who leads you up to the correct tree, and to a desirable conclusion.

The story has unfolded still further. Once we had the new technical momentum developed during the Lafora body study, we could next plunge into an entirely new field—aging of the brain. For example, when we modified our earlier methods, we could then proceed to isolate and analyze other round structures such as amyloid bodies (corpora amylacea),[4] senile plaques and cores,[5] and finally Lewy bodies.[6] Our hope is that when we know more about the chemistry of each of these

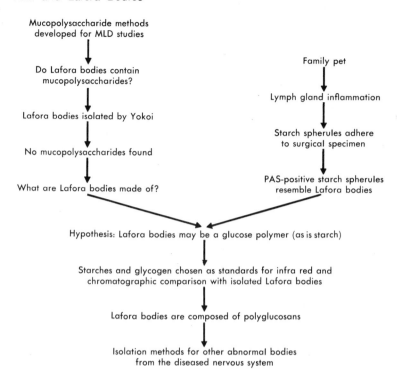

Figure 9. Evolution of the Research in Lafora's Myoclonus Epilepsy

structures, we may understand why some cerebral functions dwindle as the brain grows older. Now, we have become fully engaged in aging research. We are there not only because our own technical capabilities have carried us in, but also because a former graduate student, Donald Armstrong, made the interesting observation that a model disease of aging was associated with a reduction in soluble peroxidase enzyme activity.[7]

11.

Finger Prints on the Window; Filling in the Hole

Every child knows that prevention is not only better than cure, but also cheaper.

Henry Sigerist

Whether he is an archaeologist, chemist, or astronomer, at heart the researcher's goal is very much the same. Basically, he looks for facts that interest him and then tries to arrange them in meaningful sequence. The researcher in any field is an *"adverbial man."* He defines *what* happens, then figures out *where, when, how,* and *why* it happens. His adverbial search for cause and effect, for the basic order in things, is primal, compelling, and satisfying, quite apart from practical considerations.

Who does research in medical schools? It depends on where you look. If you look in the laboratories of basic science departments (e.g., biochemistry), the vast majority, 73 percent, are Ph.D.'s, whereas 18 percent are M.D.'s and 9 percent hold both the Ph.D. and the M.D. degree. However, in the clinical departments (e.g., neurology), an even greater percentage, 89 percent, are M.D.'s, only 5 percent are Ph.D.'s, and 6 percent hold both degrees.[1] Overall, there are over twice as many M.D.'s as Ph.D.'s in medical schools, but more Ph.D.'s (11 percent) are involved solely in research than are M.D.'s: 2 percent. Still, it is the rare Ph.D. or engineer who actually goes into the *medical* sciences. For example, only 5 percent of a total number of 265,500 doctoral scientists and engineers were, in fact, in the field of medicine.[2]

A young physician makes a substantial financial sacrifice if he pursues an academic career in a medical school. If, for example, he takes a two-year fellowship to learn research after his residency training, his net loss could range from about $48,000 if he is a psychiatrist, to $137,000 if he is a radiologist.[3]

To such a physician responsible for the daily care of his patients, his role as a laboratory researcher brings more than its share of conflicts. Can he really justify long hours spent in the laboratory, when caring for patients at the bedside has so many other advantages, both tangible and intangible?

A favorite anecdote of Dr. Alan Gregg provides an illuminating answer.[4] One day, Dr. Henry Forbes told Gregg of a vision he had of a long line of patients waiting to see him—a line extending far out of his office and into the street. He already knew what their diagnosis was: each had sprained an ankle stepping into a deep hole in the sidewalk outside. Forbes felt keenly the source of his own dilemma. It was simple: he was just so busy seeing patients in pain with sprained ankles that he never had the opportunity to go out and fill the hole.*

Why research? To fill in the hole.

But not just any kind of research will do. There is a great call nowadays for research that is "relevant." If his studies in the laboratory become too impractical, the experimentalist is soon brought back to reality by the stark human tragedies he faces in the wards and clinics. The world seems all too close when we follow children who were previously normal and see them slowly crippled by diseases of the nervous system. The following lines taken from the letter of a mother whose child developed MLD illustrate the situation:

> Can you imagine the anguish connected with wiping little finger marks from a window—knowing that the hand which once put them there still wants to touch the window but now cannot? Can you imagine the impact of seeing one's own bright and beautiful child stop developing and then regress to nothing?

I can imagine it, but not of course to the same degree. My encounters with pneumonia, accidents, meningitis, cancer, and myocarditis either in myself or in members of my family have been far too close for comfort. It is as the worried patient or relative that one learns best what illness really means in human terms. Indeed, I believe a physician who has never experienced a major illness in himself or in his family has missed a crucial part of his medical education. It pays to be sick some-

---

* The chance conversation that Alan Gregg had with Henry Forbes that day led young Gregg to a momentous decision—he would go into public health and preventive medicine. Shortly thereafter, Forbes, too, changed his orientation from private practice and went into neurophysiological research.

times, both as a reminder of what illness is and of how lucky we are to be healthy.

12.

Overview: What Next? So What?

Again I saw that under the sun the race is not to the swift, nor the battle
to the strong, nor bread to the wise, nor riches to the intelligent, nor favor
to the men of skill; but time and chance happen to them all.

Ecclesiastes, 9.11

Time and chance have a way of deciding things: such as which project our laboratory is going to take on next and how far we're going to go with it. The future isn't clear. You can appreciate some of the reasons for this uncertainty by glancing at figure 10. Here is one schematic version of how in the past the growing points of research have budded out, grown into branches, and how one field of study proliferated into another. Clearly, there is a conceptual link between research in metachromatic and globoid leukodystrophy. But there is no rational way to link hypertrophic neuritis (lower left) with Lewy bodies (top right) except by tenuous meanderings and chance encounters through five other intervening disorders.

What is all this work leading up to? What are the ultimate goals? Let's step out from among the branches and take a look at the tree as a whole. In general our laboratory has been concerned with inherited diseases caused by an inborn metabolic error. We have been working at the interface between molecular biology and medicine. Three themes have been under investigation: polyneuropathies, deposition disorders, and aging of the brain (figure 10, at top). None of these themes or interrelationships was preordained; each has grown haphazardly by a certain curious, inconsistent, internal logic of its own. In broad outline, these have been more meanderings than searches, more peregrinations (wanderings) than trips.

And none of our work is completed. Some of the task will be taken on by subsequent generations of investigators. How do we define comple-

	DEPOSITION DISORDERS			AGEING OF THE BRAIN
POLY-NEUROPATHIES	SULFATED MUCO-POLYSACCHARIDES	LIPIDS	POLY-GLUCOSANS	

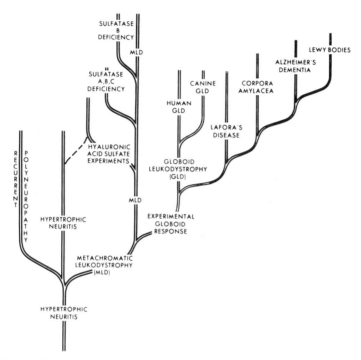

Figure 10. Evolution of the studies starting with hypertrophic neuritis.

My early interests in hypertrophic neuritis (lower left), proliferated into several new and seemingly unrelated lines of research. The headings at the top indicate the general category of molecule or disease that was studied.

tion? The pragmatic physician must define it in terms of total eradication or effective treatment of disease. Only in one disorder, recurrent polyneuropathy (figure 10, at left), has our research yet led to a treatment. Even then, the treatment with adrenal cortical hormones has only suppressed the disease, not cured it. The discovery was empirical; the treatment just happened to work. It then took five long years of controlled study before we were certain it did work.[1] We still have no solid conceptual understanding of what causes this illness, why it recurs, nor do we understand, in precise molecular terms, why the treatment with corticosteroid hormones helps the nerves. Currently, the cause and ultimate treatment of hypertrophic neuritis is also unknown.

What next, then, in the diseases in which molecules are deposited—the deposition disorders? Better to understand what must come next, it will first be useful to review some steps leading up to the causes of diseases that are genetically determined. Here an awesome realization confronts us: we must be dealing with an enormous number of diseases. For example, some first-order approximations have been made of the number of enzymes in man. Here, we may venture a figure of 100,000 enzymes for purposes of discussion (estimates range from 50,000 to 150,000). The cell produces each enzyme according to the blueprint lodged in a specific gene unit of DNA (deoxyribonucleic acid). In theory, whenever this DNA changes (as a result of mutation in its chemical structure) then its corresponding enzyme would change; *each altered enzyme could have its corresponding disease.* A tiny change in DNA can be a blueprint for disaster. To sum up:

normal DNA $\xrightarrow{\text{mutation}}$ abnormal DNA $\longrightarrow$ abnormal enzyme $\longrightarrow$ metabolic disease.

The medical implications of these metabolic diseases become staggering. At present, perhaps only 2,000 genetic diseases are known to exist. We may know a few facts about these 2,000 disorders of enzyme and other proteins, but that still leaves a potential 98,000 more still to be discovered and understood. We are barely on the threshold of this problem; our medical mission is perhaps 2 percent accomplished! The collective impact of the genetic disorders to be added to this list will have an enormous influence on biomedical sciences and on the future of mankind in general.

Does the possibility of having an abnormal gene seem too remote for the reader to consider? If so, it may be noted that, on the average, each seemingly healthy person carries an abnormal "genetic load" of perhaps four deleterious genes. We are all carriers of inborn metabolic diseases.

In preceding chapters, we have seen how an understanding of an inborn metabolic disease evolves through the following sequences: clinical description, pathological description, histochemical clues, chemical identification of the corresponding enzyme that is decreased in activity.

Here, we must apply the "so what?" test. Well, so what? Now that we have this information, what practical value, if any, does it have? Let us consider four examples:

Turning back to MLD, it now appears possible to diagnose MLD in the unborn fetus. Fetal cells show the sulfatase A deficiency.[2] This means that the informed parents can decide, if they wish, to end the pregnancy. If they do, they will be spared the heartache and expense of rasing a child soon to die of a progressive neurological disorder, and can later go on to have normal children if they choose.

Now, one can also identify seemingly normal carriers, who may transmit the disease, even before they have children.[3] The technique is called genetic screening. If each parent carries the recessive gene, and if they have four children, then one child (on an average) will come down with the disease. Two of the four would be carriers, but like their parents, would be symptom-free. One of the four children would not be a carrier and would be both genetically free and clinically free of the disease. The ultimate hope of eradicating MLD lies in identifying and saving this entirely normal child.

Some patients will not develop the symptoms of MLD until later in life. What of them? Some day, we may have a drug which will increase the biochemical activity of their deficient enzyme. This statement of faith hinges on three recent observations. First, we found that the sulfatase A enzyme is *not* absent in MLD. The enzyme protein is present,[4] but its structure is chemically altered in a way that renders it inactive.[5] Now that we know the enzyme protein is present, we have something to work with, something to improve.

Second, we found, to our astonishment, a way to increase the activity and stability of the normal enzyme. This increase occurred when we combined sulfatase A with another molecule that reacted intimately with it. (This other molecule happened to be an antibody to the enzyme.) What we hope to do now is design still another appropriate molecule, small enough to enter the nervous system, that will combine there with the abnormal enzyme and enchance some of its low activity. The two important findings above were made by Dave Stumpf and Ed Neuwelt, two outstanding medical students who have done extraordinarily fine research in MLD in our laboratory.

Third, it has been shown that the activity of an abnormal enzyme can be increased by using the kind of approach just described. For example, a biochemist, Dr. Norman Radin, and his colleagues recently found that they could increase the activity of the normal enzyme, cerebroside galactosidase (figure 6), when they combined it with a smaller molecule.[6] I happened to run into Norman at the meeting at which he first presented his work. He and I have now collaborated in a study carrying this observation one step further. In test tube experiments, he found that the same small molecule could also increase the trace amount of activity of the abnormal cerebroside galactosidase that occurs in globoid leukodystrophy (GLD).[7] We can now see whether this or some related molecule will work in a living patient with GLD. And we don't have to experiment in humans to do so; there exists a precise animal model for GLD: the West Highland and Cairn terriers that have the same galactosidase enzyme deficiency found in humans.[8]

Once we know which molecule is increased in a disease, there are several ways to bring its levels down to normal. For example, it isn't necessary to focus only on the enzyme that normally disposes of the molecule. We might be able to inhibit the enzyme system producing the molecule. This would be another way to reduce the elevated levels of sulfatides in MLD. Some years from now we might even try to correct the abnormal DNA itself using appropriate drugs or even viruses. If its DNA were restored to normal, the cell could then go on to produce a normal enzyme. I cite these "science fiction" approaches to indicate how molecular biology has opened up an exciting range of therapeutic possibilities in what seemed to be only yesterday a hopeless field of medicine.

In the interim, what other function do deposition diseases serve? They serve as models—as prototypes. Progress in understanding, or in diagnosis or therapy in any one disease, makes it much easier to advance in other similar diseases. For example, years ago we developed a simple inescapable hypothesis. Given the sulfatase A deficiency in MLD, there ought to exist another disease caused by a deficiency of sulfatase B. We searched for a long time. Now, Dave Stumpf, the same exceptional medical student who worked on MLD, has finally pinpointed such a disease[9] (Type VI mucopolysaccharidosis; Maroteaux-Lamy Disease) (figure 7). These patients accumulate molecules of sulfated mucopolysaccharide because they lack sulfatase B and thus cannot split off sulfate groups. Given the backlog of experience with MLD, it should now be possible to understand and, ultimately, to treat this disease more effectively.

In overview, medical scientists can now visualize many of the storage diseases in their broader biological perspective. We have this greater conceptual understanding because of the pioneering work begun in 1949 by the Belgians, de Duve, Hers, Van Hoof, and their collaborators. These investigators characterized small particles, called lysosomes, in living cells.[10] Lysosomes contain many enzymes that collectively break down all major constituents inside our cells: lipids, carbohydrates, proteins, and nucleic acids. Such digestive enzymes normally help the cell avoid abnormally high concentrations of these molecules. Sulfatase A, sulfatase B, and cerebroside galactosidase are included among these lysosomal enzymes. In short, lysosomes can be viewed as the digestive apparatus of the cell. If lysosomes lack one digestive enzyme, then the molecule they normally would digest builds up in the cell and stays there. We can visualize MLD as a disease in which lysosomes lacking sulfatase A cannot dispose of sulfatide molecules. In this sense, MLD is a "lysosomal" disease.

In most of the other diseases at the right in figure 10, we now have a general idea which molecule is increased, but still do not know what this means in enzymic terms. If not in our own laboratory, then elsewhere, someone personally interacting with some equally incredible circumstances, will come up with the answers sooner or later.

We have spoken of mutations in the medical sense, as though they were all bad. But as biologists we realize that the genetic accidents we call mutations have been the basic fact responsible for the evolution of mankind up to Cro Magnon man and beyond. Monod emphasizes this fascinating point about mutations: "Since they constitute the *only* possible source of modifications in the genetic text, itself the *sole* repository of the organism's hereditary structures, it necessarily follows that chance *alone* is at the source of every innovation, of all creation in the biosphere."[11] Anything this important deserves our attention. Let's look next at chance, and then at creativity.

TWO

The Varieties of Chance

What is life but a series of inspired follies?
The difficulty is to find them
to do. Never lose a chance:
it doesn't come every day.

George Bernard Shaw

13.

Chance and the Creative Adventure

But if adventure has a final and all-embracing motive, it is surely this: we go out because it is in our nature to go out, to climb the mountains and sail the seas, to fly to the planets and plunge into the depths of the oceans. By doing these things, we make touch with something outside or behind, which strangely seems to approve our doing them. We extend our horizon, we expand our being, we revel in a mastery of ourselves which gives an impression, mainly illusory, that we are masters of our world. In a word,we are men, and when man ceases to do these things, he is no longer man.

Wilfred Noyce

If you are completely candid with yourself, you will soon discover how much your discoveries hinge on contingencies. Every now and then, when you happen to combine both boldness and skill, you may be able to exploit a few of the lucky situations that arise. But skill alone will not be enough, for much of the novelty in creativity is decided only when you are bold enough to thrust at chance.

At this pivotal moment, research is more than all the things we have discussed thus far. In essence, it is an adventure. To be fully creative, you must respond positively to the risk and the challenge of exploring new frontiers. This mobilization of self to seek out and confront a new situation, whatever its primitive origins and subsequent refinements, is a powerful agent of creative discovery. One of my teachers of neurology at Columbia, Professor Houston Merritt, used to say, "Behold the turtle, he makes progress only when he sticks his neck out." Like the lowly turtle, we too will only lurch forward if we first stick our necks out to look around, then chance the consequences. We must take the chance.

We do need a sense of adventure in our lives, and adventurous impulses may appear in some other form if they are not channeled off into our work. Why do I think this is so? Each summer when I stop work and go on vacation, we head up into the mountains for two or three weeks of camping and fishing. Two days after camp is set up, I start becoming very relaxed and "loose." At this time, I develop what I have called for many years "adventure dreams." Vivid and colorful, they involve me either as an awed participant or spectator in some extraordinary situations. The plot involves adventure and exploration almost anywhere on the surface of the earth; the tone is one of excitement without fear. Most locales I have never visited or seen in photographs, nor are the experiences those I have lived or read about before. I became so engrossed in the story that as the dream fades with wakefulness, I try vigorously to steer it back, while still remaining astonished at the range of situations portrayed. Rarely do I have adventure dreams in the city, and then only after two or more days of respite from the usual work-filled routine. Surely one of our deeper needs in life is to find a daytime occupation that satisfies the innate thirst for adventure we find out about in our dreams.

Dreams do tell us who we are and what interests us. If you are a person who does better on open-ended tests requiring imaginativeness and mental fluency, you will also tend to specialize in the liberal arts rather than in the physical sciences. You will probably recall more dreams, they will more frequently involve people and animals,[1] and your dreams will also involve you in more frequent and more aggressive interactions with other persons. If you are a biomedical investigator, hope that your personality contains a generous blending of the elements in both the arts and sciences, for you surely need to meld the attributes of each in your work.

But let us now return to the investigator on the job during the daylight hours. He is in a reflective mood at his laboratory bench. He may still be chasing the elusive possibility of finding something new, yet he knows there is more to research than this—more than simple curiosity, more than the fun of solving problems, more than occupational therapy. As he looks back, he feels a positive thrust of many years' duration in his work, sees it operate on a sweeping scale throughout the course of his lifetime. To him, biomedical research is taking one step after another into pitch darkness—not a fussy rearranging of familiar furniture in a floodlighted room. He senses the depth of his commitment to an entire life of uncertainty, testing, and challenge, to an acceptance of failure far more often than success. Yet he will take the chance.

No ground the researcher really wants to explore is secure underfoot.

The shaky nature of his footing was summed up well by the American painter, Albert Pinkham Ryder, when he said:

Have you ever seen an inchworm crawl up a leaf or twig and there, clinging to the very end, revolve in the air feeling for something to reach? That's like me. I'm trying to find something out there beyond the place I have a footing.[2]

The investigator groping away at a major problem knows he is engaged in a trial and error business, and freely accepts its implicit "back to the drawing board" philosophy. Only in his readiness to generate hypotheses is he well-prepared when he begins his search. Thereafter, he must remain ready to change tactics (always), strategy (many times), and policy (less commonly, but whenever the situation warrants). The worm does turn. It must.

At the beginning, the researcher will send up as many trial balloons as he can, having little immediate knowledge of their validity or, indeed, of their final destination. Most will pop; a rare one soars to an unforseen height, drifting in the winds of chance. Surprisingly, he finds himself aboard, aloft, jettisoning old certainties, patching holes in his new craft with the tattered fabric of previous failures. Like as not, he will wind up in some other county, and if he's lucky, in a foreign country, where other unexpected adventures will await him.

In his quest, the investigator is kin to other explorers, pioneers, and mountain climbers. He begins his journey not realizing its full implications. Beginning, he is swept along by an exciting chain of contingencies. Rewards, apart from the stimulation of the search itself, come more as an afterthought. In the risking, he is most alert, most alive; *in the seeking, he has found*. He needs to take the chance.

What else does he find, as a by-product? No permanent satisfaction for his innate curiosity, for it is insatiable—instead a way to ensure that it is constantly engaged. No path that reveals the outside world alone, for each new project is also self-revelatory; each adventure involves a voyage of self-discovery. Anyone as consumingly curious as is the investigator about his external world is also curious about how his own internal world came to grow up and function. And, bit by bit, glimpses of this, too, will be revealed to him in one guise or another. If but for this reason alone, he cannot afford not to take the chance.

14.

On the Trail of Serendipity

This discovery indeed is almost of that kind which I call *serendipity,* a
very expressive word. . . . I once read a silly fairy tale, called *The Three
Princes of Serendip:* as their highnesses traveled, they were always
making discoveries, by accidents and sagacity, of things which they were
not in quest of. . . . you must observe that *no* discovery of a thing you *are*
looking for comes under this description. . . .

Horace Walpole

We use the word often nowadays. But what does serendipity really
mean, where did it come from, and who were the three princes ex-
emplifying it? If we dig down through many layers, we find a term
deeply rooted in antiquity. The tale of the three princes in Walpole's letter is at least 700 years old! Indeed, parts of the legendary story probably
go back more than 1,500 years to old folktales told around the campfires
at night when camel caravans were resting (figure 11).

It was in 1557 that Christoforo Armeno* gathered together and published a number of the ancient stories that originated in Persia and
India. He focused on the story of three princes, and, possibly to lend a
still more exotic note to his tale, he placed their home on the island of
Ceylon. However, he still preserved the flavor of Persia, where many of
the stories originated, for he called Ceylon "Serendippo." In doing so, he
was thinking of the medieval Arabian name for Ceylon. It was Sārandib,
or Serendīp in later Persian.[1]

Many persons, physicians and chemists in particular, have become
fascinated by the magic in the word, serendipity, and have come under
the spell of its alluring connotations. Most have done so without ever
having read the original tale about the three princes, for it is elusive and
not easily found in the library. To any generation, the story of the
princes' meanderings is instructive, and it is not without its spicy Arabian
Nights moments. But for our present purposes, the English translation

---

*Christopher the Armenian

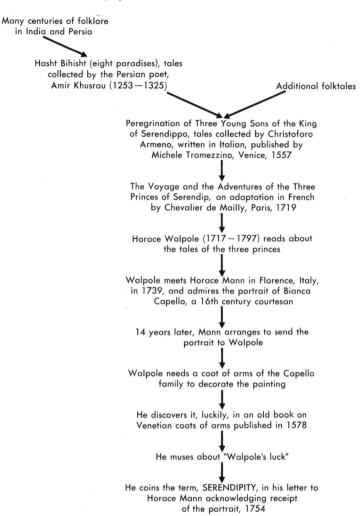

Many centuries of folklore
in India and Persia

Hasht Bihisht (eight paradises), tales
collected by the Persian poet,
Amir Khusrau (1253—1325)

Additional folktales

Peregrination of Three Young Sons of the King
of Serendippo, tales collected by Christoforo
Armeno, written in Italian, published by
Michele Tramezzino, Venice, 1557

The Voyage and the Adventures of the Three
Princes of Serendip, an adaptation in French
by Chevalier de Mailly, Paris, 1719

Horace Walpole (1717—1797) reads about
the tales of the three princes

Walpole meets Horace Mann in Florence, Italy,
in 1739, and admires the portrait of Bianca
Capello, a 16th century courtesan

14 years later, Mann arranges to send the
portrait to Walpole

Walpole needs a coat of arms of the Capello
family to decorate the painting

He discovers it, luckily, in an old book on
Venetian coats of arms published in 1578

He muses about "Walpole's luck"

He coins the term, SERENDIPITY, in his letter to
Horace Mann acknowledging receipt
of the portrait, 1754

Figure 11.

of Armeno's *Peregrinaggio*[2] can certainly be shortened, and I have done
so in Appendix A.

Let us pick up the trail of serendipity when Horace Walpole read, at
some unspecified time, Chevalier de Mailly's French adaptation of Armeno's *Peregrinaggio*.[3] Who was Walpole? He was a small frail lad born
into a distinguished family. His father, Sir Robert, was Prime Minister
of England under George II. Young Horace was educated at Eton and

Cambridge, where he became a friend of the poet Thomas Gray.[4] At the age of twenty-two, he and Gray set out on a grand tour of Europe. Walpole spent much of his trip from 1739 to 1741 immersed in the lively social and cultural whirl of Florence. There he stayed at the home of Horace Mann, British Minister to the Court of Tuscany. The two soon became fast friends and thereafter carried on a life-long correspondence that has been carefully preserved.[5]

More than a social chronicle of eighteenth-century England, Walpole's letters to Mann and others form a self-portrait unique in the history of English letters. It is largely through his correspondence that the legacy of Walpole's wit and worldliness has gathered momentum over the past two centuries. Perhaps nowhere is this more finely distilled than in the term serendipity—the happy word he coined and passed down to posterity. For in literature no more intriguing example is to be found of the way chance interacts with creativity than in the way this one word, serendipity, weaves together the threads of the life and times of its inventor (figure 11). A piece of art, interestingly, figures prominently in the story.

Growing up in a politician's home, Walpole was steeped in the political history of Europe, and was continually exposed to paintings of many famous historical persons. When he was in Florence, still a young bachelor, he became enamored of one portrait in particular.* It was of Bianca Capello (1548–87), a sixteenth-century courtesan who became Grand Duchess of Tuscany by marrying Francesco de Medici. Her life soon ended on a tragic note, for she died within eleven hours of her husband, both presumably of an overwhelming infection. But because of the tarnished reputation of the Medici court, it was widely believed that they were both poisoned.

Some fourteen years after Walpole first saw the portrait of Bianca, Mann purchased it and sent it (minus the original frame) to his old friend in England. Walpole needed a new frame, and he also had to find a coat of arms of the Capello family to decorate the frame appropriately. Luckily, he happened to find the coat of arms in an old book. He then sat down with his goose-quill pen to write a thank-you letter to Mann acknowledging the receipt of the painting. Included are the following key passages:

---

* Attributed to the artist Giorgio Vasari (1511–74).[6]

Arlington Street, Jan. 28, 1754

"Her Serene Highness the Great Duchess Bianca Capello is arrived safe at a palace lately taken for her in Arlington Street: she has been much visited by the quality and gentry, and pleases universally by the graces of her person and comeliness of her deportment" . . . this is the least that the newspapers would say of the charming Bianca . . . The head is painted equal to Titan, and though done, I suppose, after the clock had struck five and thirty, yet she retains a great share of beauty. I have bespoken a frame for her, with the grand ducal coronet at top, her story on a label at bottom, which Gray is to compose in Latin as short and expressive as Tacitus (one is lucky when one can bespeak and have executed such an inscription!) the Medici arms on one side, and the Capello's on the other. I must tell you a critical discovery of mine *à propos:* in an old book of Venetian arms, there are two coats of Capello, who from their name bear a hat, on one of them is added a flower-de-luce on a blue ball, which I am persuaded was given to the family by the Great Duke, in consideration of this alliance; the Medicis you know bore such a badge at the top of their own arms; this discovery I made by a talisman, which Mr. Chute calls the sortes *Walpolianae,* by which I find everything I want *à point nommé* wherever I dip for it. This discovery indeed is almost of that kind which I call *serendipity,* a very expressive word, which as I have nothing better to tell you, I shall endeavour to explain to you: you will understand it better by the derivation than by the definition. I once read a silly fairy tale, called *The Three Princes of Serendip:* as their highnesses traveled, they were always making discoveries, by accidents and sagacity, of things which they were not in quest of: for instance, one of them discovered that a mule blind of the right eye had traveled the same road lately, because the grass was eaten only on the left side, where it was worse than on the right— now do you understand *serendipity?* One of the most remarkable instances of this *accidental sagacity* (for you must observe that *no* discovery of a thing you *are* looking for comes under this description) was of my Lord Shaftsbury, who happening to dine at Lord Chancellor Clarendon's, found out the marriage of the Duke of York and Mrs. Hyde, by the respect with which her mother treated her at table.[7]

It isn't easy to understand serendipity from this original source, but let us try to decipher his meaning. What was going on inside Walpole's mind when he created the word? It is noteworthy that he invented it in the visual context of a painting—one, moreover, that he was especially fond of. It is also interesting that he started his letter to Mann by using the word "Serene" to describe the lady of the portrait. We may also observe that throughout Walpole's writings words such as "posterity" and "futurity" flowed from his pen with ease. So, the beginning of the word—serene—and its ending—ity—were there somewhere in his brain, waiting to be linked together.

He then goes on to note that he was "lucky" to be able to enlist the aid of someone like his old poet friend, Thomas Gray, to compose an inscription for the portrait. Next, he says that he just happened to discover the Capello coat of arms for the frame in an old book. He adds that his good friend, John Chute, uses the term, "Walpole's luck" (sortes Walpolianae) to describe his penchant for finding everything he wants in the nick of time (à point nommé). Walpole describes this gift as a talisman, a charm bringing apparently magical or miraculous effects. Musing on the subject of luck, his associations led him, happily, to the story he once read about the lucky Three Princes of Serendip. Starting with serene, then Serendip, there remained but one short playful link to the new term, serendipity.

The first example Walpole gives of the princes' experience (with a camel, not a mule) leaves much to be desired. It emphasizes only that one needs sagacity to discern the real meaning of the observation that grass differs in height on the two sides of a trail. (The meaning is more clear in the condensed plot in the appendix.)

Walpole's second illustration is somewhat better, but it too requires historical explanation. It should, however, interest psychologists and psychiatrists, because it extends the scope of sagacity well beyond that of the length of grass to include a discerning sensitivity to the nuances of interpersonal relationships. Walpole is referring to Lord Shaftesbury (Anthony Cooper), who was invited over for dinner one night at the home of Lord Chancellor Clarendon (Edward Hyde, 1609–74). At the dinner table, Shaftesbury was keen enough to observe that his host's daughter, Anne Hyde, was now treated by her mother with unusual respect. From this, he shrewdly concluded that Anne Hyde had recently married the Duke of York.[8] This would mean that Anne, as a potential Queen of England, indeed had a new and higher social standing. In fact, Anne's new husband, the Duke of York, did later succeed to the throne of England, Scotland, and Ireland as James II (1685–88).

In his later writings, Walpole even anticipated the title of this book, for he elaborated on the roles that chase and chance play in creative invention. To anyone curious about the many origins of discovery, it is fascinating to see how clearly he appreciated that accidental discoveries occur, not only when the alchemist pursues gold, but also when man searches for immortality. This, his second say on the subject of serendipity, will interest chemists in particular:

> Nor is there any harm in starting new game to invention; many excellent discoveries have been made by men who were *à la chasse* of something very different. I am not quite sure that the art of making gold and of living forever have been yet found out—yet to how many noble discoveries has the pursuit of those nostrums given birth! Poor Chemistry, had she not had such glorious objects in view.[9]

What did Walpole mean by serendipity? We might begin with what he excluded from the definition. His own facility, finding what he was looking for, what he *wanted,* was not serendipity. Instead, he regarded serendipity as a quality—a gift for discovering things, by *accident* or *sagacity,* while hunting for something else. In today's parlance, we have usually watered down serendipity to mean the good luck that comes by accident—a result, not an ability. We have tended to lose sight of the element of sagacity, by which term Walpole originally wished to stress that some distinctive personal receptivity is involved. The archaic meaning of sagacity is acuteness of smell, if we need further testimony of the word's entirely sensory connotation.

And we have also slighted another obvious fact about the Princes of Serendip. They were not simply dallying their lives away in luxury in Ceylon on some convenient palace couch. They were out on the move, exploring, traveling widely when they encountered their accidental good fortune. Kettering, as we shall soon see, would have approved.

To sum up, serendipity is the facility for encountering unexpected good luck, as the result of accident, sagacity, or general exploratory behavior. But chance has a fourth element in it and the principles underlying all its elements bear closer scrutiny.

15.

The Kettering, Pasteur, and Disraeli Principles

Keep on going and the chances are you will stumble on something, perhaps when you are least expecting it. I have never heard of anyone stumbling on something sitting down.

Charles Kettering

Chance favors only the prepared mind. (*Dans les champs de l'observation, le hazard ne favorise que les esprits préparés.*)

Louis Pasteur

We make our fortunes, and we call them fate.

Benjamin Disraeli

In the past, the role that sudden flashes of insight play in the process of discovery has perhaps been overemphasized. Much, also, has been said about the need for plodding, methodical work both before and after these creative moments. Now, let us present the case for chance. What is chance?

Dictionaries define chance as something fortuitous that happens unpredictably without discernible human intention. *La cheance,* in Old French, is derived from the Old Latin, *cadere,* to fall, implying that it is in the nature of things to fall, settle out, or happen by themselves.

Chance is unintentional, it is capricious, but we needn't conclude that chance is immune from human intervention. Indeed, chance plays several distinct roles when humans react creatively with one another and with their environment. I use the word "roles" in the plural, because chance comes in four forms and for four different reasons. The principles involved affect everyone, and it is time we examined these principles more carefully.

The four kinds of chance each have a different kind of motor exploratory activity and a different kind of sensory receptivity. The varieties of chance also involve distinctive personality traits and differ in the way one particular individual influences them. I have summarized these various aspects of chance at the end of this chapter in table I.

In Chance I, the good luck that occurs is completely accidental. It is pure blind luck that comes with no effort on our part. No particular personality trait is in operation. If, for example, you are sitting playing bridge at a table of four, it's "in the cards" for you to receive a hand of thirteen spades, but statisticians tell us it will occur on an average only once in 635 billion deals (635,013,559,600).[1] You will ultimately draw this lucky hand, but it may involve a rather longer wait than most have time for.

In Chance II, something else has been added. Motion. Years ago, when I was rushing around in the laboratory working on sulfatides, someone admonished me by asking, "Why all the busyness? One must distinguish between motion and progress."

Yes, at some point this distinction must be made. But it cannot always be made first. And it is not always made consciously. True, *waste* motion should be avoided. But, if the researcher did not move until he was certain of progress he would accomplish very little. There's no "standing pat" in research; the posture of creativity is forward-leaning. A certain basal level of action "stirs up the pot," brings in random ideas that will collide and stick together in fresh combinations, lets chance operate. Motion yields a network of new experiences which, like a sieve, filters best when in constant up-and-down, side-to-side movement. Consistent motion is what distinguishes Chance II; its premise is that *un*luck runs out if you persist.

An element of the chase is implicit in Chance II, but action is still your primary goal, not results. The action is ill-defined, restless, driving, and it depends on your basic need to release energy, not on your conscious intellect. If later on, you harness the energy toward a visible secondary intellectual goal, the goal must be one impossible of success without the basic persistent drive that moves you forward. Of course, if you move around in more likely areas, Chance II may enter in to influence your results more fruitfully. For example, if orchids were your only goal, you wouldn't want to go out tramping around for them in the harsh desert. (That would be *too* chancy.)

So Chance II springs from your energetic, generalized motor activities, and, with the above qualification, the freer they are, the better. It involves the kind of luck Kettering, the automotive engineer, had in mind when he said, in effect, "keep on going, and you'll stumble on something." When someone, *anyone,* does swing into motion and keep on going, he will increase the number of collisions between events. If you link a few events together, you can then exploit some of them, but many others, of course, you cannot. Still, we return to the basic fact that in medical research, as in Kettering's engineering research, if you're not already in motion, you probably won't stumble on something. Press on. Something will turn up, as indeed it turned up for the three princes after they set out on their travels. We may term this kinetic principle the Kettering Principle. It deserves special emphasis.

In the two foregoing examples, a unique role of the individual person was either lacking or minimal. True, the mantle of chance can fall indiscriminately on anyone, but sometimes it seems almost to bear the personal name tag of the recipient.

Now, as we move on to Chance III, we see blind luck, but it tiptoes in softly, dressed in camouflage. Chance presents only a faint clue, the potential opportunity exists, but it will be overlooked except by that *one person* uniquely equipped to observe it, visualize it conceptually, and fully grasp its significance. Chance III involves a special receptivity and discernment unique to the recipient. Louis Pasteur characterized it for all time when he said: "Chance favors only the prepared mind."

Pasteur himself had it in full measure. But the classical example of his principle occurred in 1928, when Sir Alexander Fleming's mind instantly fused at least five elements into a conceptually unified nexus. He was at his work bench in the laboratory, made an observation, and his mental sequences then went something like this: 1) I see that a mold has fallen by accident into my culture dish; 2) the staphylococcal colonies residing near it failed to grow; 3) therefore, the mold must have secreted something that killed the bacteria; 4) this reminds me of a similar experience I had once before; 5) maybe this new "something" from the mold could be used to kill staphylococci that cause human infections.

Actually, Fleming's mind was exceptionally well prepared.[2] Some nine years earlier, while suffering from a cold, his own nasal drippings had found their way onto a culture dish. He noted that the bacteria around this mucous were killed, and astutely followed up the lead. His experiments then led him to discover the bactericidal enzyme, lysozyme, present in nasal mucus and tears. Lysozyme itself proved inappropriate for medical use, but think of how receptive Fleming's mind was to the penicillin mold when it later happened on the scene!

It is appropriate that we recall Pasteur's name in the same context as Fleming's discovery, because back in 1877, Pasteur and Joubert made a similar observation that airborne microorganisms could inhibit anthrax bacilli.[3] They fully grasped the therapeutic significance of their finding but had neither the time nor the technology to pursue it further.

We observed earlier that serendipity included good luck coming as the result of an accident, general exploratory activity, or sagacity. Somehow, the list is incomplete. Something, we sense, is missing. What is lacking?

The motor counterpart to sagacity. *Chance favors the individualized action.* This is the fourth element in good luck—an active, but unintentional, subtle personal prompting of it. Indeed, there may even seem to be an element of courting involved, to the degree that chance is still referred to as "Lady Luck" or "Dame Fortune" in many cultures.[4] But if it is courting, the result is surely unforeseen.

Let us pursue this proposition for a moment because it helps us visualize the fourth element of good luck in a little different perspective. We recall that in the true *affaire du coeur* the lady sought will not bestow her favors indiscriminately. The suitor may be a mover and a shaker who diffusely smothers her with attentions, or he could be a prince from a foreign land in all his finery. But the queen of India yields to the blandishments of neither (appendix A). She responds instead to another suitor with whose particular personal qualities she herself finds a special deeper affinity. These qualities may appear trivial to the onlooker, but they take on a special deeper meaning to the two persons involved, who may themselves be quite unaware of their significance. He who pays court will express these qualities unconsciously, by word, gesture, and deed—each a highly individualized motor activity revealing his own temperament and special motivations; each the product of the unique experiences of his lifetime.

Chance IV is the kind of luck that develops during a probing action which has a distinctive personal flavor. The English Prime Minister, Benjamin Disraeli, summed up the principle underlying Chance IV when he noted that, as persons, "we make our fortunes and we call them fate." Disraeli, the practical politician, appreciated that by our actions we each forge our own destiny, at least to some degree. Chance IV comes to you, unsought, because of who you are and how you behave. It is *one-man-made,* as personal as your signature. Being highly personal, it is not easily understood by someone else the first time around. The outside observer may have to go underground to see Chance IV, for here we probe into subterranean recesses that autobiographers know about, biographers rarely. Neurologists may be a little more comfortable with the concept, because so much of the nervous system we work with exists as anatomically separate sensory and motor divisions. So, some natural separation does exist in our brains and underlies the distinction: Chance III, concerned with personal *sensory receptivity;* its counterpart, Chance IV, involved with personal *motor behavior.*

There is no mystery about Chance IV, nothing supernatural about the way it generates an uncommon discovery. But you do have to look carefully to find Chance IV for two reasons. The first is that it operates in an elliptical unorthodox manner. The second is that some problems it may help solve are uncommonly difficult to understand because they have gone through a process of selection. We must bear in mind that, by the time Chance IV finally occurs, the easy, more accessible problems will already have been solved earlier by conventional actions, conventional logic, or by the operations of the other forms of chance. What remains late in the game, then, is a tough core of complex, resistant problems. Such problems yield to none but an unusual approach, much as does the odd lock in an old door open only to the rare key. Under normal circumstances we won't be able to state what shape such a key should take, because we are not familiar with the contours of the tumblers it must fit inside the odd lock. What makes Chance IV even more unpredictable is that the kind of personal behavior it requires—itself the key to the solution—lies hidden out of sight, unidentified, until the moment it is called into play.

The situation bears some analogies to the way a mutation acts. For example, we have learned since Gregor Mendel's day how it happens that a rare but helpful mutation enables a bean plant to survive unusually difficult extremes of temperature. But, until we have exposed the plant to such extremes, the potential effect of its mutation lies hidden, dormant. The special kind of activity within Chance IV is adaptive in a similar way, and also has survival value. It also waits, invisible, until summoned by unique external circumstances that correspond to it precisely.

Unlike Chance II, Chance IV connotes no generalized activity, as bees might have in the anonymity of a hive. Instead, it comprehends a kind of discrete behavioral performance focused in a highly specific manner. Whereas the lucky connections in Chance II might come to anyone as the happy by-product of a kind of circular stirring of the pot, the links of Chance IV can be drawn together and fused only by *one* quixotic rider cantering in on his own homemade hobby horse to intercept the problem at an odd angle. As we shall see in a subsequent chapter, Chance IV resists straight logic and takes on something of the eccentric flavor of Cervantes' Spanish fiction.

What psychological determinants enter into the varieties of chance? Chance I is completely impersonal. You can't influence it. Personality traits only start to enter in the other forms of chance. To evoke Chance II, you will need a persistent curiosity about many things coupled with an energetic willingness to experiment and explore. To arrive at the discernment involved in Chance III, you will need a sufficient background of sound knowledge plus special abilities in observing, remembering, recalling, and quickly forming significant new associations. Chance IV favors those with distinctive, if not eccentric hobbies, personal life styles, and motor behaviors. The farther apart these personal activities are from the area under investigation, the more novel and unexpected the product of the encounter.

Table I summarizes the varieties of chance. With some of these distinctions in mind, let us now go back and review the origins of chance in Part I of this tale.

Table 1

Various Aspects and Kinds of Good Luck

Term Used To Describe the Quality Involved	Good Luck Is the Result Of	Classification of Luck	Elements Involved	Personality Traits You Need
	An Accident	Chance I	"Blind" luck. Chance happens, and nothing about it is directly attributable to you, the recipient.	None
	General Exploratory Behavior	Chance II	The Kettering Principle. Chance favors those in motion. Events are brought together to form "happy accidents" when you diffusely apply your energies in motions that are typically nonspecific.	Curiosity about many things, persistence, willingness to experiment and to explore.
SERENDIPITY				
	Sagacity	Chance III	The Pasteur Principle. Chance favors the prepared mind. Some special receptivity born from past experience permits you to discern a new fact or to perceive ideas in a new relationship.	A background of knowledge, based on your abilities to observe, remember, and quickly form significant new associations.
ALTAMIRAGE	Personalized Action	Chance IV	The Disraeli Principle. Chance favors the individualized action. Fortuitous events occur when you behave in ways that are highly distinctive of you as a person.	Distinctive hobbies, personal life styles, and activities peculiar to you as an individual, especially when they operate in domains seemingly far removed from the area of the discovery.

16 .

Personal Encounters with Chance I-IV

The way of fortune is like the milky way in the sky; which is a number of small stars, not seen asunder, but giving light together: so it is a number of little and scarce discerned virtues, or rather faculties and customs, that make men fortunate.

Francis Bacon

The younger the scientific field, the more it responds to the human, subjective elements of chance; the older, well-defined field has less room for open-field running, requires a more disciplined, objective conscious effort. I know I have chosen to work in areas of medical biology that are regarded as "softer" sciences from the perspective, say, of an advanced nuclear physicist or mathematician. Yet the principles underlying the lucky art of novelty seem likely to remain the same, and if there are differences, they would appear to be more of frequency and degree than of kind. In any event, Chance has usually been a welcome guest in our research. It was pure luck of the type appreciated by Claude Bernard that I happened to encounter the patients with hypertrophic neuritis and MLD in the hospital at the right time. Later, when Frank Witmer intervened, his infrared expertise in the sulfatide story was both timely and decisive, yet it came about with no initial effort on my part, but rather through the agency of Roy Swank and his patient, Frank's wife.

The origins of Chance II are seen in my restless probing during the flawed hyaluronic acid sulfate experiments (chapter 6). These studies stemmed from curiosity, from muddled ruminations about metachromasia which could best be externalized by a broadly focused experiment. The by-products of the experiment were all fortuitous and quite unpredicted.

As for the discernment of Chance III, I could grasp the importance of the experimental globoidlike response to cerebroside when I saw it in the rat because I had earlier observed that the same microscopic appearance was the distinctive feature of human globoid leukodystrophy.

The sequences involved in Chance IV are more personal and are difficult to perceive and unravel unless one has known for a lifetime the person involved. When Bimal Bachhawat's group teamed up with our group, we could go on to discover that sulfatase A was deficient in MLD. But that connection hinged on events that brought me all the way to India to meet Bimal. We can trace the steps in this back to the cold war setting, and to friendships in Oregon with the Danas and the Finegolds. These were the circumstances that started my meddling in politics. Thereafter, in a curious kind of inevitability, they shaped my decision to become actively involved in India (figure 7). Such are the turning points that decide major issues. Hidden from view, they are subtle but telling. And usually untold.

In the Lafora body episode, the outcome depended on recognizing the similarities between a starch granule and a Lafora body. Yet, again, the story doesn't begin there. For we must go back to ask: what steps led up to the presence of the starch granule, and why in a hunting dog? If this line of questioning points to the man who followed his dog afield, it is only a temporary answer. For footprints in the snow ultimately lead us back to the *kind* of boy who tried to narrow the gap between the rabbit and himself; beyond that, I dimly sense an atavistic kinship with a cave dwelling ancestor on the game trail in the distant prehistoric past. All this is not to imply that Chance IV is predestined or violates physical laws, but rather to suggest that if it takes on a quality of being instigated, it is by remote events too subtle and far removed to be under conscious control.

Chance also occurs in mixtures. Thus, elements of Chance I through IV occurred in my work as a result of my lifelong attraction to colors in general, and my curiosity about metachromatic colors in particular. These prompted my diffuse reading in the literature, and led me to appreciate that a disease existed—MLD—in which color was the salient feature. The special interests in colors in childhood and with the microscope in summer camp preceeded by years the crucial experiment designed to stain urine sediment in the MLD patient. Because I didn't really know then exactly what I was looking for, it was my long-standing concern for color and form which made it possible to single out the golden-brown granular body of MLD.

I glanced recently at the date on my first watercolor painting of the

New York skyline as viewed down the Hudson River. The year was 1955. Only now do I grasp that it was painted during the "red and blue period" at Columbia.[1] I was then staining the urine with toluidine blue and was swept up in the question: what did all these metachromatic colors mean? Now, in retrospect, I can perceive how the scientific problem stimulated my artistic interest, in the same way that my earlier childhood curiosity about the "cause" of colors itself led on to the scientific search. Colors . . . . to research . . . . to water color painting; the connections to and fro were not at all clear to me at the time.

A few months ago, I glimpsed a personal correlate of red-purple colors. I was on sabbatical leave in Kyoto, Japan, and, as a fringe benefit, took the unique opportunity to learn how to meditate with my eyes open at a Zen Buddist temple. After two months of practice, I regularly entered into stages of meditation when associative thoughts had largely melted away, and relaxation was complete. Twenty minutes after starting meditation in a dimly lighted room, after a prelude of yellow-green color, I consistently went through a phase in which a luminous orb of vivid, complementary red-purple colors glowed in the darkened central portion of my vision. The phenomenon waxed and waned without my conscious control, and was accompanied by a pleasant feeling of relaxation. Here was a spontaneous emphasis on red-purple springing from the depths of my own brain![2]

But personal experiences aside, we need a new general term something like serendipity to convey the elusive quality of the workings of Chance IV. Moreover, it would help to have an illustrative story something like the *Three Princes of Serendip* (but not as difficult to locate). At this moment, we have neither the word nor the tale.

We don't have to turn to ancient Persian history for the exotic, or go as far as Ceylon for a name. A true story already exists, and in its twists and turns it illustrates a happy reunion between art and science. A curious feature of the tale is that it not only involves a dog, but either parallels or reflects an inverted mirror image of some other personal events in the narrative in Part I. The scene opens in Spain only a hundred years ago, but its distant origins sweep us back four hundred or more generations, back to the time of our Cro-Magnon ancestors.

17 .

The Spanish Connection

Papa, Papa! Look! Painted bulls!
        Maria de Sautuola

When you visit the hill, there is nothing externally distinctive about it, nor is it really as high as its name might suggest. Still, it does afford a good view of the rolling farming countryside that extends around it, of orange-roofed houses basking in the warm Spanish sunshine. Perhaps that is why, for as many years back as local records go, the hill has always been called Altamira.

Altamira lies inland between the northern seacoast of Spain and the base of the Cantabrian Mountains. The land immediately around it was but a minute portion of the extensive estates of a cultured Spanish nobleman, and there seemed no good reason why he should ever pay closer attention to this particular parcel. For its owner, Don Marcelino, Marquis de Sautuola, was more familiar with his own locale some twenty miles away on the Bay of Biscay. He had grown up there around his ancestral home in the old Castillian seaport city of Santander. As he grew up, Don Marcelino developed many hobbies to occupy his time. He became a bibliophile, a horticulturalist, a genealogist of the noble families of his province, and as chance would have it, a student of its geological and archaeological features.

One day in 1868, a hunter was afield chasing foxes near Altamira. Suddenly, to his astonishment, his spaniel vanished into thin air. The puzzled hunter whistled and searched but to no avail. Finally, he stumbled upon a crevice in the ground near a rocky outcropping. Putting his ear to the hole, he could hear the dog whimpering and barking underground. Pulling rocks aside, the hunter widened the aperture, eased himself down into the cold dark hole, and hauled his grateful spaniel out. His own native curiosity then impelled him to look around, and in the dim light he perceived something surprising. He had discovered a cave.

It took seven more years before the cave of Altamira was reexplored. It happened only because a friend, knowing of Don Marcelino's geological interests, told him he had a cave on his property. Some days later, Don Marcelino first visited the cave with some workmen, widened the opening, and crept down the slope by its entrance until the cavern became high enough for him to stand. In the flickering torch light, he soon discovered many large bones, frequently split lengthwise. He later showed these bones to his friend, Spain's greatest prehistorian of the time, Don Juan Vilanova, professor of geology at Madrid University. Professor Vilanova pointed out that the bones came from a bison, a wild horse, and an extinct giant stag. He observed that a *man* must have split the bones to remove and eat the marrow.

Thoughts of the cave incubated in Don Marcelino's mind for another four years before he returned to it. In the interim, he meandered elsewhere, made field trips to other caves in Spain, and found out how to excavate them. Then, ten years after the hunting spaniel disappeared from view, de Sautuola, while on a trip to Paris, paid a rewarding visit to the International Exhibition of 1878. He was enormously influenced by displays of prehistoric arrowheads and other flint tools found recently by explorers in cave sites in France. These stone artifacts had been discovered among the same kind of split bones that he had found earlier at Altamira. He was so stimulated by his trip that he determined to reexplore his own cave for similar stone tools. So he went back again the following year, when he was forty-eight years old; and found a number of stone artifacts, their edges so worked that he was certain prehistoric man had inhabited his cave.

Don Marcelino continued to excavate for several days, and then, as one does, grew tired of digging alone in the damp earth underground. At this point, the indulgent father could readily agree when his nine-year-old daughter Maria asked if she, too, could come along to look at the cave. So it happened that while he dug in the dirt near the entrance, his daughter played and crawled about farther down in the cavern.

Suddenly she cried out in astonishment: *"Papa, Papa! Mira! Toros pintados!"* He hurried over to a nearby chamber, and followed her open-mouthed gaze upward to the ceiling. Up there, in the flickering lamplight, his own startled eyes saw the colored paintings of a herd of snorting, charging, great bison! As he peered more closely at the ceiling, he could see how the artist had cleverly used the existing bulges on the cave roof to give a three dimensional bas-relief quality to the natural contours of each animal. His aesthetic sensibilities could only marvel at the keen powers of observation of the artist who, with the bold sure touch of a master, had not only captured the natural grace of each bull, cow, and calf, but had gone on to render it with a unique style of his own.

The paintings stretched on to cover the entire ceiling of a part of the cave beneath which he had passed many times. Naturally enough, he first looked where he had always found heavy objects before, on the *floor* of the cave, and he never leaned back to look upward. But Maria, unhampered by any such preconceptions, looked not only at the floor but all around the cave with the naive open-eyed wonder of a child.

He moved closer to touch the warm reddish-brown flank of the nearest bull. Some of its color came away on his finger tip, and it felt greasy. Trembling with excitement, he and Maria looked throughout the cave. Painted animals nearly six feet long appeared almost everywhere on the ceiling and even, in places, on the walls. Don Marcelino must soon have felt an eerie sensation creep into the very marrow of his own bones. Both a hunter and a student of natural history, he knew only too well that animals such as these had not existed in Spain for many millennia. And as the genealogist of his family and of his district, he must quickly have sensed that he was in the presence of artistic masterpieces created by primitive men who could have been his own distant ancestors. Anyone who has found even a fragment of worked flint can imagine the excitement of that day, let alone the mind-stretching thoughts that surged and tumbled as the father and his daughter tried to sleep that night.

Soon thereafter, Professor Vilanova hurried up from Madrid, and the excitement multiplied. Examining some 150 figures, they could finally reconstruct the technique of painting. The reds came from iron oxide and red ocher; the golden-yellow from lighter ocher; the browns from mixtures with charcoal. These pigments, moistened with water and mixed with grease and animal blood, were then ground into the porous rock by marvelously talented finger tips. Lighter color tones of the animal's coat were blended subtly into darker tones with extraordinary skill. Preserved by the grease and the cool darkness of the cave, the colors were fresh and vibrant as though they had only recently been applied.

Reasoning from the age of the implements lying on the surface, the two men dated the paintings to the Magdalenian era of the Old Stone Age. We can now date them back somewhere between 15,000 B.C. and 12,000 B.C.

The spaniel's search,* Don Marcelino's quest for tools of stone, and Maria's open-minded curiosity had culminated in the discovery of what would later be called "the Sistine Chapel of Prehistory," the first known painted cave of Paleolithic Europe. Passionately pursuing his hobby of archaeology, de Sautuola, to his surprise, determined the discovery of man's first paintings. In quest of science, he happened on art.

The discovery at Altamira forms a classical example of scientific exploration in yet another sense. For, like many another scientific discovery down through the ages, Altamira revealed too much too far in advance of its time. Don Marcelino's treatise, published locally in 1880, was scholarly, and understated, and he noted with becoming modesty that his own efforts were intended to prepare the way for more competent observers.

But the keenest minds of the outside scientific world were not prepared to accept his report. In fact, he and Professor Vilanova were widely suspected of having engineered a hoax. Professor Virchow thought the episode was a deliberate fraud, and his judgment was openly concurred in by all prehistorians at the International Archaeological Congress in Lisbon in 1880. The opposition was particularly fierce from Cartailhac, a professor of prehistory at Toulouse University. To this Frenchman, it was preposterous to think that Ice Age man, with primitive methods, could have produced these works of art, comparable in style and execution with those of contemporary French painters. Indeed, so deep was the skepticism of all the scientists of his time that Don Marcelino was refused admission to successive congresses of French prehistorians in Algiers, Berlin, and Paris. De Sautuola died in 1888, his work ignored if not wholly rejected. A year later the name Altamira still connoted a forgery comparable to Dawson's Piltdown man of our own era, and was not even accorded a single mention at the archaeological Congress in Paris.

---

* The cave paintings of Lascaux were also discovered by accident in 1940 when four French boys followed their terrier who had vanished into a crevice in the ground.

Like other scientists, archaeologists would never consider something as real evidence, let alone proven, until it was confirmed by another person somewhere else. The tide began to turn only when the Abbé Henri Breuil, a young French priest, could show Professor Cartailhac identical paintings on the walls of a proven prehistoric cave in southern France. To his credit, Cartailhac then published in 1902 his complete conversion under the title, "La Grotte d'Altamira: Mea Culpa d'un Sceptique." He also made a pilgrimage to Altamira to apologize in person to Maria. Twenty-four years after his epoch-making discovery, Don Marcelino was finally vindicated in his grave.

With the discoveries at Altamira, our vision of our ancestors could never again be the same. Creative minds were at work 15,000 years ago! Henceforth, one could go on to wonder: if so much creative ability existed at the dawn of man, how much is present in each of us today, waiting only to be unearthed, cultivated, and channeled![1]

18.

Altamirage

The dog that trots about finds a bone.
                Spanish Gypsy Proverb

Go forth to seek: the quarry never found
Is still a fever to the questing hound,
The skyline is a promise, not a bound.
                John Masefield

No boundary line, the horizon. It never really fences in our adventurous questing selves. For the skyline always holds forth the promise of unusual and interesting things. Take mirages, for example. A mirage is defined in encyclopedias and dictionaries as one of several images formed when light rays are bent by passing through air of unusual density. As a result, distant views may be magnified as if a telescopic lens were in the atmosphere, and real but remote objects, ordinarily beneath the horizon, may become visible as an inverted mirror image. The usual basis for the phenomenon is a strongly heated layer of air, less dense than usual, and lying next to the earth. A mirage is elusive, as anyone knows who has tried to walk toward a flat shimmering pool that looks like water. It ebbs as fast as you approach it, and advances forward as you retreat.

If we look more closely, we find some interesting analogies between Don Marcelino's Spanish odyssey and a mirage. For Altamira resurrected something hidden beneath the earth's surface, and when it did so, it completely reversed our old erroneous views about our ancestors.

A century ago, no one had the remotest idea our cave man ancestors were highly creative artists. Weren't their talents rather minor and limited to crude flint chippings? But the paintings at Altamira, bursting forth like a mirage, quickly magnified this diminutive view, brought up close and into full focus a distant, hidden era of man's prehistory, revealed sentient minds and well-developed aesthetic sensibilities to which men of any age might aspire. And like a shimmering mirage, the events at Altamira took shape when de Sautuola's heated personal quest interacted with the invisible forces of chance we know exist yet cannot touch. Accordingly, one may introduce the term *altamirage* to identify the quality underlying Chance IV. Let us define it as the facility for encountering unexpected good luck as the result of highly individualized action. Altamirage goes well beyond the boundaries of serendipity in its emphasis on the role of personal *action* in chance.

What role did de Sautuola himself play in the paintings' discovery? After all, a dog did "find" the cave, and the initial receptivity was his daughter's. Still, the pivotal reason for the cave paintings' discovery hinged on a long sequence of prior events originating in de Sautuola himself. When we dig into the background of this amateur excavator, we find he was an exceptional person. It was he who was sufficiently stimulated by his trip to Paris to start searching thereafter for prehistoric artifacts. Few indeed were the Spaniards out probing into caves 100 years ago. The fact that he—not someone else—decided to dig that day in the cave of Altamira was the culmination of his passionate interest in his hobby. Here was a rare man whose avocation had been to educate himself from scratch, as it were, in the science of archaeology and cave exploration. This was no simple passive recognizer of blind luck when it came his way, but a man whose unique interests served an active creative thrust—someone whose own behavior and personality would focus the lens that led circuitously but inexorably to the discovery of man's first paintings.

Then, too, there is a much more subtle matter. How do you give full weight to the personal activities that imbue your child with your own curiosity, inspire her to ask to join you in your own musty hobby, and then agree to her request at the critical moment? For many reasons, at Altamira, more than the special receptivity of Chance III was required— this was a different domain, that of the personality and its actions.

Now, this kind of formulation is susceptible more to intuition than to proof, and to some casual onlookers it may take on almost a mystical nebulous quality that invites disbelief. "A Spanish Gypsy's tale," they might say. Others may agree that, yes, something is definitely there, but it is difficult to get a firm grip on the phenomenon, for it retreats as one pursues it, and advances as one steps back. But you who have observed altamirage firsthand through the heat of a uniquely personal interest know that the phenomenon itself is a real one. And to you, moreover, the reason for the new image is clearly understandable: when you warm up the air, the atmosphere rarifies, new things happen. Light does bend—it doesn't always follow a straight line. Once you appreciate that fact, then you join the viewers of the mirage in being simply grateful for any natural phenomena that bring in a larger vision of new worlds beyond the skyline.

To be sure, elements of the other kinds of chance are embedded in the Altamira story. The spaniel's search, the hunter's persistence, the critical meeting between the Don and his friend, whoever he was, who first told him about the cave, the rewarding naiveté of Maria as she, alone, looked *all* around—the intervention by a friend who was a skilled specialist—we have seen examples similar to these once before in earlier chapters. These are the will-o'-the-wisp, but crucial coincidences linked and drawn along by the active personal momentum of altamirage.

19.

The Fleming Effect. Examples of Chance in Biology and Medicine

There are thousands of different molds and there are thousands of different
bacteria, and that chance put that mold in the right spot at the
right time was like winning the Irish Sweepstakes.
                                        Sir Alexander Fleming

Things do not happen in this world—they are brought about.
                                        Will H. Hays

Science has its taboos. Scientists operate under strictures. It is never
entirely in fashion to mention luck in the same breath as science. By
convention, the investigator is constrained to put his work in the foreground, himself in the background, avoid the personal pronoun at all
costs. Still in the firm grip of the Protestant or other work ethic, he is
supposed to make his discoveries for rational reasons by virtue of his
own intellectual hard work, and he feels guilty if he does not live up to
the code.

Perhaps for all these reasons, good examples of Chance I (pure blind
luck) do not leap out from the medical literature. In fact, they are very
difficult to tease out from formal reports in scientific journals and identify by themselves. However, we can again rely on Fleming, this time
for his candid statement about his own "Irish Sweepstakes" luck. To
find a statement by Fleming now associated with Chance I should not
be too surprising, if we keep in mind that a good example of this form of
luck is easily lost sight of among the other varieties of chance, unless
the investigator himself points it out.

Many investigators are as energetic as bees, so their fast mental and
physical pace stirs up in the pot a certain amount of Chance II for this
reason alone. Examples of Chance II are surely all around us, but it is
difficult to prove with scientific certainty that they exist, because studies of twins would be required. No researcher seems to have a twin who

is indolent, but equal in all other abilities, to serve as a basis for comparison. Perhaps in Paul Ehrlich do we begin to see the impact of a persistent willingness to try something, to keep on going, until the right combination finally occurs. In the beginning of Ehrlich's career he looked for a treatment for bacterial and parasitic diseases. Later, he was diverted from this, his main work, by the prospect of finding a treatment for syphilis. Trying literally hundreds of different compounds, he finally succeeded with salvarsan (arsphenamine) on the 606th try.

Although the number 606 is quantitative and easy to remember, Chance II starts in this case with an earlier number no one ever noticed then and no one now recalls. At some blurred spot in our consciousness, the things we start out seeking fade away; from then on things *found* are empirical and utterly unpredictable. Therefore, Chance II begins, not in Ehrlich's boyhood, not even when he first started to look for a potential "606" compound, but at the hazy moment later on when his intellect really abandoned all rational hope of ever finding such a suitable compound. We don't know whether he passed this point at compound 106, 306, or 506. But the index of Chance II in his discovery would be how much he was astonished, not how much he was relieved, when 606 turned out to work.

You may rightly observe that because Ehrlich was trying to find a treatment for syphilis, his search was intentional, and therefore compound 606 was arrived at more by design than by accident. But Kettering might reply that after anyone makes 605 negative attempts to find something, the odds are almost nil that he will encounter it on the next try. When that far removed from the beginning of the quest, you're just "going through the motions"; you don't logically expect a solution. At this late date the outcome—always subject to the luck of the draw— would depend on whether or not a chemist happened to synthesize an effective compound that Ehrlich might then happen to try. In any event, in Paul Ehrlich, who always kept on going from his childhood until he stumbled on 606, we at least have a numerical, almost quantitative, expression of a persistent willingness to try until chance turns up a lucky combination.

As one example of Chance III (the prepared mind), we can turn to Conrad Röentgen's discovery of X rays. One day in 1895, Röentgen was experimenting with cathode rays in a darkened room. Some barium platinocyanide happened to be nearby. Suddenly, he noticed that the barium salt seemed to emit its own light—to fluoresce. No ordinary light rays could have been generated by the cathode tube and then been transmitted across the room to light up the barium, because a solid piece of cardboard blocked the path of light between the tube and the barium. Röentgen concluded that he was in the presence of something—that powerful invisible rays generated by the cathode tube had gone *through* the cardboard.

The discovery of the cause of puerperal sepsis by Ignaz Semmelweiss marks another example of Chance III. One day in 1847, a male laboratory assistant contracted a skin infection from infected pathological material. The infection spread and the man died. Semmelweiss was present when the autopsy was performed on the assistant, and recognized how closely his fatal disease resembled the infection occurring in mothers soon after childbirth ("childbed fever"). He perceived that obstetricians, who in those days used neither gloves nor other sterile techniques, were moving on from the room where one mother lay sick or the autopsy room where one mother had died to the delivery room of another. In so doing, they were spreading the disease to pregnant women undergoing delivery. Semmelweiss was severely attacked for his conclusion, but years later it would be proven that the disease was contagious, as he had predicted, and streptococci would be shown to be the bacterial cause.

On analyzing any given discovery, it may be a thorny matter to draw an arbitrary line between the contributions of Chance I through Chance IV. No need to—it is not an either/or matter. Another part of the problem resides in our lack of biographical or autobiographical information. If we only knew more about the background and life history of various scientists we might then find that their luck originated not in the sagacity of Chance III per se, but that it was in fact provoked by Chance IV, by distinctive personal actions highly specific for each man. Given this more personal insight, we might wish to add some further contribution of Chance IV to their discovery.

Take now, for one example of the subtle workings of personality in Chance IV, the background of Alexander Fleming. In his background was a boyhood shaped by the frugal economy of a Scottish hill farm in Ayrshire. Later, we find that much of his decision to train and work at old St. Mary's Hospital in London was not based on the excellence of its scientific facilities. Laboratories there were primitive by today's standards, damp and readily contaminated by organisms swirling in out of the London fog. Instead, Fleming's decision hinged on the fact that he liked to play water polo; St. Mary's had a good swimming pool. Without the *hobby*—swimming—that drew him to St. Mary's, Fleming would never have gone on to discover the bactericidal action of the penicillin mold! Among the several elements that entered into the penicillin story, this is one crucial personal item we tend to overlook. Still later, when he is forty-seven, let us visit his laboratory at St. Mary's and observe this same thrifty Scot at his work bench. It stands beneath a window open for ventilation, and its surface is buried under a clutter of old culture dishes. Why? Because Fleming won't throw any dish out until he is certain that everything possible has been learned from it. He then picks up one culture dish of staphylococci that, with ingrained thrift, he has hoarded for many days. The delay has been crucial. Had he thrown the dish out earlier, on schedule like the rest of us, the penicillin mold might not have had the opportunity to develop. But there it is now, growing in the overage culture dish, and he alone now has the prepared mind, the sagacity, to realize its implications.

We have now seen Sir Alexander Fleming's modest comment about his Irish Sweepstakes luck under Chance I, and can infer that Chance II entered his life by virtue of his many industrious years in the laboratory. These years, of course, involved generalized motions, common to most of us whose activities have been far less fruitful. We later observed how receptive he was (Chance III) and finally how his hobby and his thrifty habits coalesced in Chance IV. Anyone who has ever recovered from an infection with the aid of penicillin will realize how major was the impact of Fleming's discovery. This was not only the "magic bullet" against syphilis that Ehrlich moved toward all his life, but also a treatment for the streptococcal infection that Semmelweiss had shown was so contagious. Fleming's discovery earned him the Nobel Prize in physiology and medicine in 1945. (He shared it with Florey and Chain, who achieved the large-scale production of penicillin.) In Fleming's life, then, we see a fusion of all four forms of chance, and from this there follows a simple conclusion: *the most novel, if not the greatest discoveries occur when several varieties of chance coincide.* Let us call this unifying observation the *Fleming Effect*. His own life exemplifies it so well, and it deserves special emphasis.

A personal element of Chance IV also entered into Paul Ehrlich's discovery. When he was only eight, he already had enough motivation toward medical chemistry to persuade the town pharmacist to make cough drops for him after his own prescription. Even as a child, Ehrlich had this passionate hobby to find a treatment for something. But when he started out as a child, he really didn't know what he was looking for. What he would find would be decided to some degree by the luck of the draw—by what drugs a chemist could synthesize for him. For what influenced his discoveries beyond that point, we ourselves must explore the personality of Ehrlich, the man, and the modest expectations of the age in which he lived. Ehrlich stands out among his contemporaries because he was a very special man in the grip of a special private obsession: the idea that dyes which stained microorganisms would selectively kill them. Other researchers in those early days would try out dozens of compounds in many different experiments, and even in our own day, some still do for other goals on an even more sweeping scale. But the rest of us would stop at a hundred trials, and a few investigators might go on to test two or three hundred, and then give up. How many would be compulsive enough to try out hundreds more—and then insist that his associate, Hata, go back all over again to *retest* an apparent failure? The astonishing thing is that a laboratory error, which obliterated the beneficial effects of the drug, had occurred without Ehrlich's knowledge when "606" was first tested two years earlier. How many would later have retested compound 606, working beyond all rational hope that something useful might turn up? It is in this sense that some elements of Ehrlich's discovery seem to move beyond the ordinary limits of the curiosity and exploration in Chance II and enter the personal domain of Chance IV as well.

Why do we still remember these men? We cherish them, not as prize-winning scientists alone. There is more to it than that. The fact is that, as men, their total contribution transcends their scientific discoveries. Perhaps we remember them, too, because their lives show us how malleable our own futures are. In their work we perceive how many loopholes fate has left us—how much of destiny is still in our own hands. In them, we see that nothing is predetermined. Chance can be on our side, if we but stir it up with our energies, stay receptive to its every random opportunity, and continually provoke it by individuality in our hobbies, attitudes, and our approach to life.

20.

Never on Monday;
The Unhappy Accidents

A fisherman must be of contemplative mind, for it is often a long time between bites. He is by nature an optimist or he would not go fishing; for we are always going to have better luck in a few minutes or tomorrow.

Herbert Hoover

Up to now, I have emphasized the beneficial aspects of chance. But research is defeated as well as helped by circumstances. Chance is not always a welcome guest in the laboratory. "Fisherman's luck" rarely happens. And whimsy is also part of the picture. The purpose of this chapter is to redress the balance.

The snags and backlashes of bad luck are everywhere. It is a hard fact that in laboratory research unpredictable circumstances are more often arrayed against you than in your favor. For example, I have learned from long experience never to do major experiments on Mondays. It is just too difficult to pull everything "together" on Monday, and get it to work smoothly. Gremlins also thwart experiments on Tuesdays through Sundays. Test tubes crack, equipment breaks down, fuses blow, communication problems arise, etc. Each researcher has had a full quota of these misadventures—of the bad luck, or no luck, which serves to more than balance out his good luck. Years of these experiences breed a philosophical attitude. The investigator comes to know, as a fisherman does, that if he isn't occasionally soaked by water spilling over his boot tops then he isn't fishing aggressively enough in the deeper streams where the big trout lie. Moreover, a certain perverse optimism also creeps in. Indeed, some with a wryly humorous bent have handed down timeless maxims that deal with these unpredictable situations. These sayings, "Murphy's Laws," have since found their way into many laboratories and offices.

I have not been able to track down the origins of these proverbial truths.[1] They are worth noting, however, because they give an idea of how many different things can go wrong in an experiment, and tell us—as humor does—where the anxieties lie.

I. MURPHY'S LAWS AND EXTRAPOLATIONS THEREFROM:

   a. If anything *can* go wrong, it will.
   b. Left to themselves, things always go from bad to worse.
   c. If there is a possibility of several things going wrong, the one that will go wrong is the one that will do you the most damage.
   d. Nature always sides with the hidden flaw.
   e. If anything seems to be going well, you have obviously overlooked something.

II. PATRICK'S THEOREM:

If the experiment works, you must be using the wrong equipment.

III. HOMER'S FIVE THUMB POSTULATE:

Experience varies directly with the equipment ruined.

IV. FLAGEL'S LAW OF THE PERVERSITY OF INANIMATE OBJECTS:

Any inanimate object, regardless of composition or configuration, may be expected to perform at any time in a totally unexpected manner for reasons that are entirely obscure or completely impossible.

V. ALLEN'S AXIOM:

When all else fails, read the instructions.

VI. SPARE PARTS PRINCIPLE:

The accessibility of small parts that fall from the work bench varies directly with the size of the part and inversely with its importance to the completion of your work.

VII. THE COMPENSATION COROLLARY:

The experiment may be considered a success if no more than 50 percent of your observed results must be discarded to obtain a correlation with your hypothesis.

VII. GUMPERSON'S LAW:

The probability of a given event happening is inversely proportional to its desirability.

IX. THE ORDERING PRINCIPLE:

The supplies necessary for yesterday's experiment must be ordered no later than tomorrow noon.

X. THE ULTIMATE PRINCIPLE:

By definition, when you are working in the unknown, you know not what you will find.

XI. FUTILITY FACTOR:

No experiment is ever a complete failure; it can always serve as a bad example.

XII. GORDON'S LAW:

If a research project is not worth doing at all, it is not worth doing well.

XIII. PARDEE'S LAW:

There is an inverse relationship between the novelty of an observation and the number of investigators who report it simultaneously.

XIV. GUMMIDGE'S LAW:

The amount of expertise varies inversely with the number of statements understood by the general public.

XV. LOEB'S LAW:

If it works, keep on doing it.

XVI. THE HARVARD LAW:

The experimental animal, brought up under strict genetic and environmental conditions, still reacts as it damn well pleases.

Despite all the setbacks, researchers still press on in the laboratory. If, in their muddled ignorance, they see through a glass darkly, it will still appear as a glass half full rather than half empty. Vulnerable everywhere, experimenters persist in their contrary, buoyant optimism about the future. Part of this attitude reflects their sense, as Bruce Barton once phrased it, that: "Nothing splendid has ever been achieved except by those who dared believe that something inside them was superior to circumstance."[2] But most of their approach acknowledges a simple fact pointed out by Pogo when he said with greater whimsy and far greater accuracy: "We are confronted with insurmountable opportunities."[3]

THREE

The Roots of Creativity

The problem of creativity is beset with mysticism,
confused definitions, value judgments,
psychoanalytic admonitions, and the
crushing weight of philosophical speculation
dating from ancient times.

Albert Rothenberg

21.
Some Dimensions of Creativity

Many of the ideas which have been developed and rooted in the earlier literature on creativity are poorly conceived, frequently unsupported, and largely untenable. More rigorous treatment of the subject suggests that there is no one creative process and that indeed, the creative process is any thinking process which solves a problem in an original and useful way. Since the creative process and creativity itself are recognizable only through the creative product, the creative product must be original and useful and, if the creative product is an idea, it must be communicated or implemented.

H. Herbert Fox

In the foregoing chapters we have seen examples of how chance and a persistent creative meandering helped solve problems in molecular medicine. With these illustrations in mind, let us now examine creativity itself. My purpose in this third part of the book is briefly to summarize something of what is known, and not known, about creativity in the biomedical sciences. In a very real sense we will consider both the ecological and the neurophysiological determinants of the creative process, exploring the ways creativity springs from interactions between the person and his environment and speculating about the ways the brain functions in this process.

Most chapters that follow are largely in the essay form. They are still a personal commentary, though they necessarily differ in style from earlier portions of the book and differ from each other. In fact, I have selected only those observations from a sizable literature justified in terms of my own experience. It follows that this statement is what I think creativity is all about. My perspective is that of a biomedical investigator, but you will find most points apply broadly to creative activity in general. There are really *many creativities*, far more than illustrated here, and if I seem arbitrarily to define creativity in ways that fit myself, I ask the reader's forbearance and apologize in advance.

Obviously, there will be some connections between the personal illustrations in the first part and the discussions in the third part, but I am hesitant to join them. My preference is to let you establish links when you can, and make the connections for your own reasons, not for mine or anyone else's. More will be gained by giving free reign to your own imagination than by my trying to force, prematurely, a tight sense of literary, psychological, or scientific unity.

What is creativity, anyway? As Rothenberg and Fox have indicated above, the field doesn't abound in certainties. Creativity not only starts as a composite phenomenon, as clusters of abilities, difficult to tease apart, but its elements thereafter have a quicksilver quality. No two people look at the creative experience exactly the same way. I believe this diversity of views means at least three things: 1) a "pure" definition of creativity differs from person to person, and from people in one discipline to those in another; 2) the creative experience itself differs among individuals; 3) creativity is not always the same even in the same person.

Many traits go into creativity. Therefore, if you lack one ability, you can compensate for it with an excess of another. This slippery quality makes creativity an elusive target to define by psychological tests, because no one ability correlates with it 100 percent.

Some would restrict creativity solely to the flash of creative inspiration. I can't agree. I would emphasize that these brief moments are rare, that they have a long prelude, and that they must be followed up if they are to be productive. Still, whenever you have an intense episode of illumination, you know that it is a profound and very special experience. To my knowledge, no electroencephalographic studies using electrodes applied to the scalp have yet been made of human "brain waves" during a major moment of inspiration. (Who would be a normal volunteer for a study in which the recording was made from wires placed deeper in the brain where most of "the action" is?)

Clearly, our present knowledge of the creative process is still incomplete, but perhaps, one hundred years from now, some conceptions will emerge that are much more factual than those considered here. For the moment then, it will serve our purposes to be somewhat flexible in our definition of terms.

Creativity. I will use the word to refer in a general way to the long and complex series of interactions between an individual and his environment that culminate in something *new*.

Creative process. This may be thought of in two ways. The dichotomy illustrates the nature of our problem with definitions. A neuroscientist would regard the creative process as the basic, still unknown, set of internal neurophysiological and neurochemical events which determine creative activity and go on during it. Currently, however, the term is chiefly used in the descriptive sense to convey imperfectly in words the series of mental events culminating in a novel idea or other new product. We are still talking about "the mind" when we ought to be knowing more about the brain.

Creative experience. Creativity is perceived in oneself and observed in others. Still, our central source of information will always be what one individual experiences within himself during his own creative activity. Unfortunately, through the years, this personal information has become intermingled with the educated guesses of others about what the creator is experiencing. Moreover, hypotheses about the mechanism (or mechanisms) which might underlie the creative experience have also added their subtle influence. We inherit more of a hodgepodge than is generally appreciated.

Creativity in science. This may be considered the creative ability associated with something new, reproducible, and significant in a scientific field.

One distinction is worth examining: that between a discovery and an invention. A discovery implies that something already exists, that it has been uncovered and brought to light. An invention, on the other hand, implies that something new has been created. We should not, however, assume that an invention is inherently a more creative act than a discovery. It is the specific operational details in each instance that are important. Suppose, for example, that you happened to discover a biological principle in 1978. A minor matter, it might seem, for surely it had existed since time immemorial. Still, in order to formulate the principle you might first have had to make a complete break in your traditional patterns of thinking and then develop a brand new concept. Thus, it could be said that Einstein "only" discovered the basic principle $E = mc^2$, for it was "there" all the time. Yet this does not detract from the immensity of his achievement, nor does the fact that to express his vision he borrowed five symbols, in use for centuries, and arranged them into a sequence never used before.

Let us go back still further to 1492. We know that Columbus didn't "invent" the New World. It was already there; he had "only" to discover it. But to do so, at the age of forty-one, he had to trust in the relatively new notion that the earth was round, sail west with the assumption that he would not fall off the sharp edge of a flat earth (and first, incidentally, raise funds from Ferdinand and Isabella to finance the whole enterprise).

Certain inventions can be relatively trivial modifications of existing technologies; others, such as the invention of the wheel, can have enormous impact on mankind. Whether discovery or invention, we assess it as a creative act by the length of the leap of imagination and the extent of progress involved. Even then, our value judgments tend to be inexact; we don't know precisely what thoughts were going on inside the brain of the person at the moment he had the idea nor do we usually comprehend how difficult was the state of the art at the time he began.

As we survey what we don't know about creativity, some of the problems confronting us are analogous to those encountered in trying to understand an unknown disease. That is, much of what we now know about creativity is still down at the primitive clinical level of symptoms and signs. Impressive as symptoms and signs are, they do not constitute the "disease" in the medical sense. Similarly, in creativity, we do have some preliminary information but it is still quite descriptive. Take for example, the major sequences identified by Hughes[1] in the creative process:

$$interest \longrightarrow preparation \longrightarrow incubation \longrightarrow illumination \longrightarrow$$
$$verification \longrightarrow exploitation$$

(In practice, investigators jump back and forth from one to another, so the steps do not necessarily follow in sequence.)

It is useful to have words to describe these stages, for they remind us, at least, that the brain does not function the same way throughout the whole process. Earlier, we also saw that it does help us begin to understand a disease if we have a few words to describe it in clinical terms. But a description is not an explanation, and an understanding of symptoms still leaves us many steps removed from knowing the ultimate neurochemical and pathophysiological causes of a disease. Similar gaps block our understanding of creativity. As Fox has observed, *not until we understand the basic mechanisms and elements of thinking itself will we be in a position to understand the creative process.*[2] This, then, is a major problem.

How might we proceed from where we are to where we want to be? Let us consider one way: a naive experiment that might be designed to study "creative thinking." Impressive hurdles, both technological and ethical, stand in the way of this kind of experiment in man. But bear with this heuristic approach for the moment, if only because it gives a view of the magnitude of the problem.

Start with a chimpanzee, a banana beyond his reach, and a stick long enough to retrieve the banana. A moment of creative illumination would be defined when the chimp discovers he can use the stick to get the banana. Weeks earlier, fine wires (recording electrodes) would have been inserted into discrete regions of the brain. Similar wires attached to the body would also permit heart rate, blood pressure, and breathing to be monitored. All these wires would lead out to a special small box which would be so attached to the chimp that it would not hamper his movements. This box would then transmit all the physiological information about which of his nerve cells were firing, and when, to a distant recording instrument.[3] Note that we can already anticipate a problem in interpretation, for we would like, if possible, to distinguish between two things: one, the processes that link up a variety of facts to form a new idea; the other, the chimp's subsequent reactions to this new idea.

Biochemical changes would also be looked for. During the earlier operation, small tubes would also be inserted into the fluid normally bathing the spaces inside and outside the brain. These tubes would wash and drain the fluid into outside receptacles. Fresh fluid would be collected at regular intervals and later analyzed chemically for several neurotransmitter substances. These chemical substances, normally passing out of the brain into the fluid, would provide some general idea of the biochemical events corresponding with those that are neurophysiological. The routine neurochemical and neurophysiological events that occur during the chimp's routine daily activities would be recorded and later contrasted with those taking place during his special moment of "creative thinking," thus defined. Given this battery of information, we would hope to learn more about what goes on during the creative process. The experiment need not end at this stage, for one day we may safely be able to add newer drugs or superimpose psychological conditioning to enhance the effectiveness of the creative process.

The chimp experiment, reasonably naive, direct, and primitive, lies within the technological and conceptual limitations of today. Yet, even by present standards, it does not begin to measure the complexity of the creative process. Creativity, as we shall soon see, involves incredibly more than the fresh idea that the stick can reach the banana.

22.

The Creative Personality: Pro

Creativity may be conceived of as an exercise of the configurative powers of the whole psyche, involving all its substance, the play of its entire energy.

Brewster Ghiselin

Everyone wonders, introspectively, "how did I get that way?" I have never been able to identify one element in isolation in myself. Nor have there been two, or three. Instead, a multiplicity of elements have interacted: *the whole life style participated in problem-solving.*

I have been curious to know which ingredients, in combination, make up a creative personality. Searching the literature, I encountered four groups of characteristics. Lists have the disadvantage of breaking up a narrative flow, and you may wonder why they are included here. My reasons are threefold. First, I find that each characteristic rings true, although for me, some are more valid than others. I have indicated the traits that I weigh highly by an open star (⋆). Second, as you look over these traits, you can clearly see that *a spectrum of characteristics is involved.* Third, no one list is complete in itself. This probably means something. It suggests that each of the different authors has emphasized those characteristics closest to his own modus operandi or those which he believes others use. If you are someone who is stunned by long lists, by all means skip over them in this and subsequent chapters. But if you are not, and wish to linger, you will find your creative self defined here and there. For everyone is creative, even though the kind and degree of creativity varies observably from person to person.

We begin with the observation that creative traits can be identified early in life. Witty, Conant, and Strang[1] suggest that creative people have, when they are still children, the following major characteristics:

A sensitive perception of details in the world of nature and the world of man;

☆ an awareness of and concern about unsolved problems—the attitude of inquiry;

☆ fluency of thought. Ideas come readily; later they are evaluated for quality and logic;

☆ concentration—ability to enter wholeheartedly and personally into an experience;

☆ integration—ability to find unity in the diversity of nature, to discover unexpected likenesses, and to relate or connect things not previously related or connected;

☆ flexibility and spontaneity guided by a goal or purpose;

☆ originality and individuality. The creative person has the courage and inner directedness to resist conformity. Not content with what is *now* accepted, he looks forward to what *may* be accepted;

☆ ability to analyze and abstract;

☆ ability to synthesize;

☆ ability to go beyond the facts and discern new implications, to imagine more than evidence obviously shows, to speculate on relations that may not at present be verifiable;

☆ keen satisfaction in creative activities;

☆ vivid imagery;

Superior abstract and verbal intelligence.

Flexibility is noted above, but we must distinguish between two kinds of flexibility.[2] One is the tendency to shift from one category of meaning to another, from one kind of logically defined entity to another. This logical approach is regulated both by the structured rules of concept formation, and is limited by what we can absorb from our culture. Not surprisingly, it involves the kind of flexibility that correlates with general intelligence. The second type of flexibility is much more loose or even unstructured. It involves a meandering of attention, a readiness to free associate, to daydream, to unleash one's thoughts into broad unclassified paths only tangentially related either to the starting point or to each other. This latter kind of flexibility correlates with the rapid production of original ideas. In the former, the word "dog" might lead to "bark" (as a vocalization). In the latter, the word "dog" might lead to "bone," thence to "cave," and from there on perhaps to "painting" or even to a variety of chance.

It is no simple matter to disentangle "pure" creativity from general intelligence using psychological tests. What the more creative have is the ability to generate large numbers of ideas.[3] The more ideas there are, the more unique some of them will be. But, if some of our ideas are to prove useful, our ideational fluency (our ability to "ride associative currents") must sooner or later be coupled with yet another capability. For we must rapidly discard irrelevant ideas, however original, that simply won't fit. It is not enough to generate a spectrum of novel possibilities; we must sift out the good ones, next make our trial and error mistakes as fast as possible,[4] and, finally, like a bulldog, hang on to what seems to be the most practical solution. (When this, too, proves inadequate, we have to be willing to go back, pick up the pieces, and start again.)

Wallach and Kogan also point out that the creative tend to have a playful attitude and view their job more as a game than a task.[5] They may be on the most serious quest and experience many agonies along the route, but many creative persons still are aware, at least at some point, that they are joyfully engaged in a kind of a game, one in which they have at least a sporting chance.

Thus far we have talked about creativity in general. What about creativity in science? Here, we find ourselves adopting a more restrictive point of view. *For in science, we see the creative process sustained in relation to a product—one that is novel, significant, completed, and reproducible.* And, often as not, chance can play a key role in determining the novelty. What sort of person becomes creatively engaged in scientific activities? How well does he conform to the popular image of the "mad scientist" portrayed in the cartoons by Lichty or Dr. Suess? Is he a middle-aged eccentric, bald and bespectacled, with a crazed gleam in his eyes, surrounded by bubbling vats at his laboratory bench? Well, yes and no.

Common observation tells us that scientists as a whole do tend to share certain characteristics. What we really want to know is precisely which characteristics determine the most fruitful final outcome, and which are irrelevant. This means that we ought to know much more than the demographic and psychological characteristics of a few scientists judged to be outstandingly creative. We must also find out which of the many characteristics relevant to creativity are the ones that sharply separate these most creative individuals from their less successful cohorts—from that much larger number of other scientists born at the same time, raised and educated in the same favorable setting, who have not gone on to make such major contributions. This latter kind of information, called cohort analysis, is very difficult to come by. It requires carefully controlled research on large numbers of scientists of varying degrees of creativity. Still, this information will be fundamental to our total understanding of the creative process.

A composite creative American scientist emerges from the existing literature on creativity somewhat as follows. His roots are sunk in the soil of a liberal era, dynamically oriented toward science and technology. It is this yeasty cultural milieu that has stimulated him to seek out new experiences in scientific fields. He tends to be of middle to upper middle-class Anglo-Saxon–German origin, and has a Protestant religious affiliation. He may have a father in one of the professions for whom his feelings are more those of a high regard than of love. Both parents have probably completed high school, may have gone to college, and have maintained a wide range of intellectual interests. This family setting has encouraged him to undertake almost any kind of exploratory activity. Whether as a first-born son or one much older than his next siblings, he tends to be placed early on his own resources.[6] Somewhat late in developing socially, he is on the shy side, belongs to few clubs except those related to science, and may not date steadily until well into college. He spends much time in a systematic pursuit of his own areas of interest, mostly alone, but sometimes with another boy or two of similar interests. He is an avid reader, poor at maintaining family ties, and this general orientation towards ideas and things rather than people appears early and changes rather little.[7] In contrast to the natural scientist summarized above, the social scientist has an early interest and involvement with others. It seems possible that the physician-investigator may reflect a mixture of the two.

What about the scientist being middle-aged? (a period that seems to expand in both directions). Prize-winning scientific work *is* performed later in life than one might think. For example, American Nobel laureates performed the work that earned them the prize in medicine and physiology at an average age of forty-one. Physicists, on the other hand, were younger, averaging only thirty-six years.[8] Still, a disproportionately large percent of all laureates did their work even later—when they were forty to forty-four years old, bearing in mind the age of their cohorts in the general run of all American scientists at the same time. In terms of patentable work, the peak output comes between the ages of thirty and forty, and by forty-five most inventors tend to be "over the hump" on the downhill side.[9] We remember the exceptions.

Beyond their great emotional and motivational diversity, research scientists tend to be complex, independent types who can control and focus a wide variety of emotional responses in areas related to their work. They are sensitive both to self, to others, to sensory stimuli from the outside world, and clearly fascinated with scientific and intellectual pursuits.

To me, among the decisive traits, one stands foremost. That trait is ✩✩ curiosity. I doubly emphasize it because the research lines I have pursued almost always emerged from a simple, naive wondering about something. If we allow that necessity is the mother of invention, then curiosity is surely the father.

I would agree with Taylor and Barron[10] that several other traits delineate the productive scientist:

✩ a high degree of autonomy, self-sufficiency, and self-direction;
✩ a preference for mental manipulations involving things rather than people; a somewhat distant or detached attitude in interpersonal relations; and a preference for intellectually challenging situations rather than socially challenging ones;
   high ego strength and emotional stability;
✩ a liking for method, precision, exactness;
   a preference for repression and isolation as defense mechanisms in dealing with affective and instinctual energies;
✩ a high degree of personal dominance, but a dislike of personally toned controversy;
✩ a high degree of control of impulse, amounting almost to over-control: relatively little talkativeness, gregariousness, impulsiveness;

☆ a liking for abstract thinking, with considerable tolerance of cognitive ambiguity;

☆ marked independence of judgment, rejection of group pressures toward conformity in thinking;

superior general intelligence;

an early, very broad interest in intellectual activities;

☆ a drive toward comprehensiveness and elegance in explanation;

☆ a special interest in the kind of "wagering" which involves pitting oneself against uncertain circumstances in which one's own effort can be the deciding factor;

☆ an unusual appreciation of the intuitive and nonrational elements in human nature;

☆ A profound commitment to the search for aesthetic and philosophic meaning in all experience.

I have been especially interested in the psychological findings[11] that investigators in the biological sciences rely heavily on their visual imagery, insist on rational controls and share with artists many of the same styles of thinking. I usually think, at times exclusively, in visual terms. Sometimes the image is clear, sometimes murky; either may seem loosely attached to words as I talk, or to a tumble of vague thoughts. When the internal images—the thought-visions—are especially clear, they preempt my conscious awareness of objects in the external world. External vision no longer registers, seems almost to be disconnected, and fades from my memory of the moment.

To me, research has many analogies with painting. First you imagine in your mind's eye what it is you might do. This inner seeing is all nonverbal activity. Then, you sketch in the bare outlines of the scene. Next come the broad, bold brush strokes, later, the fine details. In between the two last techniques you may swing back and forth many times from one color to the other. Or, putting it another visual way: at the bedside or in the laboratory, you operate very much like a "zoom" lens, set on low power magnification for scanning much of the time, shifting freely to ultrahigh magnification when minute details are important, then back to medium power for items of intermediate size.

The visual element of creativity is not a single skill, but one separable even in children into at least three components: a preference for complexity, a skill at handling complexity, and an ability to complete what is unfinished.[12] Beyond these gifts the adult researcher needs a special permissive attitude, one that enables him to "see" deeply into a problem, then to find relationships between many seemingly unrelated items, and finally to forge links that connect them. He is not only adept at recognizing a cluster of facts, but he is utterly transfixed when he notes an exception to the rule. Incongruity in a situation snaps him instantly to attention. Charles Darwin's son described this quality in his father as follows: "There was one quality of mind which seemed to be of special and extreme advantage in leading him to make discoveries. It was the power of never letting exceptions pass unnoticed. Everybody notices a fact as an exception when it is striking or frequent, but he had a special instinct for arresting an exception."[13]

Walter Cannon's[14] many years of pioneering laboratory experience led him to include the following abilities among those necessary for the creative investigator:

☆ Resourcefulness;
   a forward look;
   a philosophical approach;
☆ a faith in the importance of his present and future scientific efforts;
☆ willingness to take risks—including the regrettable risk of losing time and reputation;
☆☆ curiosity;
☆ ability to design an experiment;
☆ imaginative insight—the projection of an idea—the ability to ask the proper questions;
☆ a critical attitude to keep imagination in check;
☆ a variety of experience—which gives insight into diverse methods;
☆ ingenuous honesty—readiness to surrender to adverse facts;
   technical skill and knowledge of equipment;
☆ good groundwork in the basic sciences, including a knowledge of statistical methods;
☆ keen powers of observation;
   retentive and facile memory;
   patience;
☆ willingness to take infinite pains and to record carefully;
   an attitude of humility.

We may wonder why humility is so rarely cited. It is there. Certainly, it can't dominate the scene in anyone who has strong inner needs to master his environment,[15] but it is still there. Humility seems to have both primary and secondary origins. Primary humility stems from the researcher's original sense of awe as he looks at the natural world around him. In me, this feeling deepens and results in an inferiority complex of cosmic proportions whenever I weigh the dust of my puny advances and place it in the vast perspective of the whole universe. The numbers alone are mind-bending: as a first-order approximation, there may be a hundred thousand million sunlike stars in our galaxy, the Milky Way. And in the rest of the universe, there are at least a thousand million other galaxies!!

Secondary humility evolves from outright failures; from being wrong; from measuring one's own small successes against what should have been possible, and also from measuring them against what others have accomplished. This feeling also grows rapidly and is quickly reinforced by other experiences. The introspective investigator soon realizes how precarious his positions are. For example, it was a humbling experience indeed to find that my dog, Tom, would provide the most crucial instruction to a distinguished colleague like Susumu Yokoi, who came all the way from Japan to learn in my laboratory. Smugness doesn't last long in research.

Koestler[16] identifies five characteristics of the outstanding scientist:

☆ an oceanic sense of wonder;
☆ a curious mixture of skepticism and credulity
  precocity;
☆ dual abilities, both to generalize and to concentrate on the particulars;
☆ multiple potentials—enough to succeed in any one of several careers.

In research, aptitude can only go so far, for as we have seen, true creativity and intelligence are not synonymous.[17] Indeed, creative persons seem distinguished far more by their interests, attitudes, and drives than by their intellectual abilities, as conventionally measured. Given a basic IQ of about 120, a further increase in measured intelligence is not necessarily associated with a significant increase in creativity.[18] Beyond that point, what seems to determine creativity is a person's motivational and stylistic variables. For example, those whose profession is creative writing tend to show a "moral attitude" and to be committed to larger meanings of an aesthetic and philosophical sort. They are individuals constantly involved in creating their own private universes of meaning: "cosmologists all."[19] Indeed, we can almost view some creative persons as missionaries on both an external and internal quest. Their well-rationalized quest may appear to be for an elegant answer, one that will throw a new light of understanding into a dark corner of the impersonal cosmos. But their internal quest is for a highly personalized, idealized interpretation—one that brings order and meaning to their *own* universe. Such a private interpretation must satisfy their own symbolic needs and aesthetic concepts.

The creative personality certainly tends to be aesthetically sensitive. Perhaps this is best appreciated in the visual sphere. Some would regard the brief measurement of aesthetic preference termed the Barron-Welsh art scale as a test of great value in predicting creative potential.[20] High scores on this scale, reflecting an intrinsic visual preference for complex form and design, are believed by some to correlate with creative potential not only in the arts and literature but in the physical sciences and engineering as well.

If I were to limit myself to the five most important traits, I would quickly select: *curiosity, imagination, enthusiasm, discrimination, and persistence.* But this would be like trying to define the complex operations of a whole human being in terms of his five most vital organs: nervous system, heart, lungs, adrenals, liver. They are essential, but they, too, are only part of the total picture.

23.

The Creative Personality: Pro and Con

If a man does not keep pace with his companions, perhaps it is because he hears a different drummer. Let him step to the music which he hears; however measured or far away.

Henry Thoreau

Given all the foregoing requirements, you might conclude that a creative investigator should be a kind of innovative super Eagle Scout who delights in problem-solving and helps little old ladies to cross the street in his spare time. Actually, more unconventional and eccentric qualities are required; the investigator must be, in every sense of the term, an opportunist at heart, wrapped in layer after layer of paradoxes. Let's now look at the other side of the picture.

It has been repeatedly stressed how nonconformist the more creative are.[1] Other socially downgraded traits that go along with the disposition toward originality include rebelliousness, disorderliness, and vanity, if not exhibitionism.[2] Hans Selye has classified the scientific personalities he knows into sixteen types whose features one should either avoid or emulate.[3] The litany is too long to reproduce here, but as Selye, too, confesses, most of us will admit to at least traces of every one of the sins it enumerates. Mea culpa.

An interesting kind of fluid intellectual instability has been noted by Barron, who finds that the effectively original person is one who can regress very "far out" for the moment, yet still be able quickly to return to a high degree of rationality.[4] As he does so, he can take back with him the fruits of his earlier regression to fantastic modes of thought. If the person is basically confident of his own ability to discern reality accurately, then he can afford to give free rein to his powers of imagination. Thus, the creative person "may be at once naive and knowledgeable, being at home equally to primitive symbolism and to rigorous logic. He is both more primitive and more cultured, more destructive and more constructive, occasionally crazier and yet adamantly saner, than the average person."[5]

I hope that the reader who feels, simultaneously, the tug of these same struggling opposites in himself has fully experienced them in what to me is one of the supreme turning points in the theater. It may come as no surprise that I would refer to the play, *Harvey*. (It just happens that the author's name is Mary Chase.) Up to the end of the second act of the play we have become convinced that Elwood P. Dowd, its lovable eccentric, is probably hallucinating when he converses with his invisible friend, Harvey, whom he describes as a white rabbit, six feet one-and-a-half inches tall. Indeed, the logical part of our mind resists any notion to the contrary. Then, as the play approaches its culminating moment, the action suddenly stops, the actors exit, and the empty stage is deserted and lifeless. Or, is it? For the door knob now rattles at stage left, the door opens and closes, as if by an unseen hand, and after an appropriate interval, the door at stage right opens and shuts, as if by an unseen . . . paw? Then suddenly, we grasp the enchanting certainty that Harvey *does* exist, even though he's invisible to us. Our fantasy becomes *real*. With a giant hop, our imagination propels us into a delightful new fantastic reality. It is this delicious, incongruous juxtaposition of reality and fantasy that captivates us not only for the remainder of the play, but also far on into a lifetime. A good new idea in research has something of the same quality—satisfying us by combining in a flash, old, richly personal symbolism with a fresh vision of reality.

Kuhn makes an important point when he observes that "very often the successful scientist must simultaneously display the characteristics *both* of the traditionalist and of the iconoclast."[6] He regards this age-old tension between tradition and innovation as the essential tension in scientific research. This readiness to break with convention is well-illustrated in Thomas Edison's saying: "There ain't no rules around here! We're trying to accomplish something!" Equally strong tensions, as described by Gregg, arise on the threshold of discovery: "To me, one of the surest evidences of probable ability in a research man is this—that when he feels near to a new truth he is overwhelmed with excitement and elation and yet almost paralysed by cautious skepticism and self-imposed dubiety."[7]

The investigator is forever in quest of the new. He is always curious, unfulfilled, intellectually restless, not satisfied with what is already well known. Indeed, to the extent that the old constricts the new and prevents it from emerging, he finds himself in rebellion against it. To this extent, creativity is the natural enemy of dogma and conformity. Because he knows this instinctively, the creative person feels a piercing shock when he recognizes that "the enemy exists within the gates," that dogma and orthodoxy still linger within himself. In fact, he will discover more than a few rigid rods within the structure of his own personality around which he molds zones of concrete conformity. Not until he consciously readjusts to this fact will he start to be truly open and even-tempered, responding as objectively to the ideas of others as he does to his own.

The evidence that creative men demonstrate a high degree of "masculine-associated" traits such as assertiveness, confidence, determination, ambition, and drive for power, while at the same time having a greater than average incidence of "feminine" interests, suggests that it is a wedding of the necessary sensitivity and intuition together with purposive action and determination that is conducive to creativeness.[8] The creative man may be less constrained to deny the side of his nature, viewed as feminine in our football-oriented culture, that reflects an openness to emotions and feelings and considerable self-awareness.

We see, then, that the creative personality includes some unusual executive abilities—if not to reconcile contradictions then at least to manage to live with them. I have presented a representative field of these opposing traits in figure 12. No single one of the characteristics on the rim of this field is all good or all bad. It is important that there be a balanced spectrum of opposing traits, and an inevitable tugging tension between each polar pair of them. Moreover, each trait serves creative ends—sometimes one way, other times another way. The creative person not only lives with the pull of these contrasting centrifugal forces, but goes on to resolve them in creative endeavor.

Some may feel they can accurately locate the epicenter of their personality in one well-defined spot. I have not been able to manage this. I have always had a strong inner sense of operating at many points that merge along a whole series of spectral bands; of having a variety of interests and traits that seem more and more compatible as the years go on even though they may be quite opposite. My inner feeling is not of being bivalent, or ambivalent, but of being polyvalent. Pledged to establish facts and biological truths, I still worship no final conclusions, but tend to look beyond toward an infinite complexity of things. Perhaps one reason my favorite movie is "Roshomon" is because it exemplifies so well the view that truth itself differs depending on the perceptions of those who look at facts in the light of their own internal needs.

No one is easy to live and work with who has as many contrary characteristics and implicit tensions as does the creative person. Consequently, he may not be able to achieve his creative goals unless he learns to adopt or at least simulate the prevailing norms of civilized behavior. The scientist soon discovers that his colleagues expect him to follow a certain code of social behavior. We observe, in Stein's summary

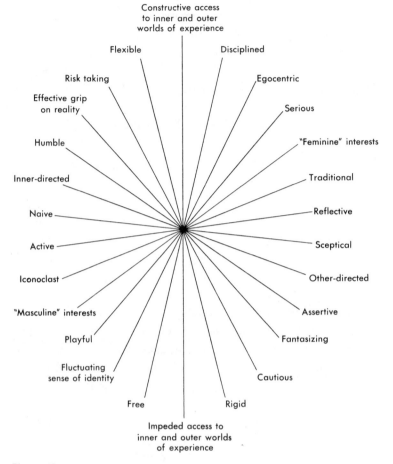

Figure 12.

of this code, something of these expectations. They, too, carry their own intrinsic contradictions. My own pragmatic side has to agree with all of them:

The researcher is expected to be assertive without being hostile or aggressive; he must speak his mind without being domineering; he is to be aware of his superiors, colleagues, and subordinates as persons, but he is not to get too involved with them on a personal basis; with superiors he is expected to know his place without being timid, obsequious, or acquiescent. He may be a lone wolf on the job, but he is not to be isolated, withdrawn, or uncommunicative. If he is any of these, he had best be so creative that his work speaks for itself. On the job he is expected to be congenial but not sociable; off the job he is expected to be sociable but not intimate. On the job, as he tries to gain a point, more funds, or more personnel, he can be subtle but not cunning; in all relationships, he is expected to be sincere, honest, purposeful, and diplomatic, but not unwilling to accept short cuts or to be inflexible and Machiavellian; finally, in the intellectual area he is to be broad without spreading himself thin, deep without being pedantic, and "sharp" without being over-critical.[9] It seems unlikely that any strong personality would ever succeed 100 percent in all of these areas, for if he tried, he would be busier than a chameleon in a kaleidoscope, far too occupied to be fully creative.

Hallucinogenic drugs have become so much a part of our present culture that no look at creativity today would be complete without passing mention of their pros and cons. The cons outweigh the pros by a wide margin, because the medical reasons for not using drugs are impressive enough to deter even the most curious.[10] Experiments in *certain* subjects, however, have given results that seem germane to creativity, and the findings should be noted. For example, relatively low doses of LSD or mescaline have been given to stable, responsible professionals whose usual occupations involved problem-solving.[11] These subjects were not representative, then, of habitual drug users in the usual street-scene drug culture. The volunteers were carefully prepared for the experiment and began their "trip" with a positive air of expectancy. While on the drug, their visual performance improved objectively and their ideas increased in fluency. Moreover, their subjective reports showed improvement in many other key areas essential to creativity. Inhibition and anxiety were reduced, the ability to see the whole problem and its solutions in larger perspective was increased, and new ideas poured forth. There was an increased capacity for visual imagery and fantasy, improved concentration, and enhanced empathy with other persons, external processes, and objects. Forgotten data in the unconscious became more accessible, dissimilar elements were associated in meaningful new ways, and there was a heightened appetite for elegance. Moreover, problems solved under the influence of the drugs proved to be of practical use, and the subjects reported a long-lasting plateau of enhanced creative ability for at least two weeks afterwards.

On the other hand, in a different study, subjects given LSD improved only in their ability to give unique responses on word association tests, but did poorly on other tests requiring visual attention.[12] Although LSD made them more open to unique associations, it did not help them narrow their attention on a more delimited perceptual field. The authors concluded that if LSD were used indiscriminately in a relatively unselected group of people, it would not be likely to enhance creative ability.

Certainly, no one familiar with all the other dismal escalating liabilities and uncertainties of the drug scene would wish to use LSD or other hallucinogens to enhance creativity outside of an experimental format. Few, indeed, would volunteer nowadays even in such a format. Not only do we have ample evidence that hallucinogens can, in fact, shift the perceptual performance of many subjects on tests in a direction consistent with "brain damage",[13] but there is still no single coherent explanation of exactly how and where the drugs work in the complex circuitry of the brain.[14] In the interim, the actions of someone who would repeatedly use a drug to tamper with the fantastic transmitter chemistry of his own brain seems not far removed from the behavior of a person who would shoot a high voltage pulse of electricity into the wiring of his expensive color television set hoping to get a more interesting and meaningful image. The results might be more interesting for a moment, perhaps, in that they would be novel and, indeed, rapidly changing. But as a message, the results would be confusing to interpret, obscured by static, and the set might never work quite the same thereafter, for it could lose some of its fine-tuned circuitry in the process. The challenge to us, individually, and to our society, is to lead more creative lives without drugs.

The creative personality, as far as our present understanding of it is concerned, has many facets, some polished, others rough, some superficial, others deep. In a sense, the many traits considered above many be viewed as the individual brush strokes and local colors in a painting. They will define the edges and the substances of the trees, the grasses, and the clouds. But let us now turn to some deeper and more basic motivations underlying the creative temperament. For they have shaped the overall subject matter, mood, and composition of the painting from the beginning, and they will suggest its symbolic meaning.

24.

Motivations Underlying Creativity

Some split between the inner world and the outer world is common to all human beings; and the need to bridge the gap is the source of creative endeavour.

Anthony Storr

It takes more than a certain kind of engine in a certain kind of chassis to make your automobile move forward; you constantly need fuel in the tank. So it is with creativity. It helps to start with a good brain and diversified experiences, but thereafter, some high-octane psychic fuel is essential. These psychic roots underlying creativity are perceptively examined by Anthony Storr, who blends psychoanalytical insights and common sense in a compelling way.[1]

Storr observes that we are each frustrated by the constraints of infancy and early childhood. Our dissatisfactions soon evolve into a rich fantasy world. This is not something to avoid, for from this inner world will spring the divine discontent that will compel us later to seek our symbolic satisfactions in creative achievement. Our creative efforts will help us not only to master our external world, but also to come to terms with our inner world. Children deeply imprinted by earlier experiences may well be the ones later impelled toward creative outlets.

As a young child, I was forever asking "why?" Many questions a child asks can be satisfactorily answered to some degree or other, but when I asked the question, "why is a color *colored?*", there were no satisfying answers. I was hung up on this question for well over a week, and I remember passionately asking others about colors at every opportunity I could get. My parents didn't know; my teachers didn't know. *Nobody* really knew. There was a huge information gap about colors. This lack of completeness in my knowledge made a strong imprint on my young imagination—one of the strongest I can remember.

Now shift the scene to New York City twenty years later. The fellow in neuropathology at Columbia is seated at a library table reading about how a blue dye changes color when it meets an unknown substance in tissue. At that moment, I was not aware of any connection at a conscious level between the two episodes. Now, writing this forty years later, it finally has occurred to me that the two events are linked at some deeper level. Moreover, when the gap connecting the child with the neuropathology fellow was closed, the result was a high voltage circuit in terms of psychic energy. Such a moment of closure is usually unforgettable.

Motivations depend on a lot of activity blended in from many neuronal circuits: the amount of "drive" from the hypothalamus, the degree of general arousal coming from the reticular core of the brain, the "push" from internal signals that signify something is lacking, and the "pull" of external incentive stimuli.

Creative endeavor serves as a remarkably useful way to express each of our motivations even though we differ widely in temperament. It can be not only a way for us to sublimate, and a means to fulfill wishes, but also a defense against our internal anxieties. Creative activity defends against anxiety if we are introverted and of schizoid temperament, distressed by our feelings of alienation and a lack of meaning. (Einstein serves as a prototype in this regard.) If, for example, you are an introvert, and bury yourself in solitary creative activity, you relate in this way to something meaningful both to yourself and to society. At the same time, you can avoid the many problems caused by direct interpersonal relationships. In creative work, you can finally communicate on your own terms, because your work will establish your own kind of private world, one in which your own inner reality becomes more important than that of the external world. Moreover, you can overcome your own sense of the unpredictability in life through creative expressions that help structure a rational, established order of things.[2]

Suppose you are of manic-depressive temperament. Creative efforts provide you both recurrent boosts of self-esteem and outlets for submerged aggressive feelings which cannot be openly expressed. Indeed, a creative achievement may also help atone for the guilt involved in this type of aggression. A new work may also give you a legitimate way to rebel against parents and other authoritarian figures both in the past and present.

If you are an obsessive person, creative activity may represent a vehicle by which you can transcend tight obsessional control and escape from other rigid personal limitations. Problem solving will also afford you a constructive way to displace internal hostility. Because you have a particular need for order, logic, and symmetry you will be well-equipped to discern the imperfect, to formulate better hypotheses than now exist. You, in particular, will savor the refreshment of your spontaneous, inspired moments, contrasting so sharply as they do with your other endless hours, so full of willed working over as to seem contrived. Indeed, your delight, as well as your need is to "stay loose." To you, even the need for tidiness can facilitate creativity if it serves as an introductory, ceremonial function to the task ahead and not as a time-wasting compulsion.[3]

Whatever our temperaments, we can be reassured that a satisfying sexual life and creative activity are not mutually incompatible, because the one does not necessarily substitute for the other. The creative adult is still impelled to create even when he enjoys a happy, fully satisfactory heterosexual relationship. He is driven to do so, in fact, because he still carries a passionate residue of dissatisfaction from his childhood, one that will not be resolved in his adult life except in symbolic ways. "It is not the suppression of *adult* sexuality that leads to creativity, but of its childhood precursors."[4] Whereas genuine love between mature adults does not interfere with creativity, a childish infatuation that promises a deceptively complete answer to life might make creative pursuits seem superfluous for awhile.

Storr disposes of the notion that creativity necessarily involves a substantial love for power, fame, or honor. To him, the desire for fame is but one part of an artist's motivation; the motive is linked with the success *of the art itself* and not with fame for its own sake.

An important aspect of motivations is revealed in questions of scientific priority: who discovered it *first*? Bystanders tend to view this kind of concern solely as a personality conflict between two or more fame-seeking persons as to which will emerge with the glory in the eyes of their contemporaries or in those of posterity. This can be so obvious that it is easy to overlook another consideration. The fact is that the inner-directed creative investigator (like the composer or the artist) also defines his territory in order to establish who *he* is, so that he himself will clearly know. The territorial imperative in animals is clear enough, and it obviously also exists in man. But creative man is far more complex. I would propose that one aspect of what has been viewed as the territorial imperative may, in creative man, be focused as much at his internal boundary as it is externally.

The strong inner pressure to stand apart, to innovate, is exemplified by one physicist who said: "The only ideas that I will pursue are those I choose specifically because it is unlikely that anyone else would have approached them in the same way . . . I'm not going to waste my time on a standard way. The other guy can do that. I'm always trying to do things in a way that's different or original."[5]

Why should a researcher need such a clear sense of his own identity? Because, for one reason, no one functions well as a vague blur without a foundation, without some firm point of reference, some substance or outline. To act decisively in complex situations, it helps to be physiologically well-defined somewhere, unique in something, an actor in the spotlight center stage, not an extra in the shadow of scenery on the set. The issue is more than one of self-confidence in the psychological sense. It is one, indeed, of personal body image in the neurological sense. If you are going to enter into any form of stimulating contacts with your environment you first have to define quite literally where you leave off and your surroundings begin. A personal identity is a necessity for everyone, but it is more difficult for one who is not only various and multipolarized, but shifting. For, like the versatile actor who performs in multiple roles, an investigator, too, may have difficulty in figuring out "which one is the real me?" But if his work represents something definite and tangible, if its ambivalences and ambiguities are resolved, then so too will the researcher be resolved in the process. It is through his work that he becomes evident to himself. He will invest so much of his time and energy in it that he comes to identify with it in his own mind. It is this externalization of self in one's work that makes the basic assertion at the territorial boundary line as much "that's *me!*" as "that's mine!"

I find it instructive when giving a seminar on a research topic to write nothing down in the way of notes but rather to use slides and improvise the words of the talk as I go along. This way I can find out, from my spontaneous remarks and improvisations, what I really have been thinking about. I understand myself much better when my thoughts are out where I can verbalize them and then listen to them.

Joseph Conrad expressed it this way: "I don't like work—no man does—but I like what is in work—the chance to find yourself, your own reality—for yourself, not for others—what no other man will ever know. They can only see the mere show, and never tell what it really means."[6]

But suppose someone else turns up with the same ideas or with exactly the same finding. Where is the researcher's unique sense of identity? Imagine the comparable situation in painting: two artists independently turn up with the same composition, same colors, same frame; the paintings hang side by side in an exhibit. For the inner-directed scientist, the central issue will not be so much the loss of time or of the drop in recognition from the outside. These are external layers. The problem, instead, will be the confusion and devaluation of self, the vague sense of floating adrift without a compass fix, the other face in the bathroom mirror asking: "who *are* you if you haven't created something unique in your work?" If the parentage of his creation, this "child" of his, is not only disputed but the child is adopted by someone else, then his intimate identity with his work becomes ambiguous, and his own inner sense of clarity is further blurred.

Let us be certain about one point: creativity need not imply neurosis. The passionate tensions that fuel creative expression do not necessarily constitute a sickness. In fact, the reverse is true, because true creative effort represents a constructive adaptation to our past experiences, an adaptation that becomes an integral part of our universal human heritage. Neurosis, on the other hand, clearly implies that this adaptation has failed.[7] In brief, the best creative work represents passion fulfilled, whereas a neurosis may be thought of as passion thwarted.[8] The liberal expression by creative individuals of obvious neurotic traits need not be taken too seriously, for in their very openness is implied the existence of a useful degree of freedom. True, psychological illness can coexist with creativity, and interact with it, but the role the malady plays (even if it lingers on) will differ from individual to individual.

Pickering observes, for example, that a neurosis may play no real role (as in the case of Elizabeth Barrett), or it may provide both the novel idea and the necessary drive that helps see the idea through to completion (as in Joan of Arc, Mary Baker Eddy, Sigmund Freud, and Proust).[9] Moreover, the creative work of Eddy, Freud, and Proust was useful in that it served as the mental catharsis that aided their cure. Finally, a psychological illness—like any other illness—may shield the invalid for truly creative work, relieving him of the everyday chores that would otherwise waste his time and energy and defeat his purpose.[10]

We now have, I hope, a truer, more charitable vision of the creative artist—no longer does he fit the popular image of one who exorcises his private demons, wielding a brush in one trembling hand, while fingering the bandage over his ear with the other.

One private demon will not go away; indeed, it draws ever closer. Infinitely more than other animals, man confronts one inescapable fact. He knows his life span is finite. Death is out there, sooner or later. Like other biomedical investigators, I live daily with a sharpened perception of this naked fact. But to me, creative activity provides not so much a way to postpone or avoid thinking about death as a way to anticipate it and make a deliberate adjustment to it. Rollo May summarizes one prevailing attitude when he says, "Creativity is not merely the innocent spontaneity of our youth and childhood; it must also be married to the passion of the adult human being, which is a passion to live beyond one's death."[11] The key point is to get the right things done so that something useful continues to *live* beyond one's death. For me, this does not mean a flattering "time capsule" or a granite headstone. I have always been too awed by the infinite reach of astronomical time to believe that either is valid. For me, rather, death has become a fact of life, useful because it lends a motivating sense of urgency to my creative efforts. My time is running out, but time in general is not, and never will.

The inevitable will come, soon enough. To comfort the biologist in me, I arranged long ago for my ashes to enter a swiftly running stream, thence to return to the sea from which the evolutionary climb started eons ago. I hope that some speckled trout or silver salmon will benefit in the process, in return for all the nourishment and hours of enjoyment these lively creatures have given me over the years. I need this idea of leaving something behind—something that reenters into life in an organic vital way.

This, too, is not enough. Though the naturalist in me may find solace in finally contributing to the nitrogen or mineral cycle, the approach gives me no positive lasting inspiration as a philosophical base. My humanistic goals incline me toward creative work that will make life a little better for future generations. John Masefield expressed this thought in the following way:

Adventure on, and if you suffer, swear
That the next venturer shall have less to bear;
Your way will be retroden, make it fair.[12]

Not really altruistic, this attitude. I sense that I need to live in this style as much for my own present self-esteem as for the welfare of future generations.

Different writers evaluate at different levels other motivations leading people into science. Some would include curiosity; the delights of ambiguity and uncertainty; the contest with nature; escape from the boredom and crassness of everyday experiences; aesthetic pleasure; and the sheer joy that comes from exercising the intellect.[13] In contrast, if we adopted the critical view of Hardy, the mathematician, we would conclude that the three motives foremost in leading men to research are intellectual curiosity, professional pride, and ambition.[14]

Power, if sought consciously, is sought not for its own sake, but more for the shield it may offer against circumstance or against the exercise of power by other persons in ways that might block one's own best creative efforts. However, creativity soon falls prey to the net of responsibilities that cling, inevitably, to positions of power.

We find, therefore, that creative expression is ultimately a highly personal matter, that it is nourished by many roots, both superficial and deep. If it is to flower as a perennial for an entire lifetime, its tap root must plumb the deepest, most personal human satisfactions, whatever and wherever they are.

Good role models are absolutely essential. Because we are motivated in many ways to live up to our models, no one is ever a "self-made" man. Examples of how to do something and—fully as important—how *not* to do something, exert their pervasive influence during one's formative years. The key figures in my own early years were my father, my physician uncle, Gibby, and later on Drs. Raymond Adams, Derek Denny-Brown, and Roy Swank. As personalities, they are as different as men can be, but they each held something in common: a practical grasp of the present, an orientation toward the big new concepts of the future, and a bedrock respect for ideas that had stood the test of time. For these men, time extended in all directions.

It is usually difficult to find factual data on the subject of role models, because one's retrospective view of them changes over the years. However, an exception can be made in my case, for I have preserved an unabridged glimpse of how one model looked to me when I wrote about him thirty-five years ago. Perhaps in the following chapter you will be able to perceive some outlines of the real father through the fanciful tongue-in-cheek hyperbole of his teenage son.

25.

Flashback: Life with Father, 1941

The following essay was written at age 16, shortly after seeing the play of the same name by Clarence Day. It appeared in *Proem*, a high school literary publication.

I am a modern Clarence Day. I am one of those rare individuals who have a Superman for a father.

Not that I belittle the home I have, the fine principles instilled in me these past sixteen years, or the future foresightedly prepared for me. I hope never to become such a thankless child that all these gifts go unappreciated. It just is hard for a grown-up of sixteen to find his natural childish search for affection and his flair for the spectacular continually subordinated to a parental "tout-puissant", whose varied life combines all the attributes of Tarzan, Einstein, Clark Gable, and John Kieran, with a dash of Clarence Day, Sr., for explosiveness and disciplinary good measure.

Yes. Father lacks nothing and is certainly not undeserving of praise. He is a perfect example of a well-rounded individual.

In the mind's eye of youth, a focal point in the evolution of an individual's character is athletics. First and undoubtedly foremost, Father at forty-eight is an athlete's athlete. Admittedly he is a Jesse Owens at track, Babe Ruth at baseball, Joe Norris at bowling, Sammy Snead at golf–the list is endless. Father is the answer to a coach's prayer, one to make any mentor go into veritable paroxysms of joy. Unfortunately (and very conveniently), however, Father's stiff knee, sprained little finger, sciatica, and lumbago prevent his all-out indulgence in these sports, such as he used to enjoy back in the earlier days; though as proof that his physical prowess of yore is not all confined to reminisc-

*ing in the depths of his favorite (and private) armchair, he still ven-
tures occasionally forth to bludgeon as beautiful a booming brassie as
ever furrowed a fairway.*

*Invariably my drive stops in back of Father's. I have given up hoping
for more. Not far back, you understand, but back just enough to create
a mental hazard on the next shot. Consequently, after this happens
eighteen times in as many holes, I usually trail Father by ten strokes
when the eighteenth pin is behind us forever. A contributing factor to
Father's success is his uncanny luck. He makes the ball do things—
things no self-respecting ball ever created should do. When a ball that's
heading for a water hazard and a two-stroke penalty, suddenly decides
to hit a lily pad, skid out, hit a tree, and ricochet off to stop eight feet
from the pin, it makes it rather tough for a beginner at the game to end
up anywhere near a hundred. The casual "that's-the-way-I-planned-it"
look on Father's face is also very demoralizing.*

*Truly, Father has relegated luck to the status of mathematical
science. Dame Chance certainly regards him as her favorite pupil. I
repeat: Father is both gifted and lucky. With natural ability and luck
taken into consideration, his amazing versatility in sports is beyond
comprehension. There is no use evading the fact that in athletics, Father is well nigh invincible.*

*Father is also a mental giant. I base my conclusions first on the "A"
that he gleaned for me single-handed out of sixth grade arithmetic, on
his record in college (which bears scrutiny well), and on the occasional
flashes of genius that come from his storehouse of knowledge to throw
light on some of the most varied subjects. Cross-word puzzles are no
longer a pastime—they are a visit; give him a physics problem, and like
as not he will stumble across the right answers; ask him who the
"brain" of the Italian Revolution was, and he will reply "Cavour." It's
astounding—and* very *perplexing.*

*Coupled with his mental abilities, Father has a natural aesthetic
sense and a real talent in the Fine Arts. Music? He worked his way
through college writing songs, musical comedies, and playing the piano.
Art? Several of his oil paintings have been on exhibition at the Alger
House.*

*To the writer, who must fall back on "Chopsticks" for his salvation as
a musician and whose only claim to being a Grant Wood are crude stick*

drawings, Father's artistic accomplishments come as quite a shock, though through the years I have learned to pass them off in a spirit of resignation.

Father was, and still is, undoubtedly good looking for his age; even the older alumni who haven't seen him for years comment upon it, and though he occasionally waxes a bit Jack Bennyish in recognition of his handsomeness, the praise is noticeably apparent in his walk and general bearing the rest of the day.

Most men between forty and fifty pass through a period in which they try to prove, if not to the world, at least to themselves, that they have lost none of their youthful tastes and charm, and that senility is merely a taunt of jealous youth. With Father it is the green suit. Words are non-existent that would describe this as a sartorial masterpiece. Every time Mother sends it to be pressed, she breathes a silent prayer that somehow, something will happen. To date, the cleaner's service has been unfortunately excellent, and Father still wears it—blissfully.

Father's exploits as a youth are multitudinous. They range from the grandiose scope of Halloween escapades of the old days to the unpleasant reminders that he mowed lawns, chopped cord after cord of wood, and had to walk through miles of snow and stormy weather to get to school. Another of Father's many confused talents is his ability as an all-around mechanic and handy man. He can repair anything. With Father, any household appliance not operating at full efficiency stands a fifty-fifty chance. Either it will be repaired permanently, or it will most certainly be unceremoniously tossed into the ash can, a hopeless wreck, and since Father's tools are likely to be scattered anywhere from attic to basement, the traditional "pre-repair" hunt for the hammer or screwdriver has assumed the status of an institution in our household.

Father's occupation of the bath room from seven in the morning to his emergence a half hour later is undisputed, and nothing more need to be said save that Mother, after twenty years of marriage, has finally given up hope that Father will ever pick up his bath mat.

To preserve somehow the balance of power at 16834 Cranford Lane, a coalition has been set up to prevent any unreasonably dictatorial actions. Through this agreement it is possible for Father to be in the proverbial dog house. Father is usually adept at seeing the handwriting on the wall, however, and never goes so far that he arouses Mother's wrath, *for if there is one thing in the world that Father fears above all, it is Mother's anger.*

With his many talents and interests, the remarkable thing about Father is that he has taken time out to become a genuine person—a fine parent and companion.

When he borrows my ties and socks to appease his vanity, when I am soundly criticised for some breach of etiquette, I still can bear no grudge; for in spite of his exterior peculiarities, numerous and just as extensive as those of Father Day, my Father is different at heart. As in the play, it takes hurt or illness to change him, but it is there, *inside.*

With the attainment of that manly, fuzzy-cheeked age when I can begin to assert my independence, it would seem that Father's position would be theoretically in jeopardy. Actually, Father stands as firm and rocklike as Gibraltar, undaunted and unchanged by the effects of age. It shall ever be so.

For Paul W. Austin is an individualist in the very fullest sense of the word with a charm and personality all his own; and life with Father years from now will be very much as it is today—explosive, unparalleled, rather wonderful—a real and unforgettable experience.

It is still stimulating, even thirty-five years after the lines were written. For Father not only lives on vigorously himself, but I literally find him living on in me. I'm now old enough sometimes to hear his exact inflections in my own voice, to catch echoes of a borrowed phrase that ring back, decades back.

Life with Father is still going on.

26.

The Search for Novel Stimuli

Whether our work is art or science or the daily work of society, it is only
the form in which we explore our experience which is different; the need
to explore remains the same. This is why, at bottom, the society of
scientists is more important than their discoveries. What science has to
teach us here is not its techniques but its spirit: the irresistible need to
explore.

Jacob Bronowski

The need to explore is not confined to man and certainly not to scientists. It is a deeply rooted instinctual response found throughout the
animal kingdom. It can be readily observed in the lowly ant, as anyone
knows who has gone down on his hands and knees in the dirt to observe
an ant hill. Living things do have their antennae out, so to speak, constantly asking questions of their environment. To search, to explore, is
part of life.

Why? Why do we ask questions of the outside world? One conse-
quence of exploration is that the organism encounters various new stimuli, and these continually vary the sensory input into its nervous system.
The known is not nearly as attractive as the unknown, for new stimuli
create a climate of change, bringing in new impulses that vary both in
their kind and intensity and in the pattern of their relationships one to
the other. In higher animals, no other rewards are necessary to keep the
exploratory drive going, so long as exploration continues to furnish an
adequate supply of fresh stimuli. For example, when rhesus monkeys
are exposed to a simple mechanical puzzle, they persist in trying to
solve it for the inherent satisfactions of problem-solving per se, needing
no food to sustain their strong exploratory behavior.[1] Even when the
human infant is only three to nine months old it is already poised to
seek out and fix on more complex, contoured visual patterns that give
its visual receptors the most off-on stimuli.[2]

If you show a one-year-old infant a small object of a certain size and shape, he will look at it, reach out for it, and try to grasp it. Suppose you next show him, simultaneously, both the now familiar first object and a second, dissimilar object. He will reach out for the *new* object. His preference for novelty also crosses sensory modalities.[3] That is, he will still show his visual preference for the second of the two objects if he has previously experienced the first object only by the sense of its feel on his lips and in his mouth (the object has been shielded from his vision at this time).

From such studies we can appreciate why babies will put literally anything handy into their mouths. More than that, we can also see that the preference for novelty is an innate phenomenon, hard-wired into the wisdom of our young nervous system. Such studies also show us that even the infant can process information coming from two sensory-dimensions and then integrate it into a concept that serves novelty-directed behavior. This has long range creative implications.

Children raised in a barren institutional setting clearly show that normal stimuli play a positive role in human well-being.[4] Left largely to themselves, deprived of normal maternal attention, they first cry, later become profoundly dazed and depressed. If deprived of stimuli for more than five months, they never return to normal. Adults subjected to prolonged sensory deprivation also become disturbed, confused, and lose their sense of identity.[5] Behavior is deranged more when you reduce the patterning of the input than if you reduce the amount of the input.[6] This observation emphasizes that, normally, we have a physiological need for complex stimuli, and not simply for stimuli per se.

When you change the psychophysiological input into your nervous system, there are both anatomical and biochemical consequences. For example, if young rats are reared in a stimulus-rich environment, they develop more dendritic branches on their cortical nerve cells.[7] Moreover, rats and mice not only become less competent when they are raised in a stimulus-impoverished environment, but their brains also weigh less and contain lower levels of vital chemical compounds.[8] The ideal environment then, is enriched by contrast, variety, even dissonance, and it furthers the creative enterprise two ways. First, it quite literally activates the brain in general. Second, it brings in a spectrum of new facts that permits new options.

There are other ways to stimulate our brains toward alertness and arousal. One begins to appreciate how powerful is the human need for stimulation from our consumption of stimulants each year. For example, in this country alone, the average person consumed 35.6 gallons of coffee and 7.2 gallons of tea in 1972.[9] A cup of percolator coffee contains about 83 milligrams of caffeine, and a cup of bagged tea contains about 42 milligrams of caffeine.[10] Worldwide, some 155 million drinks of Coca-Cola (each containing somewhere between 20 and 36 milligrams of caffeine) are consumed daily.[11] In the United States the tea intake was 170 million pounds in 1973. The retail value of this—$456 million—represents about one-third of the entire budget for biomedical research of the National Institutes of Health in 1972. (Their total research budget was $1.47 billion.)[12]

There is another role for stimuli, depending on what part of the brain is stimulated. Nerve cells in the brain differ in their functional impact. Some are extraordinarily influential, and when such key nerve cells are stimulated, they exert powerful effects on behavior. This can be seen in the laboratory if one implants a fine wire down in these influential nerve fibers in the brain and then stimulates them with a discrete electrical current. The external stimulus soon becomes an extraordinarily effective "reward" in itself. It is important to appreciate that the experimental animal can then be conditioned to press a lever to "turn on" the stimuli to his own physiologically satisfying nerve pathways. Thus, he will go on trying to continue the stimulus, repeatedly pressing—for many hours or days—the lever that keeps delivering the current, preferring this stimulus to food, water, and sex. The experiments show how readily the nervous system can get "hooked" when it receives certain stimuli from the outside that appear natural and physiologically rewarding.

The especially rewarding neuronal systems that mediate this phenomenon are located near the base of the brain. At first, they came to be loosely known as "the pleasure center," but they are too diffusely represented for the word "center" to be accurate. For example, the reward systems include the ascending network of cells in the brain stem called the reticular formation; its extensions into the hypothalamus, subthalamus, and certain thalamic nuclei; and the more primitive cerebral structures collectively known as the limbic lobe.[13] Some special nerve pathways are also distinctive biochemically. For example, the possibility has recently been raised that some discharge specific neurotransmitter substances, dopamine and noradrenalin, at their nerve endings.[14] These two biogenic amines are closely related to their counterpart, adrenalin, more familiar to us as the substance that, released into the blood stream from our adrenal glands, makes our pulse race and bound when we are excited.

Nowadays, we talk about being "turned on" by an idea. We may well be describing quite literally the satisfying state of alertness and pleasurable excitement triggered directly or indirectly by stimuli that fire some of the special neuronal systems deep within our brain. For it is important to note that we humans, too, have reward systems in our brains, waiting for us to find normal memorable stimuli adequate to turn them on. Stimulation experiments were done years ago in humans by means of fine wires implanted deep in the brain, and these have borne out the findings in animals. The human patients, who also developed self-stimulation behavior when given a lever to press,[15] reported that the stimuli caused them to experience a feeling of ease and relaxation, a sense of joy with smiling, and a feeling of great satisfaction. Experimenters studying both humans and animals appear to have their wires tapped into some neuronal systems that normally operate in the brain to provide natural rewards.

You don't need wires inside your brain to feel this way. For example, I've been aware for years that my temporal lobes are connected with my hypothalamus. Whenever I hear (with my temporal lobes) some musical sequences that affect me profoundly, I get not only an emotional feeling of deep pleasure, but the overflow through my hypothalamus triggers off gooseflesh extending from the back of my head all the way down to the calves of my legs.

We can only assume that persuasive reward systems exist, giving less tangible external evidence than gooseflesh, but still imprinting us subtly from infancy on with "good" internal feelings in certain environmental settings.* We may not be consciously aware every time these internal systems are engaged, but they still provide the physiological basis for motivating our behavior toward certain kinds of external stimuli. Moreover, once programmed, our brain would seem to acquire the capacity to

---

* Every parent and educator knows the power of positive reinforcement. Seven words sum up the philosophy underlying my own approach: "Speak softly, but carry a big carrot."

seek out those new circumstances, those new levers, that reinforce its own "good" behavior. This would occur even though it might be impossible fully to express in words the precise reason for our pressing the "levers" in our environment or to sense the reason for our "good feeling" when some new action is successful.

There are not only "positive, rewarding" sites that reinforce a subject's pressing a lever, but also "negative" sites that cause him to try to avoid the stimulus. Some fibers in the latter system are located more externally in the brain stem and may liberate a different neurotransmitter substance, acetylcholine, at their nerve terminals.[16] The profound implications to man, the social animal, of having both positive and negative ways to "civilize" his behavior are surely of immense practical significance in directing our creative efforts and enabling us to survive as a species.

The transcendent "high" that comes when a brand new idea hits might seem to be a stimulating state of mind so pleasurable, so memorable, that it would itself serve as an internal reward, helping to condition the exploratory drive. Yet, as a matter of personal observation, I have never been remotely conscious of seeking out anything for this "big" reason. Rather, when such a feeling arises, it seems to occur more as a by-product and not as a primary reason for a search. On the other hand, I can more readily define as a motivating influence the sustained excitement, the sense of being totally absorbed if not possessed, that comes with following up a hot lead. Being has its limitations; becoming carries an aura of excitement. Eiduson summarizes this nicely by noting that the research scientist is not swept up in the pursuit of happiness, but finds rather his "happiness in pursuit."[17] The chase itself is more rewarding than the rabbit. Perhaps that is why one lets the rabbit go, to chase again some other day.

Everyone knows that it is easier to learn and recall "cold" facts when they are "warmed up" with meaning by a good teacher and given impact by piquant metaphor or simile. Unless we do develop some extrameaningful neuronal associations in this manner, how else could one remember, for example, to palpate months after the event for enlarged nerves in the rare patient who might have hypertrophic neuritis?

How do the foregoing points relate to creativity? The neuronal set when memory traces are originally laid down has a great deal to do with how easily we later scan enormous quantities of data, then link together and retrieve only the pertinent information. For instance, we can envision the complex neuronal network that constitutes one memorable thought as something like a telephone switchboard whose connections extend all over the globe. In every country there are millions of black telephones and many white ones which carry the routine conversations, the sometimes significant but largely forgettable day-to-day chatter. Nowadays, there are also a few circuits linked by phones of another color. RED telephones. When your "hot line" rings, you're not only placed instantly on the alert, but you'll remember the conversation. (If you don't remember it, it may still be there, but repressed.) In a sense, these "red" circuits correspond to the several facilitatory systems at the base of our brain. True, memories do drift back when one achieves a certain critical mass of connections, but some surge back quickly, powered by an extra dose of psychic energy. When such memorable circuits are hooked in among the more routine ones in a complex memory loop, they capture our attention, enhance our perception, help us retain the information, and permit us to retrieve it in a flash months or even years later. One striking example serves to illustrate the phenomenon—reflect on how accurately your mind retrieves precise details of the moment when you first heard the news that President Kennedy was assassinated.

Stimuli need to vary—or your brain itself needs to change—if you are going continually to pay attention to items of information from your environment. For example, if you are constantly exposed to a ripe onion odor, you become insensitive to it. Physiological psychologists call this phenomenon "olfactory fatigue." The disposition toward novelty also has its own physiological needs—it cannot long tolerate "sameness" in its surroundings. To dispense originality, it must feed on change.

The optimal amount and kind of change you need depends on what state you are in at the time you begin. If you start in a "low" phase, you will seek out zest and vitality, for life without them is intolerably drab and unproductive. But, if you are already in an ebullient "high" phase, it is easy to become overstimulated to the point of hypersensitivity and hyperactivity. Because these, too, become both uncomfortable and counterproductive, a cycle of behavior can then occur: induced hypersensitivity first leads both to withdrawal from stimuli and to habituation to stimuli. When each of these in turn becomes associated with a sense of boredom, you finally move back out again to search for the variety in novel stimuli:

hypersensitivity $\nearrow$ withdrawal $\searrow$ habituation $\nearrow$ boredom → the search for novel stimuli

Are the creative really any more sensitive to external stimuli? In humans, inborn abilities are difficult to disentangle from those that we have learned. So, too, is it difficult to separate the primary sensitivities of our eyes and ears from the subsequent mental elaborations that take place in our brains. In many instances, creative individuals appear to excell not so much in their primary, threshold, ability to perceive a simple auditory or visual stimulus, but in their subsequent ability to process stimuli, retain them, retrieve them in new combinations, and subsequently put them to good use. Some evidence does suggest that the most creative, when defined by their fluency on visually oriented, non-verbal tests, do pick up prior cues and then use them more readily when they subsequently solve problems.[18]

Intelligent creative persons, as inferred from word association tests, also seek out word stimuli that are followed by the delivery of novel, improbable associations.[19] Indeed, the subjects appeared not only to prefer novelty, but to have a distinct need for it that could actually be reinforced. Perhaps some creative individuals like the feeling of novelty, the quality of freshness of experience, so much that they seek to perpetuate it.

Your search for novelty shuts off if you are aroused to the point of anxiety. Experimentally, a sense of anxiety was caused by first exposing subjects to a message so confusing that it produced a threat to their self-esteem. Thereafter, the experimental subjects chose fewer novel stimulus cards than they did before.[20] Experiments in animals also suggest that stimuli are more rewarding only at moderate levels of arousal and that the reward value falls off at high levels.[21] Any administrator genuinely concerned about creative output should clearly keep the anxiety level of his team below the point of diminishing returns.

Thus far, we have considered how stimuli come in to activate the brain in general. Then we observed how certain stimulated nerve cells go on in a more specific way to motivate behavior, to enhance the way the whole brain learns and recalls. It is now time to consider the ways the two halves of the brain differ from each other. For it turns out that the right and left sides of our brain complement each other, and we are now beginning to perceive many fascinating and subtle creative implications of their partnership.

27.

Eyes Left! Eyes Right!

The mind in creation is as a fading coal which some invisible influence, like an inconstant wind, awakens to transitory brightness; this power arises from within . . . and the conscious portions of our natures are unprophetic either of its approach or of its departure.

Percy Shelley

The "mind in creation" is really the brain in creation. My purpose in this chapter is to continue to suggest some ways that the brain is involved in creativity. I am speculating here, and the reader is forewarned that when anyone speculates about the human nervous system, plausibility is far removed from certainty. Let us begin with an example of a relatively simple sensory-motor task.

You are hungry. Suppose you glimpse, out of the left corner of your eye, a luscious red apple lying on a nearby table. Visual information about the apple and where it lies in the space off to your left has come in, then crossed over, and been perceived by your right visual cortex. But to see the apple clearly, you must turn your eyes to the left. At this point, aware that information is required by the right visual cortex, the eye movement center in your right frontal lobe directs your eyes to the left.* You now see, at a glance, that the apple lies within reach.

Your left arm, governed by the activity of the opposite right motor cortex, stretches out toward the apple. As your fingers touch the apple, sensory information from your skin and finger joints goes up, crosses

* The two frontal lobes are located in the front of the cerebrum: The visual, "seeing," cortex is back at the opposite pole in the two occipital lobes.

over, and apprises the right sensory cortex that you are indeed on target. After a beautifully integrated series of crossed sensory-motor interactions, the apple comes up to your mouth, courtesy of your right cerebral hemisphere.

Your left hemisphere could do the same, vice versa, if the apple had been off to the right, for in these routine sensory and motor functions like reaching or walking, one side of the brain conducts the affairs of the opposite side of the body very much the same way as does its partner.

Not so when the two halves of the mind are involved in creative activity. They do not behave as identical twins, nor is one the mirror image of the other. The inconstant wind of creativity fans different coals on the two sides of the brain. Though our conscious mind can predict the timing of the creative impulse no more readily now than it could in Shelley's day, we do know a little more now about how the coals glow differently on the two sides. Our left cerebral hemisphere "thinks" in verbal, auditory terms, is good at translating symbols, including those of mathematics as well as language, and works best when analyzing a sequence of details.[1] For these reasons our left hemisphere plays the dominant role when we talk and listen, when we actively memorize, when we recognize the conceptual similarities between a newspaper press and a radio station, or when we count each of forty-eight stars on a flag, then go on to conclude, logically, that the flag must antedate the entry of Alaska and Hawaii into the Union.

In contrast, our right hemisphere "thinks" in visual, *non*verbal terms, particularly in terms involving complex spatial relationships, and specializes in three dimensional depth perception.[2] It also recognizes structural similarities, and works best in Gestalt: that is, drawing conclusions based on a grasp of the total (visual) picture. It will instantly recognize a friend's face in a crowd, or perceive that a large skeleton key will fit a keyhole that has only a certain size and shape. Being adept at incidental memorization and the more musically gifted of the two, it may also prompt us to hum a long forgotten tune in an evocative surrounding.

Freud, delving deeply into his own associations, helped us figure out some reasons why such a tune might be prompted to leap out of the depths of the brain given its special environmental cue. But this is very difficult detective work, because the right hemisphere, however interrogated verbally, "isn't talking." It basically is *non*verbal. Here is a most tantalizing paradox for those who would wish to understand creative mechanisms and express what they know in language. Hidden away, almost out of reach of language, can be the source of intuitive insights that are of fundamental importance in solving a problem. And this hemisphere can't tell us, in so many *words,* what sequences it has been experiencing. It is mute.

Did Tchaikovsky anticipate that the musical hemisphere might not only function separately, but also at the same *time* as the speaking hemisphere? Could the right side compose music even while the left side is talking? This is what he said:

Sometimes I observe with curiosity that uninterrupted activity, which—independent of the subject of any conversation I may be carrying on—continues its course in that department of my brain which is devoted to music. Sometimes it takes a preparatory form—that is, the consideration of all details that concern the elaboration of some projected work; another time it may be an entirely new and independent musical idea. . . .[3]

Because the left hemisphere is the more vocal of the two,* its preeminent role in language has long been evident in patients who lost their speech when the left hemisphere was damaged by strokes or tumors. Only recently have the more subtle contributions of the right side of the brain caught the attention of many students of the human nervous system.[4] We now know that much of the nonverbal thinking we do depends on the way the right side perceives and analyzes the world around us. While its left partner proceeds, piecemeal, to examine the irregular bark on each tree, our right hemisphere grasps in one sweep the shape of the whole forest, relates it adroitly to the contours of the near landscape, then to the line of the horizon.

The brain waves of normal persons performing normal activities clearly reveal these functional differences between the two sides of the brain. To appreciate the differences, one must compare the amplitude and frequency of electroencephalographic (EEG) recordings from the right side with those from the left using fairly sophisticated mathematical formulae and interpretations. Suppose then, with the wires on your

*Even in most left-handed persons (about 5 percent of the population) the left hemisphere is still dominant for language.

scalp, you attempt to solve a musical task such as listening to detect the recurrences of one rare phrase in a whole Bach concerto. Or, try to solve a spatial task such as building in your mind's eye a complex figure out of a given number of disassembled blocks. Your EEG will indicate that you have engaged chiefly the attention of the regions in the back of your right hemisphere.*[5] In contrast, if you are given a verbal task, such as mentally composing a letter, your EEG indicates that the major activity is in the corresponding regions of your left hemisphere.

Recent EEG studies during sleep indicate that the two sides of our brain also "dream" differently. The findings suggest that the right side is more involved during the period when our dreams are more vivid and elaborate—rapid eye movement (REM) sleep.[6] It appears that our left hemisphere may be more engaged in the several other phases of sleep in which dreams are less prominent.[7] There may be an underlying physiological basis for the predominance of the right hemisphere in visual imagery: the right brain tends to yield the greater electrical response when light is flashed in both eyes.[8]

When cortical nerve cells are actively firing, they require a greater supply of blood. Blood flow studies in humans confirm the results of studies of electrical activity.[9] That is, during verbal tests, the supply of blood increases chiefly in the left hemisphere. In contrast, visuo-spatial tasks cause increased blood flow chiefly in the right hemisphere. These differences are enhanced when the volunteers are motivated by a $20 reward toward higher levels of performance.

Though the parieto-occipital cortex is clearly important early in visual perception, the frontal lobes, too, must be engaged when a decision is called for, as it is in visual problem solving. For this reason, it is noteworthy that when visual problems are solved, blood supply increases not only over the visual cortex, but over the frontal lobes as well.

The studies I have cited do reveal special functions of the right side of the brain, but they require fairly elaborate equipment, mathematical processing, and interpretation. Less complicated observations are also revealing. Here, perhaps the "eyes" have it. Just noticing the character-

---

*The back of each hemisphere contains three lobes: the back of the temporal lobe; the parietal lobe, which is located farther up toward the top of the brain; and the occipital lobe, which occupies the back pole of the brain.

istic direction of someone's eye movements under standardized conditions may yield very interesting information about his attitudes and ways of thinking.[10]

To test this proposition in the laboratory, the subject's eyes are observed when neutral questions are asked that might be handled by either brain hemisphere. One question might be: "If you were President, how would you deal with the Middle East situation?" Or: "What is the meaning of the proverb, 'Better a bad peace than a good war?' " One observes that the subject's eyes glance (and frequently his head also turns) in one direction as he first begins to reflect about the answer. Some look quickly to the left; others look first to the right. The direction of gaze of most persons is reasonably consistent (78 to 80 percent of the time in the same direction). The direction of this initial flickering shift, at the moment of pondering, permits researchers to classify individuals as "right movers" or "left movers."

What kinds of people glance to the left? Those who are more prone to focus on their internal subjective experiences. "Left movers" are more readily hyponotizable, more likely to have been a classical humanistic major in college, and are somewhat more likely to report clear visual imagery. It is significant to our understanding of creativity to note that the more readily hypnotizable person is one whose subjective experiences are rich, who accepts impulses from within, and who is capable of deep imaginative involvements.

Who are the right movers? They tend to major in science or in "hard" quantitative subjects in college and they are better at mathematical problems than in verbal ability. They are also quicker to identify concepts when the problem centers on words, such as, "what adjective applies to these four nouns: sky, ocean, eyes, jeans?"

What does the direction of a glance tell us about the way the brain functions? It implies a physiological bias—a preexisting "set." One hemisphere is poised to act a fraction of a second before the other. In a sense, the connections of this half of the brain will take the lead in the person's psycho-physiological functioning.

Earlier, when you consciously glanced off to the left at the apple, you had an external object to look at, and it was activity within your right frontal lobe that directed your eyes to move to the left. But when there is no external target to look at deliberately, the glance is spontaneous, unconscious, determined by internal factors. It is plausible to think, then, that when "left movers" start their movement of internal reflection, they uncover greater facility in function within their right cerebral hemisphere. This bias in favor of the right hemisphere more readily activates the eye movement connections of their right frontal lobe and expresses itself in a quick unconscious glance to the left.

How significant a glance may be as a clue to basic differences among persons in their temperaments, life styles, and the way they create can for the moment better be imagined than defined, for the basic descriptive work is still going on, and much still needs to be done before we know what is going on, and how.[11] Again, we see that an observation raises far more questions than it answers. But in the interim, the issues raised illustrate the spectrum of decisions—subjective/objective, humanistic/scientific—that our two hemispheres make every day throughout many levels in the hierarchy of creative thought.

I have touched earlier on certain specific frontal lobe activities; the chief functions of our frontal lobes, however, are far more abstract. Common to most of them is the ability to organize complex patterns of behavior and project them into the future, drawing on all the learning of the past. In short, the frontal lobes help you put storm windows on your house at winter's first chill, fertilizer on the rose bed at the beckoning of spring, and a few dollars away in the bank now for your children's future education. Your frontal lobes also help screen out irrelevant distractions. They preserve a persistent continuity of action throughout the many complex sequences involved in problem-solving. With no clicking of mental gears, your preliminary analysis flows smoothly without interruption through a definition of alternatives, discrimination among many choices, and on to final effective action.[12]

A vast chorus of internal dialogue, verbal and nonverbal, embellishes our loosest associations as we dream, or focuses our concentrated attention when we are awake. This is not performed by one single hemisphere. Communication between the two hemispheres of the brain is essential if we are to integrate our creative efforts in many dimensions— verbal and visuo-spatial, internal and external, past, present, and future. Indeed, when the two halves of our brain exchange their disparate experiences, pool their viewpoints and approaches, the resulting synthesis brings to problem-solving a whole symphony of talents.

How does this exchange occur? The corpus callosum, the great commissure of white, myelinated fibers bridging the two hemispheres, serves as the major thoroughfare for the rapid transfer of this information.[13] Through it, the left hemisphere speaks, quite literally, to the right, and the right hemisphere answers with its own repertoire of musical refrains or vivid visual metaphors, sotto voce.

Because the frontal, parietal, temporal, occipital, and limbic lobes of the brain are each paired, we begin to see the whole coordinated creative quest as a major orchestral performance, with drum beats and clashing cymbals from all the more primitive deeper structures of the brain stem contributing rhythm and passion to the score.

At certain times, the whole orchestra—both sides of our brains—needs to work in concert. But at other times, we need to shift the balance from one cognitive mode to the other, from verbal, linear thinking to nonverbal Gestalt processing. How is this possible? Galin has proposed that normal persons might do this if they were to inhibit impulses from the left hemisphere, say, from reaching the right.[14] Such inhibition could permit the right hemisphere to function for a period with an internal life of its own. While on sabbatical leave in Japan recently, I studied one of several mechanisms that might make this possible.[15] It turns out that when you stimulate certain nerve cells down in the brain stem on one side, they release norepinephrine from their terminals way up in the cerebral cortex on the same side. When this transmitter reaches cortical nerve cells, it stops them from responding to impulses that normally cross over from the opposite hemisphere. Inhibitory messages ascending from this deep brain stem system then, plus signals from other subcortical systems, could help us shift the functional balance from one hemisphere to the other either by inhibiting one side or by enhancing the other. We may have in our own brains, therefore, not only the orchestra, but also the conductor, one whose hand and baton will tell us whether the left, right, or both of our hemispheres are to be fully engaged.

28.

The Quest

The scientist does not study nature because it is useful; he studies it because he delights in it, and he delights in it because it is beautiful. . . . intellectual beauty is sufficient unto itself, and it is for its sake, more perhaps than for the future good of humanity, that the scientist devotes himself to long and difficult labors. It is, therefore, the quest of this especial beauty, the sense of the harmony of the cosmos, which makes us choose the facts most fitting to contribute to this harmony, just as the artist chooses from among the features of his model those which perfect the picture and give it character and life.

Henri Poincaré

As we ascend the phylogenetic scale, the amount and complexity of the cerebral cortex increases enormously. In man, a whole new realm, the intellect, has been added. And in man we can observe that the search for stimuli takes on a new dimension—that of a quest. The quest is both psychologically utilitarian and intellectually satisfying. Man's search to satisfy the physiological needs of his cerebral cortex now takes on a greater meaning, not only to himself but to society as well.

Beyond the need that any animal has to seek new stimuli, A. H. Maslow believes that humans have an additional instinctual "need to know." This basic yearning for knowledge is reinforced by a social environment in which freedom and boldness are encouraged.[1]

Frankl has gone on to base his whole system of psychotherapy, logotherapy (logos: meaning), on man's need to find meaning in his everyday existence.[2] In the past, man's need to identify with something constructive in life, his will to meaning, has probably been underestimated. In me, I find it exerts a powerful force, sustains a drive fully as compelling as the will to pleasure identified by Freud and the will to power noted by Adler.

The ancient Greeks, as Dubos observes, attributed inspired deeds to *entheos*, a god within, a kind of divine madness that motivates man.[3] Over the centuries the word has lost none of its magical power, for it has been handed down to us as *enthusiasm*. Enthusiasm for the quest is the elixir that pervades creativity, inspires it, frees it so that anything seems possible, and enlists others in the cause.

To me, and to other biomedical investigators, the scientific quest takes on some spiritual overtones, if it does not become a kind of religion in itself. One reason is straightforward. I start with the realization that our solar system began only four to five billion years ago; I then see increasingly the astounding complexity of all living things, the human nervous system in particular. And the gap between that nebulous beginning and the tangible present is so enormous that I am left with a reverent awe toward the creative forces in the universe, however defined, that have generated so much in such a relatively short time.

Other satisfactions which lie at the end of the quest will vary subtly from one creative field to another. The medical researcher can respond deeply to the higher artistic works of the poet, the musician, and the artist. He can sense the aesthetic delights open to the mathematician, the physicist, the chemist, and the astronomer. But he is drawn early in life to explore the interface between health and sickness. Man is his canvas, man's diseases his concern, and in helping man toward health will lie his ultimate satisfactions. Apart from his own small contributions to this end, the young men and women whom he trains and influences will also give him a personally satisfying link with what resides in the future.

I learned a lot about the pleasures associated with this process, not only from our children, but also from teaching our dog, Tom. We now have a new four-month-old Brittany Spaniel who is learning both from Tom and from me. The approach you take when you raise a good bird dog for the field is similar to that involved in trying to raise a creative child or researcher. You start to refine the chase into the quest even before the litter is conceived. First you search for the very best mental and physical pedigree you can find, balancing the sire's known assets and liabilities against those of the dam. This gives you the optimum opportunity to have the best "hard wiring" already built into your pup's nervous system at birth. Then you select the boldest, healthiest-looking pup as best you can tell from the way he stands, runs, cocks his ears, and socializes with you. Finally, you give him as much affection as you can without spoiling him. He'll not only thrive on this, but you later won't have to discipline him as much, for a word or a gesture will suffice instead of firmer measures. You'll give him as much wide open country to explore as freely as possible, graduating to tougher cover only when he's tall enough for it, always trying to achieve that happy balance between preserving his intense feral qualities and keeping him out from under your feet. You'll show your enthusiasm with praise when he goes staunchly on point on a pheasant, and your disapproval when he chases a rabbit. If you and he are especially lucky, you'll have an older, wiser dog he can imitate, from whose experience he can quickly learn the wisdom of the chase that takes years to accumulate. Gradually, he'll learn that fun and serious work are not incompatible. Ultimately, then, what you will have tried to do is to supplement his basic genetic constitution with the best "soft wiring" you can help him add from his environment—this will include behavior that he's learned for himself, from you, and from another dog. Your goal is a strong, bold, wide-ranging dog, capable of practical, instinctive action in the field and still housebroken at home, a joy to watch in the field as well as to live with. If you should ever err, your bias should be in the direction of his independence in the field.

In humans, it may be difficult to identify all the many sources of the creative quest, particularly when they are buried within the very fabric of life itself. For example, without being unduly philosophical, we can readily view the creative urge to "bear fruit" as an extension of the deepest biological urge toward reproduction. As Gutman has put it, "Man creates his outer world not only in his own image but, at the same time, he enlarges this image beyond life size. As an expression of the principal of self-duplication, creative activity is intimately related to growth and reproduction."[4] It should not surprise us too much to find creation, in the broadest biological sense, residing at the very core of what we call creativity.

29.

The Creative Setting

(The creative process) is the emergence in action of a novel relational product, growing out of the uniqueness of the individual on the one hand, and the materials, events, people, or circumstances of his life on the other.

Carl Rogers

Human creativity flourishes in certain settings.[1] In my own family, originality in music, art, writing, preposterous associations, "punning," and higher forms of humor were encouraged early, both by example and by praise. The conditioning is still going on. Even now, on my visits home to Oak Park, Illinois, my father, at eighty, may be working on a new painting, or on a tape of reminiscences about the late humorist, James Thurber. And my mother, at seventy-seven, will for the duration of my stay interrupt her substitute teaching and reduce the many visits to our home by neighbors, teachers, artists, and other high-spirited creative types. Mother today remains as interested in people of all kinds as she has for many years.

In an earlier chapter, I documented some ways in which my father provided a role model. Mothers, too, influence the creative setting. For example, mothers of creative New York State high school students were studied psychologically to determine which of their personality characteristics might have fostered creativity in their sons.[2] The prototype mother turns out to be an independent, capable woman, perceptive in interpersonal relationships, but not always concerned about the social impression she creates. Although adaptable to change and variety, she still expresses her impulses freely and is restive when confronted by rules and restraints. Confident and versatile, she is not always reliable and may not achieve a commensurate position of high community visibility. Though perceptive and tolerant of others, she also appears indifferent and detached. Biologically female, she scores somewhat lower on psychological tests for feminine interests. In short, she contains (as does my own mother) a dynamic balance of contrasting tensions not unlike those of her son.

The family setting in which scientific creativity develops has also been examined.[3] The descriptions convey a reasonable picture of the climate in my own family when I was a child. For example, my parents encouraged my independence. They were moderately affectionate, and did not become involved or intrude in negative ways. They did communicate certain expectations, however, and from these expectations, I sensed that I was trusted to make my own rational choices. This trusting attitude set the tone of free inquiry and enhanced my ability to achieve by independence rather than by conformity.

The school must play an important part in reinforcing and expanding what is learned in the home, but it is difficult to tease out this separate contribution. In Eiduson's study of forty Ph.D. research scientists, all were very diverse in their biographical data, and no crucial chemistry set, no single all-important teacher decided their vocation.[4]

Humor, novelty, freedom, and creative performance have been linked in a speculative way for many years. Some recent research provides factual data suggesting that creativity is enhanced by the release from tension that we experience as an integral part of humor. For example, in one study, the Torrance creativity test was used to assess creativity in 282 tenth grade Israeli students. Just before the test, half of the students listened to a recording of the performance of Israel's most popular comedian. These students showed much higher creativity scores in terms of originality, flexibility, and fluency than did the other half of their classmates who were not so entertained.[5]

Creative potential can be enhanced if it is considered to be important. As Plato said, "What is honored in a country will be cultivated there." Even programmed instruction can enhance creativity in children, but *it must be properly prepared so that it reinforces many different responses.* In this regard, I was interested in the results of one controlled study of Berkeley schoolchildren.[6] Some of the fifth and sixth graders were encouraged to use creative approaches to solve detective stories and mysteries; their classmates served as the control group. It turned out that the programmed learners did much better both qualitatively and quantitatively in subsequent tests of their creative and problem-solving abilities. Moreover, their improvement generalized to test materials quite different from the original problems. It was not only a few children who benefited—children at all IQ levels shared in the improvement. When follow-up tests were performed six months later, the trained children still maintained their edge in problem-solving abilities, but they no longer retained their ability to generalize to other tasks. An interesting difference emerged between solving new problems and solving those of a purely logical nature, for when they were subsequently tested for logical problem-solving skills the trained children had not improved over their controls.

Children aren't the only ones who can improve. When adult business school students were trained in creative thinking, the quality and quantity of their ideas also improved.[7] The older students (age twenty-three to fifty-one) gained as much from the course as did younger students (age seventeen to twenty-two). So we see that continuing education does make sense; we should all make a point of providing ourselves with repeated reinforcement of problem-solving abilities on a lifelong basis.

I have noted an interesting "carry-over" phenomenon in this regard. For example, I develop a creative mental "set" if I am working on a watercolor or taking a pottery course. Once in this creative frame of mind, I find that new ideas come to me more freely in my professional work in the laboratory and even along administrative lines.

Certain social environments dispose favorably toward originality. The creative spirit flourishes best in a climate all too rare: *one in which ideas are the coin of the realm, and concepts and mechanisms are held all-important.* Here are the elements in such an ideal setting: When there is freedom of expression and movement; lack of fear of dissent and contradiction; willingness to break with custom; a spirit of play as well as a dedication to work; and a sense of purpose on a grand scale.[8]

One can certainly agree with the fact that "the open system is thus the ideal, propitious environment for creativity, and anything in the environment that tends to close the system makes the environment unpropitious for creativity."[9]

The message for administrators is clear: first choose the right people and then support them fully, but don't meddle unnecessarily in their research. For in research, if there is anything worse than having too little administrative efficiency, it is having too much.

But creativity doesn't imply joyously happy researchers roaming freely like contented cows in a lush, green, unfenced pasture. There are limits to happiness. As we have seen earlier, complete inner and outer harmony is not an integral part of the creative process. Thus, in children, the greatest creativity occurs in association with an intermediate level of anxiety,[10] not among those lowest in anxiety. Similar results have emerged from a study of adult scientists and engineers.[11] These researchers were more effective when there was a "creative tension" between sources of stability and disruption, between security and challenge.

Other features of the local setting also enhance scientific creativity. They include: academic freedom; a feeling of security; access to pertinent literature; time; the freedom to contact other investigators; freedom from unnecessary harassment; generous, long-term financial support; good collaborators; and sympathetic administrators.[12]

It took very little time before my scientific colleagues—local, national, and international—became central figures in my intellectual environment. These men and women played a major role in my life, and still do. They provided more than new stimuli and facts; *they also shaped my attitudes*. During my formative years they taught me an important distinction. Growing up earlier, when I heard the question, "what's new?", the phrase seemed no more than a banal prelude to casual conversation. But now, when scientific friends ask me this question, I know they mean: "What have you found out recently that's never been known before?"

The implication is clear; this knowledge must be new not only in Portland, or Denver, but anywhere else on the surface of the earth. The basic neuronal mechanisms of creative inspiration remain independent of the value of their product. But creativity in science transcends a purely local interpretation; it operates in the international dimension. The goal is something unique within the entire realm of existing scientific knowledge. Thus, in the arts, I have a casual understanding that I can still enjoy myself at leisure on my home ground, creating music, pottery, and painting for myself or for a small circle of friends. But, beyond home ground, the rigorous demands of the scientific world call for something more. The essence of scientific creativity is a product that is brand new within the ken of the world scientific community.

Laboratories all over the world necessarily compete in the marketplace for this new scientific information. In 1958, Horst Jatzkewitz, while working independently in Germany, also reported an increase of sulfatides in MLD.[13] The discovery in our two laboratories, continents apart, came about through quite different approaches, each a separate expression of creativity. How did it feel to be a *co*-discoverer rather than a discoverer? Well, I remember feeling let down when I found the sulfatide story was to be shared, and for a while, whenever the question of priority was forced, I feebly rationalized that my manuscript was sent off two weeks before my competitor's. But these petty considerations began to evaporate within weeks, because the value of each discovery was reinforced, not diluted, by the other. Indeed, in science, one soon learns that nothing is considered rigorously proved unless it is confirmed in another laboratory, and preferably by other methods. This is good. In the forward thrust of a new field of science, the real setbacks occur when "fundamental" facts thought to be true, and acted upon as such, later turn out to be false.

The progress of each scientist depends utterly on a firm data base established by the worldwide fellowship of scientists. To illustrate this point, let us now take an abbreviated look at MLD from the international perspective (figure 13). Here, we see that contributions from at least seven different countries converge into our present concept of MLD. And I have included only five major lines of evidence. Two others are waiting in the wings. The sixth will be the contribution of biochemists who tell us what is structurally wrong with the DNA, the RNA, and the sulfatase enzyme protein. The seventh will be the contribution of the biochemical pharmacologists and clinicians who will teach us how to treat MLD. When MLD is ultimately treated, it will surely be the result of a worldwide effort involving many scientists and technicians. As José Ortega y Gasset proposed, it *is* the many who lay the groundwork for the few.[14]

This historical and geographical version of the MLD story shows us a fairly typical scientific discovery advancing not so much in a single intuitive flight of the imagination, but ripening in a series of little leaps. The discovery process surges forward almost inexorably—and occurs over a decade or two when, in the history of ideas, "the time is right." Let us examine the contributions of all those early researchers at the left in figure 13. When we do, it seems certain that their ideas and technology generated a momentum that would have caused someone to unravel the sulfatide-sulfatase-MLD story—even if all the later investigators in the center portion of the diagram had never been born.

Looking back now, in this perspective of time, I see my own work,

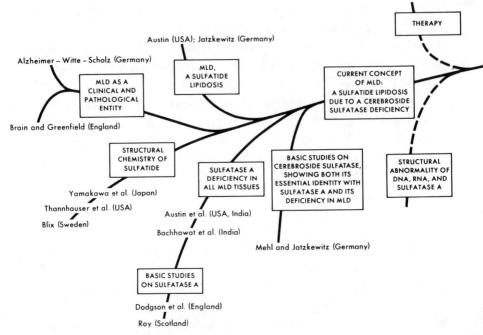

Figure 13. *International Contributions to Mld Research*

and that of our team, shrinking in significance. Surely someone else would inevitably have made the same discovery sooner or later. What do you do when you confront this sobering reality? You can rationalize. You say to yourself that in some larger sense, a research discovery resembles a painting or poem. It is not a thing depersonalized. Rather, it is both a statement of self and an expression of the vitality within a society. A society is vitalized to the degree that it first shows its members which social goals are worthwhile and then makes it possible for them to further these goals by solving problems in ways that are personally self-fulfilling. It is in this dual sense that our scientific discoveries become not only an objective fact, an end in themselves, but also become the happy personalized by-product of the Zeitgeist, of the total creative climate within our culture.

As there is a worldwide fellowship of scientists, so too there is a worldwide test for their creative achievement—the Nobel Prize. Today, Jewish eminence occurs in a number of areas, probably because selection factors, interacting in the setting of the Jewish cultural tradition combine to place a premium on creative attainment. Arieti conducted an international survey of five ethnic groups of Nobel Prize winners during the seventy-year period up to 1970. A Jew was some twenty-eight times more likely to be a Prize winner than someone else in the total world population at large. The ratio of French winners to winners from the rest of the world was 6.3; of German, 4.4; of Italian, 1.6; and of Argentinian, 1.3. Jews led especially in the fields of medicine and physics, lagging behind only in the Nobel Peace Prize.[15]

Zuckerman recently published an excellent comprehensive survey of the demographic characteristics of eminent American scientists—both Nobel laureates and members of the National Academy of Sciences. In their geographical origins, most American Nobel laureates came, as did their cohorts, from rural areas, towns, and small cities. Only a third of them came from large cities. (The interesting exception was New York City, where the proportion of laureates was almost twice that expected on the basis of population alone.)[16]

In their social origins, Nobelists resemble other elite groups in other spheres of activity (Supreme Court justices, admirals and generals, business leaders, etc.) in that they come largely from middle and upper occupational strata. Eighty-two percent of American laureates had fathers who were professionals, managers, or proprietors. This percentage is about eight times as great as the representation of their cohorts in the same occupational groups in the male labor force in the United States during the same period. However, it is largely the Protestant and Catholic laureates that account for this phenomenon; three-quarters of the Jewish laureates originate from lower reaches of the social stratification system, largely from the ranks of small businessmen and also from clerical and blue-collar families.[17]

Zuckerman looked further into the matter of the religious origins of American Nobel laureates (not their own present religious preferences). The proportion of Jewish laureates was nine times the proportion of Jews in the general population. Jews, comprising about 3 percent of the U.S. population, accounted for 27 percent of the Nobelists who were raised in the United States. The proportion of Catholic laureates was but one-twenty-fifth the proportion of Catholics in the population. Catholics, comprising 25 percent of the population, accounted for 1 percent of the laureates. Bearing in mind that Jews account for a relatively high proportion of faculty members in medicine and the biological sciences combined, laureates of Jewish origin were about one and one-half times their expected proportion.[18]

Possibly some Unitarians were comforted with much earlier data (dating from 1927) showing that they were eighty-one times more likely to be listed in the ranks of the scientifically eminent.[19] Now, half a century later, the data base on Unitarians and other faiths has undergone obvious changes, and no group appears to have room for complacency.

In terms of their own undergraduate training, the greatest number of laureates went to college at Columbia (seven) or Harvard (five), whereas Yale, Berkeley, and MIT ranked next with four each.[20]

Scientific meetings are also part of the total scientific milieu. Rarely does the researcher find everything he needs to know in a book or journal. Personal contact with colleagues is constantly stimulating. These encounters develop most fruitfully at scientific meetings that draw together investigators from distant laboratories representing a wide spectrum of disciplines. The cross-fertilizations which occur at a good meeting prompt many hybrid ideas, because new discoveries tend to occur at the interface between disciplines.

Meetings in other cities serve other needs. They afford a perfect opportunity to restore one's sense of aesthetic appreciation. I know my own limits at meetings now; after two solid days, my scientific synapses are packed full, and it's time for a break. So I go out in response to some inner need to clear the air—browsing around art museums, seeking out new exhibits, varying the menu all the way from man's ancient archaeological treasures to his groping contemporary efforts, feeling a kinship with each artist, emerging refreshed and inspired.

Big problems must first be defined in the mind, however vaguely, before they can be effectively approached in the laboratory. But, increasingly during this century the investigator has come to depend on a more intricate technology than his counterparts did even a generation ago. Our own studies would not have been successful without the international advances in infrared spectrophotometry, chromatographic techniques, and later on, radioisotope equipment. When a human has to depend on a machine, it is an uneasy alliance. I always feel more at home with results I can *see* quite literally with my own eyes than with those that come from a piece of equipment. But the fact is that, unless one incorporates the new technological approaches, few creative contributions will be made on today's rapidly advancing scientific frontiers. Technological advances do have an increasingly important impact on creativity, and we are all bound, now, to machines of some kind, with all the good and ill that this portends.

To appreciate this fact in yet another dimension, it is helpful to consider an analogy with Impressionist painting. It was from Monet's work in 1874, entitled, *Impression: Sunrise* that the term "Impressionists" was coined. But Monet's approach and that of his colleagues was greatly facilitated by the development of an array of bright new colors earlier in that century. In 1826, an extraordinarily intense blue pigment, French Ultramarine, became available. Reds and oranges of great brilliance soon followed. Another critical development occurred when the American painter, John Rand, developed the simple collapsible paint tube.[21] It was this, essentially, that freed the artist from the bulky paint pots and the north light of his garret studio, and liberated him into the countryside, *en plein air,* there to capture the ambient sunlight in all the subtleties of its spectrum. Thus, a century ago, even the spontaneity of the Impressionists rested on the firm base of the technological advances of the time.

This is not to slight the fact that research ultimately depends on people. In the laboratory, much research nowadays is really a collaborative effort. It is true teamwork; everyone contributes. A solo effort might have sufficed for some projects a few years ago when all one might have needed were some test tubes, a smoked drum, and some equipment held together with baling wire. But research today has grown exponentially more complicated, and the creative setting involves a team of specialists. One recent example shows this clearly: of ninety-seven original articles published in the *New England Journal of Medicine* late in 1975, not one had a single author. The average number of authors was 4.55.[22] (At the present rate of increase in authorship it has been calculated that in 2076, each paper might have at least twenty-four authors!)[23]

In our own laboratory now, a mere 4.55 of us get together to work out a plan of action. Our team has certain requirements. As we get to know one another better, we work together more effectively. An important ingredient is the quality of liveliness and "sparkle" in one or more members of the team. Margo had it, and it always perked up our conferences with a sense of electricity. We also need consecutive time to explore the problem if we are going to come up with better ideas.[24] This means we must firmly set aside a one- to two-hour block of time and meet in a room free from a telephone or other interruptions. When we meet an impasse, it will help to generate a lot of ideas, even if many of them are "wild ideas." At some vaguely perceived time, however, our "free-wheeling" has to stop, and at this point we need to impose a deadline in order to emerge with any worthwhile plan of action.[25]

The relationships between scientific creativity on the one hand, and gender or the sexual climate on the other, are so complex as to fall well beyond the scope of this work. It suffices to note two points. First, women face a very long uphill climb if they try to enter a scientific field. Even as children they confront a cultural setting tilted away from scientific investigation. They create in other areas. Take as one example, the Nobel Prize in medicine and physiology. If you conclude that it reflects the ultimate global test for scientific creativity in these two fields, then the award remains strictly a male preserve. Between the years 1901 and 1974, when a total of 112 Prizes were awarded, only one went to a woman, Gerti Cori, who shared it both with her husband, Carl, and with Bernardo Houssay. As the cultural milieu changes, and as more women are freer to pursue academic careers, we may see them represented more often in this and other indices of scientific creativity.

The second point to make is no more than a private hunch. I think that the creative drive and the sex drive may overlap to the degree that they share some common neuroanatomical sites in the brain. However, I do not sense that the creative drive is necessarily derived from the sex drive. Nor do I believe that they exist either in a one-to-one, cause and effect relationship, nor indeed always in some reciprocal relationship. In my own case, I was most creative musically in a setting in which I was young, in love, engaged, and sexually frustrated. But, subsequently, I have no controlled data to offer on the subject of sex and scientific or artistic creativity except to note that neither sexual satisfaction nor physical lassitude necessarily inhibits the flow of creative ideas when thoughts are really pressing for expression. Clearly, the subject is still wide open for study.

The creative setting in academic life is no insulated ivory tower. It is under constant assault from all sides. What is especially harmful is to lose your free time for browsing. The gradual death of creativity in a researcher who becomes enmeshed in too many committees is well portrayed by Carl Dragstedt. His essay is appropriately titled, "Who Killed Cock Robin."[26] And biomedical investigators of all ages would also do well to ponder Dwight Ingle's true statement:

The early years in the laboratory are the golden years for many scientists. After he becomes known, the volume of mail, telephone calls, number of visitors, organizational activities, including committees by the dozens, and demands for lectures, reviews and community activities grow insidiously and will destroy the creativity of the scientist if unopposed.[27]

Not only does my own brain operate more slowly and less flexibly as I get older, not only do the newer problems out on the newer frontiers require increasingly sophisticated technologies and colleagues versed in more highly specialized fields, but I too have become increasingly subject to all the distractions of contemporary living, swept up in a "future shock"[28] of my own and others' making. As a result, I have learned I must establish and protect my own setting, my own tropical islands of uninterrupted time—mornings in general, Saturday mornings in particular, lunch time, and travel time. Vacations are a last resort.

Yet all good work settings erode. Sooner or later their novelty wears off and the whole routine tends to become stale. Once productive grooves turn into ruts. The experimentalist worries about going "flat" just as much as the artist or composer. All feel the anxiety that "the well will go dry someday."

At this point, fresh stimuli are needed. The only way some persons can break out of this root-bound situation is to transplant themselves to a new job. True, a move will be fruitful if it involves a real pruning of useless activities and a repotting of roots into fertile new soil. For others, new projects, new friends, and new meetings will be inspiration enough if they can be supplemented by an occasional year away on sabbatical leave. Still, it is surprising how many times I have had to rediscover the elementary principle that *re*-creation is essential to creativity.

30.
The Creative Prelude

By the creative process we mean the capacity to find new and unexpected connections, to voyage freely over the seas, to happen on America as we seek new routes to India, to find new relationships in time and space, and thus new meanings.

Lawrence Kubie

Ideas often come suddenly to individuals, but they usually have a long history.

Lancelot Whyte

We start with a problem at the bedside or in the laboratory. There follows a rush of thoughts. In a few seconds, a complicated experimental design unfolds, aimed at solving the problem. Seemingly, everything happened quickly and spontaneously. Not so. The stories in Part I illustrate that my ideas evolved through long and complex pathways. Indeed, the longitudinal history of an idea extends much farther back and is much more circuitous than I realized at the time (figures 5, 7, 9, 10).

For example, when I finally start a painting, my sketchbooks show that I have usually had it "in the back of my mind" for years. My musical notebooks are filled with "stray chords" and chord sequences long before these are synthesized into a complete song. Similarly, most themes in our research today have been incubating, in one form or another, for the past five to fifteen years. Ideas, like persons, have long pedigrees.

One cannot rely on the processes of conscious or subconscious memory to pull out the right facts at just the right time. (At least, *my* brain doesn't function that way.) Instead, I supplement what is inside my head with a fairly elaborate filing system. The individual topics are listed in large, bold print, color-coded so they can be seen—a file folder full of enzyme reprints here, a folder on a certain disease there, a file of methods farther on. With luck, connections will emerge between one file and the others. Sometimes they do, but rarely.

This is only a token gesture in the direction of being organized. Actually, many ruminative and complex meanderings go into the creative prelude. My mind has no well thought out scenario. Indeed, if I'm really on a new frontier, I don't know where or how I'm going because, by definition, I've never been there before. A jumble of potentially useful facts lies scattered over the landscape of my own experience and that of others. Most of this is not in the filing cabinet. Some bits of information are years old; others only seconds old. The nascent stirrings of this prelude have been well described by Ghiselin:

> A common delusion among those ignorant of the creative process is that it begins in clarity and order, systematic understanding, and proceeds in logical advances and under pressure of will to the development of a foreseen, or at least partially foreseen, structure or system. Actually, it begins in obscurity and in some degree of confusion.[1]

The state of mind accommodating all the elements soon to fuse in a flash of creative inspiration can only be likened to organizable chaos. In order to generate and then unite all these disparate elements, it is essential to have a flexible approach. Kubie uses the term "preconscious" to describe the rapid, fluid mental processes operating during this period. Descriptively, they operate like a cross between a friendly genie and a first-rate executive secretary.[2] However defined, these scanning and sorting activities are an essential instrument in all creative activity. The goal is to liberate them. True, as Kubie points out, the unconscious does spur creativity, but it also acts as a straitjacket. It makes responses rigid and stereotyped and distorts them. On the other hand, the conscious processes that perform the important service of evaluation or correction also have their own pedestrian limitations.

During the creative prelude, my mind increasingly gnaws away at the problem like a dog at a bone, working for a solution at all levels of consciousness. It is frequently a time of intellectual turbulence and emotional frustration. When the data are all in, and one's problem is to interpret them, the frustration resembles in a sense that of trying to crack the insoluble paradox of a Zen koan. One difference is that in research, the facts themselves are usually not all at hand, and the solution is hung up on several levels at once. The answer just won't come. And, it can't be forced.

Will this be a dead end? I won't know at the time, but whenever I meet with an impasse, I find it helpful to relax into something less demanding or recreational, quite literally, to "let go" and set off in another direction. So I set aside the first problem and pick up the thread of a second one in the hope that a solution may soon arise out of the very fact of approaching the first problem afresh from another direction, from an angle at which it is more vulnerable. When I lapse into a change of pace (music, sight-seeing, manual tasks, daydreaming, sleeping) it does more than provide a refreshing interlude. It also helps "reshuffle the synapses," and gives my subconscious mental activities the freedom to work unrestrained.

Diversion, to the French painter, Ingres, meant turning to the violin as a respite from his long hours at the easel. The French not only developed a phrase, "the violin of Ingres," in recognition of the fact, but placed the violin itself on display in the museum at Montauban.[3] The phrase directs our attention to an important point—the need for a diverting hobby. In the final analysis, it didn't much matter whether Ingres' fingers played his violin well or not.* What was important was that he could shift for a while from a mental set that was primarily visual to one that was mainly musical. There is in everyone a need for a refreshing change of pace, for a "violin of Ingres."

If another person were to observe you during your creative prelude, he might conclude that it ended in one of two ways. Either you would appear actively to set off in a different direction, or you would seem to have lapsed into a quiet pause. Both would be deceptive. Appearances aside, this is not a time of complete change, nor is it one of quiet, because neuronal circuits keep working over the problem beneath the conscious surface of your brain, and neither you nor your observer need be aware of their activities. As blood flows in the heart during the phase of cardiac "relaxation," so deep in the brain unconscious thoughts keep flowing during a kind of mental diastole that precedes the next systole.

Sometimes the interruption of a good night's sleep provides the pause that helps you arrive at a solution; other times, even a poor night's sleep is no hindrance if problems are still churning over rapidly in your mind. I have never had a useful solution leap forth from a dream in the middle of a deep sleep. Kekulé did. Confronted with the chemical problem of

---

* And critics did respond more favorably to his artistic purity of line than to his skill as a musician.

how six carbon atoms could be arranged, he dreamed that a snake held its tail in its mouth, and awakened with a beautiful new concept of the benzene ring. In my own experience, the most productive free association occurs in the early morning reverie just before arising. In this fluid state, halfway between dreaming and waking, reasoned analysis is suspended. Problems, long unsolved, float up toward consciousness, and then seem easily to attach themselves to solutions, or to ideas for solutions. A few such ideas written down hurriedly and evaluated critically during the light of the next day will turn out to be very useful.

Even when we are fully awake, we still evaluate our environment through subconscious processes which we now call intuition. Although our hints and our hunches seem instantaneous, they may well mean that we have successfully forged links between scattered memories and partial solutions buried in the past and observations drawn from the present. Intuitive thinking and creative associations in general involve "thinking in loops." They differ from logical thinking in which rational sequences appear to unfold in a straight and reasonably predictable line. For example, as you stand back and watch your own thoughts, you see them go out in one direction, gather in a series of other loose associations, and then, like a boomerang, loop back sometime later from another direction.

When you solve problems over the full range of situations in life, you likewise use a wide repertoire of association loops, varying from the commonplace to the esoteric, poised at various levels of consciousness, and you connect them at some very inplausible intersections. And when I speak of "loops" in the above context, the word is quite literally correct, for the links made by free associations connect nerve cells in the cortex of the frontal lobes up in front, for example, with those back in the occipital lobes, forward from there to the temporal lobes, up from there to the parietal lobes, down to subcortical nerve cells, over to the opposite cerebral hemisphere, back again—on and on in multiple swirling successions. Indeed, to give birth to even the simplest thought, not one but multiple neuronal circuits will be involved even before the primitive idea starts to float up into the more conscious mind's eye or ear. Each circuit is unlikely to be a simple one, because each nerve cell may have up to 10,000 connections, and therefore, big clusters of stimulated cells will be drawn along and invest each association loop.

If professorial types often appear absentminded, the fact is that they *are*—off on cloud nine, preoccupied, daydreaming about something else. Daydreams are cloud-hopping trips on random looping, frequently visual, associations.

Whenever and however they come, and whatever the source, there is no need to downgrade subconscious mental activities. Scientific types tend to do so because they try to keep things "rational," "within reason" (that is, consciously workable). Moreover, it is hard for anyone to escape from the firm grip of the Protestant ethic, which holds that logical work which comes hardest (again, "conscious" work) must be the most laudable. Nonsense. Our concern is largely misplaced in time. Doubly misplaced. For, the conscious effort properly occurs during the long early period of education, self-education, and filing away. Or, as we shall see in a later chapter, there is a second extended period during which conscious processes are fully engaged—later on during the creative follow-through. During this subsequent period, any investigator will be all to conscious of his hard work. His awareness will help remove any lingering guilt feelings that have arisen when his earlier subconscious efforts were too fruitful, and produced what may seem to be an "unearned run."

One who has restored proper dignity to the unique contributions of the subconscious is the mathematician, Henri Poincaré:

The subliminal self is in no way inferior to the conscious self; it is not purely automatic; it is capable of discernment; it has tact, delicacy; it knows how to choose, to divine. Among the great numbers of combinations blindly formed by the subliminal self, almost all are without interest and without utility; but just for that reason they are also without effect upon the esthetic sensibility. Consciousness will never know them, only certain ones are harmonious, and consequently, at once useful and beautiful.[4]

With this introduction, let us go on to look more closely at the flash of creative inspiration. It will be the essence of all the symbolic possibilities in the prelude, a distillate of rare ideas from a vast memory bank, surging up—*tugged* up—because they were invested long ago with special affective connotations.

31.

Moments of Creative Inspiration

As usual, I stepped over the stretched out body. At this precise moment
the insight struck me. When, a moment later, I entered the hospital, I
held the solution to the problem.

Charles Nicolle

In these few lines, Nicolle describes how he suddenly realized, in a
flash, that typhus was transmitted to humans by a louse.[1] Sometimes, in
such seconds of rare intensity, everything falls easily, beautifully, into
place. In this state of enhanced awareness, old faint trails of facts spring
into wide open avenues of information. The mind steers itself unerringly
through all the traffic to the proper, harmonious combination.

The puzzle seems to solve itself. With only the lightest unintentional
touch of a few keys on the organ, a major chord has burst forth to shake
the cathedral. So facile is this process, so free and uncontrived, that one
almost gains the impression that the solution has come from without.
Among the accompanying feelings are an exalted sense of revelation
and a melting away of all internal tensions, an intense admixture of certainty and serenity. And this chord will not be lost in the future; it will
be replayed.

A flash of insight startles us, not only because it is abrupt, but also
because it may possess the special quality of reversing our preexisting
assumptions.[2] It thrusts up from our unconscious a quick, sharp wedge
of reorganized material that fits precisely into the focal area of our conscious mind where we fruitlessly struggled earlier, and renders obsolete
our old rational beliefs. Indeed, it is sometimes obvious that the more we
hungered earlier for a solution, the more passion we committed to the
previous intellectual struggle, the more profoundly we are relieved
when the struggle is resolved. *"Aha!"* we say. *"Eureka!"*

What really happens in a major insight? Is the depth of feeling the
result solely of a kind of cognitive relief? Probably not. What may also
occur is that our brain automatically completes the jigsaw puzzle with

one missing piece electric with symbolism—a forgotten, highly charged memory circuit in which long ago we made a heated emotional invest-ment. What we experience in the present may seem to be a fresh, shin-ing thought structure, so novel in shape that it all seems newly forged. Only rarely do we sense that in its amalgam are rusty old links of metal, heat-tempered years before.

When a major bolt of inspiration flashes into your mind, nothing remains quite the same thereafter. Your mental topography changes in two ways. First there occurs that abrupt sharpening of perception dur-ing the "peak" moment itself when, with a subtle jar, something clicks into place like a keystone into the waiting arch.[3] This moment is satu-rated from base to peak with a rare clarity of feeling lasting seconds, minutes, or more. What comes next—the second phase—is a residue of enhanced perceptual awareness mingled with a pervasive sense of awe, a serene but lesser "high" that lingers for hours or days thereafter. With the initial turning over of the mind, we felt *something* internally fall neatly into place. Now, *everything* internally shifts gracefully a bit closer toward some natural center of gravity where it seems to belong. Simultaneously, we perceive ourselves in a more open and free in-terrelationship with the external world. The delayed feeling of well-be-ing associated with inspiration may go on for two or three days; that as-sociated with revelation may last many years. When contrasted with the "sea level" feeling of ordinary existence, the lesser high can neverthe-less constitute a newer, higher plane of sustained conscious experience, a "plateau" in a sense.[4]

We invisioned the flash itself as related to the discharge of a number of nerve cells. As they send neurotransmitter messengers across innu-merable circuits, these neurons forge a very special pattern of remem-bered experience. But what explains the later ongoing residue? For at least the early part, one might turn to recent studies showing how close the coupling is between electrophysiology and metabolism. It turns out that many transmitters have metabolic effects outlasting the fraction of a second occupied by the message of a single nerve impulse. In fact, neurotransmitters from one cell turn on enzyme systems, called cyc-lases, in the other nerve cells they contact. These enzymes then synthe-size the *second* messengers: cyclic AMP and cyclic GMP.[5] These chemi-cals in turn can influence the excitability of nerve cells for much longer periods of time. New levels of perception, fresh attitudes, and, ultimately, patterns of behavior could start in motion when the cyclase enzyme systems set whole circuits of nerve cells at newer levels of excitability.

Our stereotyped view is that poets create chiefly from inspiration. Lewis Carroll describes it well:

I was walking on a hillside, alone, one bright summer day, when suddenly there came into my head one line of verse—one solitary line—'For the Snark *was* a Boojum, you see.' I knew not what it meant, then: I know not what it means, now:* but I wrote it down: and, some time afterwards, the rest of the stanza occurred to me, that being its last line: and so by degrees, at moments during the next year or two, the rest of the poem pieced itself together. . . .[6]

But this is not the only way poets create, for Edgar Allen Poe's magnificent *The Raven* was composed with the heavily reasoned systematic precision of a long mathematical equation, and Poe himself disclaimed any inspiration in it.

So, we must be careful not to attribute too much to a second of creative inspiration, for though vividly recalled, these seconds are relatively uncommon. In fact, bearing in mind the fact that there are 604,800 seconds in a week (in even a nonproductive week), these inspired moments are rare in anyone's lifetime.

And again, let us stress that the moments are not all exactly the same, either from person to person or within the experience of each person. Indeed, we see this fact demonstrated in the many different approaches described by contributors to the books *The Creative Process* and *The Creative Experience*.[7] In a sense, the titles are misnomers; they could as well be titled the Creative Process*es* and Creative Experienc*es*. As Koestler observes:

At one end of the scale we have discoveries which seem to be due to more or less conscious, logical reasoning, and at the other end sudden insights which seem to emerge spontaneously from the depth of the unconscious. The same polarity of logic and intuition will be found to prevail in the methods and techniques of artistic creation. It is summed by two opposite pronouncements: Bernard Shaw's 'Ninety percent perspiration, ten percent inspiration,' on the one hand, Picasso's 'I do not seek—I find (*je ne cherche pas, je trouve*),' on the other.[8]

---

* Poets can thrive on whimsical Snarks and Boojums, but investigators won't get very far without adding something more substantial.

The investigator must be both Shaw and Picasso, and all the men in between. He must swing back and forth from the freest flights of imagination to the most rigorous grinding logic. He may be struck by an intense flash of creative inspiration that hits with lightninglike impact. Or, he may pursue the vaguest of hunches, driven by an intuition corresponding to the faintest glow of one lone ember in the hearth. Then again, he may experience his enlightenment through a sequence of small sparks, each of lesser intensity and amplitude, which successively leap upward into consciousness. These, too, can collectively solve the problem with new ideas of all sizes and shapes which spring forth at intervals of hours, days, weeks, or longer.

Inspiration has been evoked using an astonishing range of techniques. These run the gamut from poets (Grey, Racine, Milton) who first quietly read passages from their favorite great masters, to those who compose on horseback (Goethe, Scott, and Burns), and to some who prefer different colors of paper for various types of literary work. (Dumas used blue for novels, pink for journalistic work, and yellow for poetry.)[9] If you have found, as I have, that music helps your creative performance, you will be glad to know that this has now been verified experimentally.[10]

The muse strikes at unforeseen times, places, and persists for unpredictable periods. I have learned to respect the creative spurt, whenever it arrives, to seize the moment, write it down quickly, and then be carried along making the most of it.

So there is not only a single flash—there are many variations on the creative theme. Let's look at three of several that have been identified;[11] others are listed separately.[12]

Closure. This means devising a whole new major scientific theory. An example from Part I of this book was the articulation by Hers of the general concept that deposition diseases are caused by deficient lysosomal enzymes.

Partial solutioning. This involves breaking down a large insoluble problem into smaller parts, some of which can then be solved. Most diseases, including MLD and GLD, are solved in this manner.

Transfer. Here, one applies a solution from one field to another problem in an apparently different field. The creative act lies in recognizing that similar problems may have similar solutions. An example would be the idea that a sulfatase B deficiency might explain a disease of sulfated mucopolysaccharides, just as a sulfatase A deficiency previously explained MLD, a disease of sulfated lipids.

The investigator is generally an eclectic, and his creative moments will have to be diversified. But, in addition, he will need a great deal more than a single flash of inspiration if his work is ever to bear fruit. Neither his intellect nor his passion can supply the missing ingredient. For what he needs now is that element of character termed *will,* a degree of dogged perseverance toward a finite goal that amounts to an obsession.

32.

Follow Through, a More Personal View

Neither the bounties from insight nor the bounties from chance, however, relieve the investigator from the necessity of hard labor, for the suggestion which is presented from either source still has to pass the rigorous test of critical proving before it can be admitted to the realm of truth.

                                                          Walter Cannon

A scientist must indeed be freely imaginative and yet skeptical, creative and yet a critic. There is a sense in which he must be free, but another in which his thought must be very precisely regimented; there is poetry in science, but also a lot of book keeping.

                                                          Peter Medawar

Thus, a novel hypothesis stutters forward, bounds upward, or springs fully into being. It will not be of much scientific value unless it is a *testable* hypothesis, translatable into action. In the testing, the real conscious work begins. From here on, the investigator needs all the tenacity in his makeup. His persistence is the measure of his motivation.

And time—*time* is required. In our laboratory, I have come to visualize it in terms of "the factor of three." That is, it takes at least three times as long to set up and complete the requisite experiments as the longest period that might at the outset be anticipated. Why is this so? Let's look at a few of the hurdles that can be expected: 1) it will take extra time to set up the first experiment; 2) the result must be reproduced at least two or three times before it is acceptable; 3) each experiment will bring forth new ideas to be tested; 4) things won't always work out as expected. Having considered in advance that all this should take about three months, for example, the gestation period is *still* about nine months before all the evidence is gathered together. And sometimes the factor is three cubed.

Even then, the experiments may prove the hypothesis, or they may disprove it. The investigator may be misled by the feeling that a new insight is beautiful and harmonious, only to find out in the subsequent testing that it is really worthless. He soon learns to beware of his "pet" hypothesis, and is extracritical of it himself. He sets out to " shake" it, to disprove it at least as vigorously as he tries to prove it. This self-critical facility, this ability to be completely detached from his prejudice while fully engaged in it, will prove one of his best assets. In this sense, the researcher resembles a circus rider. He stands precariously, each foot on the back of a different horse. The horses veer from side to side, and he must quickly shift his weight from one to the other to maintain balance. Here similarities end. For the path ahead of the researcher is no circle smoothed by sawdust, but raw unbroken ground; one of his steeds may be a critically trained performer, but the other—the burning new idea he'd like to prove—a spirited maverick.

Attention to fine detail is sometimes vital, but a constant preoccupation with detail is not fruitful. Dr. George Minot (who showed that liver therapy helps pernicious anemia) once put it this way: "A single hair protruding above the underbrush may be the only sign that a large furry animal lurks beneath." His statement has that instant feeling of validity, especially to old rabbit-trackers and kindred searchers.

Sensing which ideas to ignore is probably more important than generating many of them. Few are the key ideas that are worth following up. Few are the major problems solvable with the technology and other resources of the present. The time has to be ripe. So the researcher must probe for the few problems he can get a grip on—those that have "a handle," in scientific parlance. Otto Warburg's words to his student, Hans Krebs, were to the effect that research is "the art of finding problems that can be solved.[1] Too many projects can seriously drain your time and energy. I have found that an optimal number is three, each in different stages of completion.

If Chance II, in particular, is ever going to prove fruitful, you must first screen your objectives, direct your search toward a promising area. Otherwise, you'll still be flailing around in a parched desert looking for those orchids. You use many kinds of discrimination to whittle down the many options to the manageable few. Your judgment operates over an entire spectrum: starting with unconscious avoidance, extending through the vague hunch that something will not work out, and then on to fully conscious elimination. In this regard, the old saying about intuition in marriage applies equally to research: "Success in love consists not so much in marrying the one who can make you happy as in escaping the many who could make you miserable."

In this other marriage (for it is that) to his work, the medical researcher tries to escape from the trivial and the derivative. His method is to use his frontal lobes—to anticipate the result. His approach is always future-oriented. His goal: the germinal; his yardstick: the "so what?" test. This means that he will tentatively project conclusions from the hypothesis well out in front of his data. He asks: what important implications, if any, would a finding have? Is the projected goal not only original but really worthwhile? Certain kinds of information take on top priority. These priority decisions seem to be made at all levels of consciousness. In arriving at priority decisions, the researcher's humanistic tendencies will lead him to consider the needs of both patient and society. His scientific orientation will direct him toward "yeasty," provocative information that catalyzes the gathering of new information to an unusual degree. His pragmatic nature inclines him toward research that will attract financial support. These are not irreconcilable opposites, but I find myself forever wrestling with the order of my priority decisions. Fortunate is the investigator who always satisfies all his instincts in one field of inquiry.

The more novel and exciting the hypothesis, the more some colleagues will resist it. They will challenge the data on which it is based for all manner of reasons and in all manner of ways. Gradually, I have come to appreciate that these "reactionary" forces are also allies in disguise. Not without effort, I have learned to bend constructively to my advantage the energies that come from resulting conflict of ideas. Challenges guarantee the extra effort that makes for my best performance. Does the method really have a hole in it here? A gap in the logic there?

If so, they will be plugged up more quickly if firm resistance is present.

Next, there is a lot of writing to be done. This, too, seems to follow a "factor of three" time scale. If the first experiments are successful, they may justify expanding the work into a full-scale research project, which takes money. A grant application must be written. Up to now, one has been humming a catchy tune; from here on it must be orchestrated fully. The area under investigation must be extensively documented, the research budget thoroughly justified. Grant applications are a headache. Increasingly, researchers have been forced to predict and to describe *exactly* how they will proceed months to years into the future. For more creative types of research, this requirement bears little relation to reality. It is like expecting a watercolorist to draw out clearly in advance, using color coded numbers, each of the hundred or so brush strokes he will make in a forthcoming painting. The inherent rigidity of painting by the numbers bears little relationship to the fluid, creating-as-you-go-along approach of painting and of novel investigative work. However much they increasingly suffer, grant applicants bear it, and write on. They know (if bureaucrats don't) that it is the second and third generation of ideas—not even envisioned at the time of writing—that will give freshness and renewed vitality to their work.

In writing the application for funds the researcher must tread several narrow lines. How much documentation should he include at the risk of boring the reader or revealing "trade" secrets? How much enthusiasm can he convey about fresh ideas still to be tested without appearing "far out" and "unscientific"? Should he apply to several agencies for support or only to one; for two years' support or for three? If the proposal is interesting, a hard-nosed team of experts may be sent out to interview him, inspect his laboratory, and decide upon the merits of the research planned.

Later, assuming financial support is forthcoming, he will have to shift the pattern of his research. Initially, much of his work was designed to test whether his methods were good enough to answer his hypothesis. He performed his first tentative pilot experiments on the shaky framework of these early methods. This was the preamble—a time for laying the groundwork and "playing it by ear." It is something like exploring a vast swamp by extending a succession of thin planks out horizontally, each barely floating on the surface. One may visualize such early attempts as a time of "horizontal research." Later, with the foundations more secure underfoot the investigator will decide that all the methods are finally poised for the "big runs" of "vertical research." These will be the major experiments, a time of upward construction, of visible progress, of "putting it all together."

If the investigator's experiments are successful, his data and conclusions should now be good enough to share with his colleagues at large. When he then starts to prepare a paper to present orally at a meeting, he quickly find himself in trouble again. The methods still have a quirk that must be ironed out; the data really aren't conclusive; someone else has evidence that may conflict with the conclusions unless further experiments are performed. And these additional experiments, necessarily, are done.

Oral reports are perishable; they have no permanent scientific value. The investigator must finally put all the information into a manuscript for publication complete with tables, figures, and bibliography, and must try to anticipate which editors of which journals will be the most receptive. By now, he has faced the factor of three so many times that *months* have gone by. The original ideas have lost their luster. Completing the manuscript is like giving birth to a cactus that has bloomed long before.

Still later, the editors suggest some changes. Swallowing pride, he finds that most of these will actually strengthen the paper. The jigsaw puzzle is now completed. Months later, the article is published. He reads it over, reminiscing now, and knowing only too well the fragile contingencies, the incredible complexity of the whole drawn-out process, he marvels how it all ever came to pass.

But the moment of pause is soon over, because new leads have opened up, a new generation of ideas is being tested out, the cycle is being repeated.

33.

All Quiet on the Eastern Front?

The most beautiful emotion we can experience is the mystical. It is the sower of all true art and science. . . . The cosmic religious experience is the strongest and the noblest, deriving from behind scientific research. No one who does not appreciate the terrific exertions, the devotion, without which pioneer creation in scientific thought cannot come into being can judge the strength of the feeling out of which alone such work, turned away as it is from immediate practical life, can grow.

Albert Einstein

Not too many years ago, if a Westerner engaged in "Eastern" forms of meditation, he was viewed as contaminated by mental leprosy. That attitude was changed by the burst of international travel and the traffic in ideas after World War II. Now, many persons may practice various forms of meditation—a kind popularly known as "transcendental," Zen, or simple relaxation—without feeling especially unconventional. Even today's star football quarterbacks now embrace philosophical and physiological principles practiced in the East for millennia, believing that it helps their game. East *has* met West. "Far out" has almost become "far in."

Anyone who hasn't meditated can only be confused about what the basic process really involves. First of all, you aren't thinking. Nor do you absolutely need to concentrate on a word, a paradox, or an idea, though these may assist the beginner, or be superimposed later. Rather, you "let go" to enter a realm of *non*thinking. As your thoughts fall away, and breathing takes care of itself, you become relaxed and can experience at least at one stage a feeling of clear, expanded inner awareness. To me, the conventional outside world then seems (somewhat paradoxically) both closer and wider in terms of perception, yet farther away in terms of conception.

Some say that if you regularly practice a popularly known system of meditation, you will increase the fluency, flexibility, and originality of creative solutions.[1] Others suggest that teachers of this system are below average in certain standard tests of creativity,[2] yet how original these teachers might have been before they started their training remains to be determined.

In any case, meditation is increasingly used to explore and extend the frontiers of "inner space." As a result, it has progressed beyond the fad stage to become a phenomenon to reckon with, both sociologically and scientifically. What was once viewed as rare and mystical has evolved into something both commonplace and practical. Moreover, the scientist finally not only feels free to acknowledge his "mystical" depths, but knows that there should be nothing mysterious about them. He insists, indeed, that meditation and similar phenomena be studied scientifically like any others, still realizing that factual evidence and proof are going to be hard to come by.

The immediate goal of meditation is to reach a calm state of both mental awareness and physical relaxation. With practice, these states increasingly outlast the period of meditation. The next phase is to expand one's spiritual perceptions toward that feeling of enlightened transcendent "oneness" with the universe sometimes called "cosmic consciousness." The ultimate goal is to experience this not only momentarily, but to integrate it, effortlessly, goallessly into the fabric of a lifelong attitude of mind, one that facilitates personal growth and appropriate social actions as well.

We still know next to nothing about the neurophysiological basis of the various steps in the creative sequence. However, we might understand some of these steps better if we examined parts of the meditative approach, for creativity does relate to meditation in two ways. To begin with, our "civilized" world forever blizzards us with a synaptic overload of unnecessary stimuli. These stimuli not only distract us from our essential selves, but even cause mental traffic jams that clog our thinking. In such a world, meditation could free up some moments for calm observation, openminded scanning, or freewheeling rumination of the kind necessary in the creative sequence. As Alan Watts has said, "it is only when there is no goal, and no rush that the human senses are fully open to receive the world."[3]

Then, too, the flash of creative illumination bears certain analogies with that "peak" moment of revelation which can be a high point of the meditative approach. During revelation there also occurs a rare sense of clarity, of certainty, and the highest perception of being enlightened or "tuned into" something beyond ourselves. If a flash of intuition has ever sent you up to the molehills of inspiration, you know something of what it must be like to be thrust atop the Everest of revelation.

Whatever its size and scope, the fresh scientific hypothesis or the deep cosmic insight doesn't come in cool, subdued, pale green tones. It is often warm, vibrant, radiating a bright sense of value. The feeling of *rightness*—the surge of certainty associated with enlightenment—is particularly interesting. Let us look at some contours of this feeling of certainty from the point of view of the nerve cells that generate it— whole populations of special reinforcing, conditioning neurons. They will not be the primary nerve cells out in the retina that start to see, or those in the inner ear that signal sound waves. They are rather the ones deep in the brain that voice their assent if what you see or hear appears personally valid. If something about a situation feels intuitively correct to you, a few circuits of such conditioning nerve cells will react in a positive way, discharging impulses, as if to nod, "yes, that's so." For the moment, they simply outvote whatever other doubting neurons you may have. Later on, the doubting, "negative" nerve cells will have ample time to make you skeptically tilt your head and shrug your shoulders as if to indicate, "well—maybe, but I'm still not convinced; let's look at more evidence first." But at the highest peak of revelation itself, vast populations of positive nerve networks are drawn together in what seems to be the mental counterpart of an orgasm, and the whole experience is stamped by the surge of absolute certainty. Now, the whole chorus of neuronal voices deep in your brain chants, "Yes, yes, yes, that *is* so!" No doubts, no ifs, ands, or buts, disturb their unanimity. You *believe*—down in the very center of your being—pulled there by the cords of feeling you've just experienced.

Within Zen Buddhism, there have grown up two schools of thought about how enlightenment—satori—occurs. In the Soto school, illumination grows gradually, and new land masses of the enlightened mind merge and take shape in a kind of slow deep continental drift. In the Rinzai school, revelation occurs in a burst as the result of a mind-shattering spiritual earthquake. Thus, these two approaches resemble the several kinds of illumination—long and slow, short and fast—we can experience within the creative process itself.

Whether the feeling of enlightened certainty comes quickly or slowly, we ought to know more about where the feeling originates, not only from the standpoint of science, but also from that of religion and politics. This knowledge is important because one who experiences it can be transformed by it, as Saul of Tarsus was converted on the road to Damascus. Whether one is possessed or liberated as a result of such a deeply felt belief depends both on the individual and on the circumstances. We can hypothesize that the surge of certainty comes when all those smaller circuits throughout the brain that subliminally reinforce an idea with a "good and true" feeling become linked together and fire in unison. This is not an epilepsy-like firing within the motor system such as would cause a muscle to twitch. Rather, the inference is that compelling nerve cells have discharged—nerve cells normally conferring feelings of a quality we experience all too rarely—enchanted states extending between deep spiritual awareness and rapture. Perhaps we should go out of our way to encounter more frequently some of these normal states of spiritual awareness, encourage them by exercising them spontaneously through more frequent, relaxed contacts with music, art, or with a satisfying personal religion. If we did, then the feeling tones that we pull up and link with our intuitions would be deeper, more frequent, more satisfying and more memorable.

But the substance of our intuitions is one thing, and the feeling that goes along with them is another. We must remind ourselves of our splendid limitations: in our own nerve cells lies the source of our perceptions, deepest feelings, and beliefs. We hope these are fully in accord with reality, but they may not be. As long as the brain remains the organ of our conscious mind, a seductive palpitation welling up from the depths of the brain no more implies that an idea is valid, or that we have actually come into *actual* union with the cosmos, than does a palpitation of the heart. Herein lies the dilemma, not only for a scientist like Einstein, but for the rest of us. We must be as receptive as Einstein was to the mystical music of the spheres, yet ultimately we both must run each cherished belief through the gauntlet of our doubt. For the scientist in particular, this is never a guided tour carefully avoiding all obstructions, but a rigorous, self-imposed obstacle course. He can never accept as wholly true what he leaves untested. In the final analysis, what will be most important to him is not one particular belief but rather what Charles S. Peirce, the American philosopher, called a consistent "integrity of belief."[4] This, a product of time, will come only when believing is habitually bonded to testing.

If you take on a problem to solve creatively, whether you are at the laboratory bench or elsewhere in life, there are basically two ways you can proceed. You can move out into the external world, encounter random new ideas as a result of chance, and incorporate them into fresh creative solutions. Or, you can reach inward to your storehouse of memories, generating a new solution from facts and feelings already existing within. *In*sight is one word used to describe the process, for it does signify seeing inward. *In*tuition is another.

Meditation also involves tuning in to some inner dimension. Many objective physiological changes occur during meditation. Can we learn anything about creativity from these changes? Do they tell us anything about how the search within and without takes place?

We can start with the brain waves of normal persons, for we all generate alpha waves during relaxation and especially when we close our eyes to external sights. Alpha waves in the electroencephalogram (EEG) reflect a kind of mental idling. They are blocked by sudden noises. They also stop for a longer period when our attention is roused and focused, as it would be, for example, if we raced our mental engine in gear by concentrating on solving a long mathematical problem.

When normal subjects are first exposed to a noise stimulus in the form of a click, they are sufficiently aroused to stop their alpha waves for a long period. This temporary loss of alpha caused by a stimulus is known as alpha blocking. However, after repeated clicks are given every fifteen seconds, the brain finally "gets used to" the stimulus. As a result, alpha waves gradually reassert themselves. That is, after the fifth or sixth stimulus, the normal person "adjusts," and is no longer aroused by the clicking noise. It is characteristic of the normal individual that alpha waves go on to persist despite repeated stimulation, and that alpha blocking, therefore, disappears. The term habituation is used to describe this decreased blocking response to repeated stimulation. It usually implies that the organism tunes out a stimulus that seems not to have important consequences.

Experienced meditators show a quite different response during meditation. For example, the following EEG changes occur in Japanese Zen monks who have had many years experience meditating. First, alpha waves appear even though their eyes are open, next the alpha waves increase in amplitude, then they slow in frequency. Finally, as meditation deepens, there appear rhythmical trains of still slower theta waves that are not associated with drowsiness.

In Zen monks, as in normal people, alpha waves also stop momentarily the *first* time a click noise is given. But in the monks, alpha waves then reappear spontaneously after only a few seconds. Moreover, the monks don't adjust to repeated clicks. Their alpha waves recur only to be repeatedly blocked each time the same noise is repeated regularly. In other words, repeated click stimuli still get through (to arouse the EEG at least) in Zen monks during meditation. Habituation of the alpha blocking does not occur. In addition, the monks report afterwards that they clearly perceive each click stimulus, but do not respond to it because the stimulus does not disturb them. To use the "signal/noise" analogy, it is as though they register each signal more clearly when the general noise level is reduced.

Instead of using a click as a neutral sound stimulus, the researcher can use various person's names to invest the sound with meaning. If you were the subject, for example, and your emotional ties were close to someone whose name was called, the name would be distracting to you. It should block alpha waves more than a neutral name. In the normal person, the more meaningful names of one's spouse or children are more distracting and do stop alpha waves more at first. But then, perhaps as some token of their greater impact, normals again habituate to the stimulus of the distracting name. Thus, as they did to click, normal individuals will again adjust to the repeated stimulus of the meaningful name, and their initial alpha blocking again tends to disappear.

In contrast, some Zen monks show no habituation of alpha waves to names while meditating. Normals vary widely in the degree to which they are aroused by various names, but Zen monks vary less and all names keep blocking their alpha waves. After the experiment, the monks report that they heard the names while meditating and knew them precisely, but made no further associations to them. In other words, during meditation their perception remains keen, their EEG responsiveness remains enhanced, but the associative spread of each stimulus toward concepts of the conventional world seems reduced.

Some investigators studying Zen monks during meditation believe that the above phenomena imply a special state of consciousness, one characterized by an optimal preparedness for incoming stimuli and by an optimum level for excitation. They describe this state as one of "relaxed awareness with steady responsiveness."[5] Others, looking with additional tests at the range of similar phenomena in the popular system of meditation termed "transcendental" call it "a wakeful hypometabolic physiologic state."[6]

Indeed, other physiological and metabolic changes occur during meditation: respirations slow to only four to five per minute, far lower than during the normal waking state or during sleep. Heart rate falls, expirations are prolonged, abdominal breathing predominates, total oxygen consumption is moderately reduced, blood lactate falls, and the basal metabolic rate drops 15 to 20 percent.

In general, the diverse physiological changes reported during meditation suggest that the activity of many neurons has been quieted or "turned down" as their firing rate is slowed. Because meditation markedly reduces the usual associative play of ideas, it may follow that the large associative areas of the cerebral cortex are no longer fully activated.

But we must avoid one generalization at this point. For it does not follow that the firing rate of *all* nerve cells is reduced or that *all* mental activities are reduced. All is not quiet during meditation, any more than quiet prevails during sleep. In fact, we know that when we sleep many neurons must still stay "wide awake," for our dreams imply a heightened, not a reduced, level of one kind of mental activity. It has also been shown that most rapid eye movements occur during the dreaming phases of normal sleep, meaning that motor nerve cells are activated in the brain stem that trigger the muscles to the eyes. Moreover, direct experimental measurements in animals tell us that certain other nerve cells in the brain stem fire even *more* rapidly than normal during the actively dreaming phases of sleep.

As some brain activity still occurs in sleep, so too does it appear to occur during proper meditation. Not everything shuts down. The firing of nerve cells down in the core of the brain apparently keeps some perceptions keenly attuned. In addition, during meditation, the organizing functions deeper in the brain extend their influence up and out to impart a novel kind of reordering to the usual rhythms of the cortex. Now the pattern of brain wave activity from the right hemisphere becomes synchronized during meditation with that from the left. Waves from the front of the cerebrum achieve a rare degree of unity with those in the back.[7] During the tranquil meditative state, as the clutter of everyday associational noise is markedly reduced, there then flows out from the center a receptive state of calm, transparent awareness, during which the brain can continue to respond to stimuli and the novel properties of each signal persists.

Meditation may, therefore, involve tradeoffs with regard to some aspects of creativity. During a half hour of meditation, and for a variable period thereafter, the creative brain may lose momentarily the obvious benefits that would occur when the intellect harnesses the thrust of fluent, freewheeling associative play. But during the hours and days that follow the brain may gain from those attitudes of the clear refreshed mind that encourage simplicity, spontaneity, and meaningful direct experience. These salutary changes can bring more than a restful change of pace; they can also create a new sense of perspective, a feeling of being elevated on a higher plateau of attitudes. From this plateau new motivations can take off, and in this way over a period of time one expands the repertoire of styles used to solve complex problems. As May observes, "Human freedom involves our capacity to pause between stimulus and response and, in that pause, to choose the one response toward which we wish to throw our weight."[8]

In the foregoing examples we saw how the brain adjusts itself when stimuli are repeated too often by tuning them out through the process called habituation. But we have also seen that the more tranquil brain can do the reverse—block habituation and thus permit each stimulus to rouse yet still retain its novelty. How does this occur? Could it involve being tuned in to some other sensitive circuits? The question is an important one to ask, because just as it is a fundamental property of many nerve cells to habituate, so too it is a property of other nerve cells to *sensitize* the nervous system, to prompt it to respond increasingly when stimuli are repeated.[9]

Many years will pass before we have a coherent picture of the circuitry underlying habituation and sensitization within man's complex nervous system. In the meantime, neurophysiological experiments help us glimpse a few of the mechanisms involved. For example, nerve cell bodies in the midline of a rat's brain stem, in what is called the raphé system, can be stimulated electrically through fine wires. When they are, they release a neurotransmitter, serotonin, from their nerve endings some distance away. Once serotonin is released, the rat's nervous system keeps on responding to each added noise or other sensory stimulus.[10] Each stimulus causes a response. In other words, stimulation of the serotonin system produces a sustained state of enhanced reactivity during which the brain no longer habituates. This increased reactivity resembles that found in meditation, for it is not associated either with somnolence or with hyperactive behavior. Moreover, the enhanced responsiveness clearly hinges on the release of serotonin: drugs that deplete brain serotonin block the response. Even in the primitive sea mollusk, serotonin sensitizes the way the gill responds to repetitive stimuli.[11]

It would be much easier to understand the brain if serotonin had one simple action and were the only neurotransmitter that could accomplish this interesting feat, but it is best to think of the raphé system as only one complex model for the way many others can operate. In fact, our nervous system is made up of an enormous number of hierarchial subsystems, each checking and balancing out the other. The complexities of this process boggle the mind. They would confuse even the consummate politician, well-versed as he must be in the contending checks and balances of our systems of city, county, state, and federal government jousting during an election year. In fact, serotonin terminals of the raphé system probably provide only one of several ways to cause the reduced habituation described above.[12] Within most circuits, actylcholine, not serotonin, is likely to be a major neurotransmitter substance in man.[13] One can generalize further and note that serotonin is largely an inhibitory transmitter, and that it shares this same inhibitory property with other biogenic amine transmitters like norepinephrine, dopamine, and gamma amino-butyric acid (GABA). Each of these modulates neuronal events chiefly by *slowing down* the firing of the *next* nerve cell they contact. Therefore, the amine transmitters each serve primarily as a governor, not as a ruler.

How easy it is to miss the crucial importance of a slowing down of the next nerve cell. Faster means better in our Western culture. Doesn't it?

Not in the nervous system, it doesn't. If a transmitter from one nerve cell, let us call it cell A, normally quiets the next cell by slowing its firing rate, two important things can occur. Which of these predominates will depend on how the circuits are wired between cell B and the next cells farther on down the line. For the first example, let us suppose that nerve cell B normally quiets cell C, blocking its firing. Now, if cell A fires much more than usual and further slows cell B, it will follow in sequence that nerve cell C will then be speeded up as it escapes from the inhibition of cell B. Furthermore, if the normal function of cell C is to excite the next neuron, D, then the initial quieting effect from cell A will ultimately be transmuted into an excitatory action on cell D because cell C will speed up its firing rate. A somewhat analogous situation occurs in mathematics: a negative times a negative becomes a positive.

For the second example, we need to know how effective cell B is to begin with. Suppose it is chronically overloaded with too many impulses—surrounded by too much "noise," already firing so many times that its message lacks contrast, and it gets tuned out by cell C. In this situation, if we really wish to improve the effectiveness of cell B, we would want to *reduce* its excitability, slow it down to a more optimal rate, or at least vary its firing rate so the next cell on down the line will sit up and take notice that the new message represents a change. Here we see that by reducing the noise level in the background, both on cell B and from cell B, the impact of each signal on it, and from it, can be much more readily appreciated.

What the serotonin example and the last two illustrations show is that quieting down one part of the nervous system is not only compatible with increased sensitivity of another part, but that slowing one part *may actually facilitate* the speeding up, or the sensitivity, of another part. No paradox here. The nervous system just doesn't operate the same way throughout: the plus signs and the minus signs on nerve cell receptors within its myriads of circuits make for some fantastically varied combinations.[14]

What other system could be slowed during a tranquil state of meditation? The reticular activating system is a reasonable candidate. This is a long network of many nerve cells ascending from deep down in the core of our brain stem. Normally, we are aroused and alerted when the activating system and its projections fire upward toward the cerebrum. When its relay of signals reaches many sets of nerve cells located still higher, we can next start to focus our attentive behavior more selectively on the external world. Our eyes open wider, we lean forward and orient toward the stimulus that sounds or looks interesting. As we saw earlier, these alerting signals do block alpha waves in the EEG. Therefore, we can view as the opposite of conventional, alpha wave, relaxed idling the whole normal process of being aroused and focusing our attention on our external environment.

To sustain such a high level of focused attention, we depend on a constant tonic flow of impulses back and forth along the circuits between our ascending reticular formation and still other higher centers. We may speculate that after the reticular formation helps alert the brain stem, subcortex, and cortex, it is these higher levels of neuronal functioning that help us decipher the meaning of what we see, hear, or feel. Our convoluted cortex, in particular, helps us become more discriminating. Then, when the limbic system feeds in its feeling tone, what is consciously perceived can finally be understood in terms of past experience, and given a relevant emotional value on the scale of: danger-bad-good-terrific. This to and fro interplay of millions of nerve cells is what normally makes up our everyday attention to the external world and gives it internal significance.

However, the most focused attention will dwindle into gross neglect if connections are blocked between the above systems. If even a small interruption is placed on only one side of the reticular activating system of a hungry monkey, he will ignore the apple on the opposite side of his external environment. His eyes are not blind, but neither does he "see" the apple except in the most fragmentary sense, because for purposes of active behavior, it really doesn't register as an apple on the one side of his hungry brain that is disconnected and disintegrated from his activating system. As a result, the monkey pays no attention to the apple—unless it is placed on the other side of his environment toward which his reactions remain physiologically intact.[15]

Larger experimental lesions, so placed that they interrupt both ascending activating systems on both sides, not only cause neglect but also stop habituation. The animal no longer normally habituates to repeated disturbing puffs of air on his back, but continues to be startled by each repeated stimulus.[16] It is noteworthy that habituation is stopped when the continuous firing of the activating system is reduced, for this finding is reminiscent of that seen during meditation or when serotonin is increased. As a whole, the evidence suggests that some changes during meditation may reflect a tuning down of the tone of the reticular system, while also raising the possibility that some functions of opposing systems may be relatively enhanced in the process. What is unusual about meditation is that the capacity persists to be phasically, intermittently, and repeatedly aroused, while at the same time the overall background brain wave activity is slowed. The implication is that the activating system can lose some of its continuous firing activity yet maintain its ability to fire episodically. *This* quiet means readiness.

What could tuning down the tonic activity of the alerting mechanism have to do with creativity? Don't you have to be alert to be creative? Certainly, but our brains do not function the same way throughout each step in the creative sequence. For example, you clearly need to be *slightly* alert and aroused during the earlier phases of problem-solving, but success falls off in later phases of the creative response if you stay alerted beyond an optimum level. This has been clear from experiments on human subjects who became less original on word association tests when external stresses drove them toward higher levels of arousal.[17]

Moreover, suppose you start with the two abilities—one, the capacity to focus your concentration, the other the capability to browse internally in a more unfocused manner. It is not to your advantage constantly to deploy one at the expense of the other for hours on end. In fact, what you really need is to be able to shift flexibly, and repeatedly, from one mental mode to the other at exactly the right time. The ability of the practiced meditator to retain his sensitivity to the click stimulus, to shift repeatedly into just enough arousal to block alpha waves with each click, yet not so much to cause habituation, thus has an interesting parallel with the way everyone's physiological requirements must vary throughout the whole creative process. The creative do have physiological abilities to fluctuate: they have an unusual ability to suppress alpha waves in their EEG,[18] their heart rates vary more than others in response to an inkblot task,[19] and their eyes move more as they shift from the analytical stage of problem-solving into the synthetic stage when they put it all together in a new way.[20]

Highly creative subjects also generate more alpha waves in the EEG while they are actually engaged in those association tests that involve their imagination.[21] On the other hand, they tend to have fewer alpha waves at rest, and develop fewer alpha waves when, in test situations, their intelligence needs to be highly focused.[22] These two sets of findings suggest that there may be an important difference in the brains of most creative persons: they are *tight-loose types*. If they are somewhat less relaxed at rest than controls, they can later become more relaxed when absorbed in the free-wheeling, mulling over phase of the creative sequence that calls for freedom of associations.

We have noted earlier that theta waves, slower than alpha, occur in the EEG in deeper meditative states. Some evidence suggests that abundant theta waves also occur during the subliminal state of preconsciousness, termed reverie, in which sudden dreamlike images occur. It will be interesting to see whether well-controlled experiments that attempt to increase theta waves will enhance visual imagery and cause a measured long-lasting increase in creativity. Such studies are already underway.[23] In the interim, it may be noted that persons undergoing regular theta training do feel better integrated. They report, for example: "I'm getting clearer and clearer"; "I feel so put together"; "I feel so with it."[24]

The ease with which meditators can learn to let go and enter a satisfying state of calm, detached awareness does correlate with their basic ability to produce spontaneous visual imagery, to free associate, and to tolerate any unreal experiences that may occur.[25] Again we see that in the collage of mental abilities open to man, being tautly integrated and staying loose need not be mutually exclusive.

What do the many cited experiments mean? They remind us that we need several kinds of sensitivity to visual and other clues when we gather preliminary data for creative work. They also emphasize that throughout the long, tough-minded creative sequence we must still blend in moments of freshness, clear perception, novelty, and inspired imagery if we are to succeed. Finally, we begin to envision some neurophysiological basis for at least two kinds of mental processes. One kind includes the seemingly quiet periods when we can still be aware, relaxed, and responsive. The other includes those all too rare peak moments of insight that thrust us upward. It is these quiet and peak moments, each working with the other, that generate a fresh mental topography, form new troughs and plateaus, new contours of experience in the brain of creative man.

34.
Prescription for Creativity

The master word . . . . is directly responsible for all advances in medicine during the past twenty-five centuries . . . the master word is *Work*.

Sir William Osler

Your own creative abilities were inborn and made, innate and learned. You can't disentangle one from the other. You started by inheriting one-half of your creative instincts from each parent and one-quarter from each grandparent. Thereafter, the attitudes prevailing in your family and those acquired in school went on to set much of the tone. But you can add still more, whatever your field of creative endeavor. It is not too late. The question is: what to add; where, when, and how to add it?

Let us begin by reviewing some of the formal steps in the creative sequence, for we first need to insert some arbitrary structure into what seems, even at best, a very disorganized process. We recall that the sequences usually quoted are, in order: interest, preparation, incubation, illumination, verification, exploitation. Let us examine them one by one because, just as timing is important in any prescription, what is prescribed will vary, depending on when it is inserted in the sequence.

Interest. Only if you are really interested in a topic will you persist in it, see it through to completion. This holds whether the topic is colors, dogs, mathematics, law, or whatever. Therefore, you should seek out those areas that serve a deep, long-standing personal need. You won't know, in the abstract, which are your areas of special interest; you will first have to try many of them on for size. Those that fit naturally will "turn you on," and only then will you really know. The interest that strongly motivates you will be the one that enlists all your energies, and brings forth skills you would never be aware of otherwise. Your best work will be a projection of self. Trust yourself to know when you're on the right track.

Soon, you will find that you're engaged in something of a quest. At all times, seek out lively vital people—good teachers, in particular—for they will both kindle your interests and be inspiring role models in many critical ways. Get involved with them. Ask them questions. Select guides, not drivers, bright persons you can respect, mentors wise enough to help you find your own way, secure enough to keep your own best interests in mind, mature enough to let go at the right time.

If need be, adopt some active hobbies that provide contrast. If you are a verbal, precise, systematic type, get into something loose—something visual or musical that you can actively participate in, whether that means finger painting, pottery, or the guitar. Engage all the nerve cells in your whole right hemisphere in active pursuits, not just in passive listening and looking. You will "see into" art and "hear into" music much more when you have done some related work (play, really) with your own hands. The active approach will ultimately enhance your depth of appreciation and make it easier for you to be inspired by the great creative artists in any field. If the arts and crafts you are interested in involve taking an adult education course, and you haven't got the time to explore such new ground, *make* the time.

The most important interest to develop is the creative attitude itself. New ideas are worthwhile in any field. Most things in life *can* be improved. Problem-solving is challenging, and challenges are fun. You must believe in these principles, be willing to act on them, and be capable of making sacrifices for them. Seek out other persons who believe these same principles, and put up with their liabilities, as they will have to put up with yours.

Preparation. You must study to become well-grounded in your field, mastering its basic techniques until they are second nature. Then, practice your craft by solving problems of increasing complexity. Before long, you will find yourself out at some frontier of the field. Here, the new problems will be as yet unsolved. One or more of these will catch your interest. You will then have to judge which one lies just outside your abilities. It should be no trivial problem, but one important in its implications, one that captures your imagination so that you are enthusiastic about it. If you are then bold enough to tackle it, and you have judged correctly, you will grow to meet it, but you won't know that at the time. For this reason, you will seek advice from those who should know more than you do. Again, you must be a sound judge of character and information, because their replies will be both encouraging and discouraging. You must discard each when the facts warrant it. Your preparation for this critical task of discrimination has been to know so many different people in so many different situations (yourself included) that you have developed an uncommon degree of common sense. If you're going to be a maverick, you'll need horse sense about other people.

Incubation. Preparation is followed by more work. When you work on a good new problem, you will become committed to it to the point of an obsession, wrestling with it months or years before you solve it completely. Like a jigsaw puzzle, each big problem consists of a whole series of smaller problems that need to be pieced together. And jigsaw puzzles or crossword puzzles are themselves good practice in exercising the skills in visualization you need to solve other problems. Earlier, you needed time to browse; now, you must create solid undistracted blocks of time to work. These blocks of time tend to be more fruitful in the morning or in the evening.

Sooner or later you will run out of ideas. If you then persist with the intensity you should, you will become frustrated by your lack of progress. Relax at this point. Let go. Free the problem to "go underground." Set it aside to be worked over at all levels of consciousness. Here, again, other diverse interests will provide a refreshing change of pace, give you a breather while you incubate the first problem, afford other problems you can still make progress on in the interim.

Know something about the structure of luck so that at least you don't do anything to discourage it. Chance I is anyone's luck; Chance II is anyone-in-motion's luck. Chance III is luck that comes from one man's discernment; Chance IV is luck that flows from one man's actions.

As you work, the varieties of chance will operate, stirring up new options, new facts, novel perceptions prompted by actions uniquely yours. Remaining alert to exceptions, keeping an open, receptive mind, you will intuitively grasp the more worthwhile observation, whatever happens to turn it up.

Define passive activities, such as listening to music, that help you relax, unfocus your thinking, and loosen up your free associations. Seek out good comedy. Never stay so busy that you don't have time to daydream.

Maybe you'll encounter something, by accident, that you weren't looking for, that hints at a whole new problem. Make note of it. This may turn out to be the important problem you'll be working on years hence.

Illumination. Solutions do leap forth by themselves, but a clear, relaxed, well-slept mind generates more innovative ideas. Get enough sleep. Stay alert for the intuitions that flicker in from the margins of consciousness, especially during the phase of reverie after awakening. Major insights can be unforgettable, but they are rare. Most other flashes of insight are of lesser intensity, and they can vanish quickly unless you immediately write them down. Don't worry if you daydream up a new approach that appears farfetched; jot the essence of it down. It may lead on to still another idea that will turn out to be much better.

Verification. If a solution has arisen, it is still only one possible solution. If a hypothesis springs forth, it remains to be tested. Again, hard mental and physical work enters in. You will save much time at this point by shifting into hypercritical gear, deferring all leads save those most pregnant with new possibilities. Ask the "so what" question.

Design the next experiments not only to verify your hunch, but also to shake it, to prove yourself wrong. Insert enough controls into the experiment so that you won't fool yourself in your enthuasism for the alluring new idea. No matter what you think you have verified, some others will not agree. Listen to them. Swallow your pride, put the resulting energies to work to prove your thesis correct one hundred percent. Even if your insight is valid, plan to spend at least three times as long as may seem necessary in order to prove it so. But routinize the routine as soon as possible, so that you save free time for innovation.

Exploitation. Keep the emphasis on ideas, theories, and hypotheses that can lead to action. If your creative efforts are ever going to cause change, you can't stop now. You must follow through on the project, investing more of yourself to make sure that change does, in fact, occur. Reactionaries, resisting change, should again only help you redouble your own constructive followthrough. Translating your ideas into effective action means you must preserve the same infectious enthusiasm at this late date that you had in the beginning.

This is the kind of prescription I would write for myself. Maybe yours is similar, but it is probably not identical. Every prescription for creativity must be a highly individualized one. Learn to recognize what works for you.

35.

Summary

True creativity is characterized by a succession of acts, each dependent on
the one before and suggesting the one after.

                                                      Edwin Land

We have now observed something of what medical research is, and
what it is not. It is no clear, blue, inorganic crystal which grows sym-
metrically and predictably in solution. Instead, it is a live, organic
growth, a wild vine winding in and around an intellectual trellis. It ventures a tendril here, thrusts out a leaf there, proliferates in odd directions, rarely bursts into bloom. It draws sustenance both from tangible
earthly sources and, seemingly, from thin air.

Discovery is pluralistic. It springs from a dynamic interplay between
one's own life style and that of other persons, between intuition and
reason, between the conventional scientific method and chance in all its
forms. The more diversity there is among these elements the more
unique is the resulting creative product. Conceptually, there is an almost infinite distance between a dog, a bell, a starch granule, and a
Lafora body. These four random elements, seemingly incongruous,
could be drawn together and fused only when the personal life style of
one individual interacted with chance. Some kinds of chance happen,
others are stirred up, discerned, or instigated. A new word, altamirage,
has the essence of the personalized generation of good fortune, and the
form of chance it leads to is called Chance IV.

A moment of creative inspiration is rare. It has both a long incubation
period and, if it is to prove fruitful, a lengthy subsequent development.
We find that the creative experience in science begins with an unconventional person, of abilities both diverse and contrasting, who is well-
grounded and receptive in his professional field. He not only prefers but
needs novelty, for he is bored if not disenchanted by a physiological
status quo. He has grown up to be a questioning, "adverbial man"
whose curiosity is piqued to solve problems for more reasons than he is

aware of. His search incorporates some elements of the primitive chase, brings all his senses to a peak, and sweeps him up in a tangle of stimulating ideas. Soon, however, his progress is blocked, and he may appear to have abandoned a fruitless struggle. But preconsciously, his mind probes and scans for clues throughout all his sources of information and experience, rapidly discerning those that will fit, neatly discarding the others. He keeps on going.

Often, through an accident that has a distinctive personal flavor, he will finally stumble on a fresh clue. At a conscious level, the clue might appear irrelevant, but it immediately opens up wide avenues of useful information. He suddenly finds himself in a state of enhanced awareness. His thoughts steer themselves at lightning speed to a new conscious insight. The new solution is vivid and intensely satisfying both intellectually and emotionally. His visual recollection of the moment is usually indelible. The "moment" may be a major flash of insight, or it may be an attenuated "spark," or a related series of faint glimmers spread out over months or years.

In broad perspective, we see in the way the two sides of his brain create one solution an analogy with the love-hate, tug-of-war going on between romanticism and rationalism since the dawn of man. The struggle is only resolved when the two sides join forces in their common cause and go off reunited hand in hand.

For, with a fresh insight, the investigator's work has just begun. He fashions his inspired ideas into a testable hypothesis, then laboriously creates a series of increasingly rigorous experiments to prove or disprove it. Persisting in these experiments through trial and error, he ultimately meanders into an entirely new set of problems. He leans forward once more, follows the Kettering Principle of staying in motion, and his chase, his search, his quest begins anew.

36.
In Closing

Medical research is an abstraction—the realities are not the laboratories and the hospitals but the men who search and search again for causes.

Alan Gregg

A neurologist looking critically at what has been written here (or indeed, elsewhere in the literature) is acutely, painfully conscious of one thing: we still know next to nothing about the basic neurophysiological and neurochemical mechanisms underlying human creativity. We are still groping to reach a valid understanding of movement and perception, let alone of what constitutes man's mind in action. Association areas of the cerebral cortex *must* be involved in complex interactions with powerful neuronal networks deeper in the brain. But this isn't saying much. Moreover, it is still hypothesis; more data are needed. We leave to neurophysiologists and neurochemists in the future the attempt to analyze all the elements involved in the creative process. Imaginative beginnings have been made,[1] but whenever we start to localize functions, we must remind ourselves that the cortex of man contains perhaps 13 billion nerve cells—each with multiple connections. Hardly a job to be finished in this century.

The biological psychiatrist and psychologist can also make important contributions as part of the team investigating creativity. If they wish to reach a more profound understanding of the scientific researcher, they must literally live with him. They will need to study him *in situ,* in action, in the total context of all the other elements and interactions described herein, yet remain discreetly in the background, all-seeing but unobtrusive. No easy task.

If you have been both interested enough in creativity and persistent enough to have read this far, I can surely start by wishing you luck (Chance I) in your own meanderings! But more than that, I hope you have seen three other more personal ways you can influence chance yourself, and how these interactions can in turn enhance the creative opportunities all around you. It is well to emphasize this point of view as we near the end of the twentieth century, becoming more anonymous and facing an uncertain future. For our ability as humans to adapt and to survive as a species depends on our creating new solutions with few attendant problems. At such a crucial time in our evolution it needs to be reaffirmed that man is intrinsically creative. It may help to recall that at Altamira our primitive ancestors held colors in their hands and not just clubs, as far back as 15,000 years ago.

Our future is still malleable, still very much in our own hands. Nothing is predetermined. Chance can be on our side if we but stir it up with our energies, stay receptive to the glint of opportunity on even a single hair above the underbrush, and continually provoke it by individuality in our attitudes and approach to life.

Suggested Further Reading

If you are interested in scientific investigation, you can find useful points of view in the writings of Cannon, Beveridge, Selye, Koestler, Noltingk, Ingle, Watson, and Krebs and Shelley.[1] Bartlett clarifies the characteristics of experimental thinking, and Szent-Györgyi adds some warm reminiscences of his own research career.[2]

The last two decades have produced an enormous bibliography on creativity. A bibliography on *scientific* creativity is included on pages 391–407 in the book edited by Taylor and Barron.[3] Roe summarizes the results of psychological approaches to scientific creativity in a chapter with eighty-one references.[4] Guilford, Stein, and Wallach review the psychological literature and point out areas of needed research.[5] Coler's publication contains a list of thirty-four references.[6]

Claude Bernard's early descriptions of chance and of his own experimental approach are also available in English.[7] Cannon, Taton, and Beveridge also consider the respective roles of reason and chance in various classical scientific discoveries.[8]

Appendix A

CONDENSED PLOT OF THE THREE PRINCES OF SERENDIP[1]

Main Characters:

King Giaffer of Serendip (Ceylon)

His sons, the three princes of Serendip

A camel driver

Emperor Beramo of Persia

Diliramma, a beautiful musician whom Beramo loves

The virgin queen of India

King Giaffer of Serendip had three sons. He loved his sons so dearly that he wanted them to have the best possible education, not only in the ways of power but in the many other virtues which princes in particular are apt to need. And so he employed skilled tutors to train them in each of many special fields.

One day, to test their progress, the king deliberately misled each of his sons, telling them that he planned to retire to a monastery. The first prince said that he did not wish the throne as long as his father was alive, and the second and third sons added that it would not be right for them to inherit the throne as long as their older brother was alive. From their prudent answers the king knew that they had reached the peak of their book knowledge, and he was wise enough to know that the rest of their education could come only from the experience of traveling in other lands. Feigning anger at their unwillingness to take over the kingdom, he banished them, knowing that this was the only way he could send them out on their own.

In the course of their wanderings, they finally entered the distant Persian kingdom of the Emperor Beramo. Outside his capital they met a camel driver who had lost his camel. He wondered if they had seen it,

[1] Condensed from *Serendipity and the Three Princes,* ed. Theodore G. Reimer (Norman, Okla.: University of Oklahoma Press, 1965).

and purely as a joke the princes supplied the camel driver with all sorts of semicontrived details. "Was your camel blind in one eye?" "Yes," said the camel driver. And the second prince said, "Did your camel have a tooth missing?" "Yes," said the owner. The third asked if the camel were lame. "Yes," said the driver. Misled when he heard these details, the driver retraced the Princes' steps along the trail, but needless to say, did not find his camel. When he encountered them again, he accused them of deception, but the first prince said, "Your camel carried a load of butter on one side and of honey on the other." The second said that the camel also carried a woman, and the third prince added that she was pregnant. The camel driver, convinced that anyone this well informed must have stolen his camel, had the princes jailed as camel thieves.

When Emperor Beramo heard about the crime, he sentenced the princes to death. In their innocence they then confessed they had played a joke on the camel driver, and that their imaginations must have gotten the better of them because some of their descriptions happened to coincide with the truth. Later, when the real camel was found, the emperor released the princes. He then inquired how they could have guessed so many details. The brothers, in turn, confessed the following camel story:* "I thought he must have been blind in the right eye, because only the grass along the left side of the trail was eaten even though it was not as thick as that over on the right side." "I guessed that the camel lacked a tooth because the way the grass cuds were chewed indicated that a tooth was missing." "I guessed that the camel was lame because only three footprints were clearly indicated, whereas the fourth print was dragged."

They continued, "I guessed that the camel had a load of butter on one side because there were many ants on one side of the trail, and I thought he carried honey on the other side because many flies gathered along the other side of the trail." "I guessed that the camel must have carried a woman because I noted a footprint and found some female urine near where the camel had knelt." And the third prince concluded, "I guessed that the woman was pregnant because the hand prints nearby showed that she had helped herself up with her hands after urinating."

* A somewhat shaggy camel story, to be sure.

The emperor, pleased by the intelligence of the princes, asked them to remain as guests in his palace. There, one day, he overheard them as they were dining. The first prince said, "I think this wine came from a grape vine with its roots down in a cemetery." The second added, "I believe the lamb we are eating was suckled not by a sheep but by a female dog." And the third prince said, "I think the emperor is responsible for the death of one of his Counselors' sons and that for this reason the Counselor plans to kill the emperor. All three conclusions were shrewdly correct, and the emperor asked the princes how they had guessed.

The first prince said that the wine he tasted caused him to feel depressed rather than happy, and he realized that only wine from a cemetery could have given rise to this feeling. The second prince said that the meat was so salty and full of foam that he knew the lamb could only have been fed by a bitch. And the third mentioned that he happened to notice the Counselor's face one day when the emperor was talking about punishing criminals. He noted that his face changed color, that he became thirsty, and from this he concluded that the Counselor had suffered a great loss such as the death of his son in punishment for a crime.

The emperor then asked the third prince to suggest a way he might escape from the revenge of his Counselor whose son he had indeed put to death. The prince then suggested that the emperor woo the Counselor's concubine and extract from her details about the forthcoming plot. At the next banquet, the emperor, forewarned by the concubine that the Counselor planned to *poison* him, cleverly extracted a full confession from him, and banished him from the kingdom.

Now thoroughly impressed with the princes' wisdom, Beramo enlisted their help in solving a very difficult problem facing his kingdom. It seemed that the ancient philosophers of his realm in former years had possessed a magic mirror called the "Mirror of Justice." Whenever there was a trial, the contending parties had to look into the mirror. The faces of the innocent would be unaffected, but the faces of those in the wrong would turn black. Because of this, prosperity reigned in the old days. But then Beramo's father became involved in a dispute with his brother over the succession to the throne, and his brother, for revenge, ran off with the magic mirror to the land of a virgin queen in India.

Now it happened that the land of the virgin queen was beset by a calamity: every sunrise a huge open hand would rise above the surface of the sea and remain there until sunset. Then, as night fell, the hand would sweep in, clutch an innocent victim and move back out to sea. Although the magic mirror was placed on the shore to offset the hand, its power was weakened outside of its original kingdom, and the only advantage now was that the hand grasped a horse or steer instead of a man.

Emperor Beramo begged the three princes to liberate the Indian kingdom from the fateful hand and return the mirror to his own kingdom. He promised them a large treasure in reward. Shortly after they departed for India, Beramo fell in love with a beautiful slave girl, Diliramma, an exceptionally talented musician. But on a deer hunt, after Diliramma offended his manly pride, he had her taken out to the forest and left to be devoured by the wild animals. Diliramma, however, was fortunately rescued by an elderly merchant who took her back to his own country and adopted her as his daughter. Beramo's great love soon overcame his wounded pride, but though he tried to find Diliramma, his search was to no avail. Assuming that she was dead, he fell into a deep depression.

The three princes, meanwhile, had traveled on to India and there met the virgin queen. Confronted by the giant hand at sunrise, the first prince raised his own hand and stuck up two fingers, his index and third, to indicate the victory sign. This bold gesture quickly felled the hand and banished it into the depths of the sea. The queen, amazed, asked for his secret. He had discerned, he said, that the hand was only a symbol of the fact that five men united for a single purpose could conquer the world. Believing, as he did, that only two men were needed for such a task, he had thus put the symbol to shame.

By then, the virgin queen had guessed from their noble bearing that the three brothers were princes from a distant kingdom. To prevent the return of the evil hand, she wished to marry one of them and keep him on to rule her own land. But, which prince to marry? Luckily, the queen's father, before he died, had given her two tests for her suitors. One requirement was to eat an entire storehouse of salt. The second prince passed this test to her satisfaction when he consumed a few token grains of the salt, and then observed that anyone who would eat this much salt could realize the full extent of the obligation. For the next test, she invited the third prince to her palace to meet with her and her Counselor. There, she removed five eggs from a box and asked the prince to divide them into three equal parts without breaking them. The prince rose to the occasion. He placed three eggs in front of the queen, gave one to the Counselor and kept one for himself.

"The eggs are now divided into three equal parts, Madam, and none has been cracked." But the queen did not understand his solution and asked him to explain.

"The three portions are perfectly equal because, you see, both your Counselor and I already have two eggs each in the crotch of our pants and you have none. Now, we each have three, and from this you will see that my way of dividing them was correct."

The queen blushed, but was nonetheless pleased by the answer.*

Impressed by the intelligence, wisdom, and prudence of all three princes, the virgin queen pledged her hand to the second prince who had, with subtlety and taste, solved the problem of the salt. The royal wedding was deferred, however, until the prince could return the magic mirror to Emperor Beramo in Persia.

When the princes returned to Beramo's kingdom, they found him so despondent over his loss of Diliramma that he was on the verge of death. The eldest prince then prescribed the following remedy. "You should build seven beautiful palaces, each of a different color, and stay for a week in each of them."[3] And his brother added, "You should have seven virgin princesses brought forth from the seven parts of the world and entertain one a week in each palace."[4] And the third prince concluded, "You should then invite the best storyteller from each of your seven main cities to tell you their most beautiful stories."

Beramo was entranced by these suggestions. The seven palaces were constructed forthwith and a beautiful virgin and a storyteller were lodged for a week in each palace in succession. The individual garments and draperies in each palace had the same color motif, with the key as follows: silver, red, various bright colors (unspecified), yellow, green, dark brown, and gold.

We naturally hesitate to abbreviate any of the hours at Beramo's disposal, but for the purposes of this story it will suffice to skip the novellas

---

* The tale works well in any language, but the queen was perhaps especially pleased because a subtle pun would have been involved in the original Persian. The language contains two words, Khāya and baiza, that mean both egg and testicle.[2]

of the first six storytellers because they do not involve the princes. But the seventh tale was about a beautiful maiden who played the lute with great skill and who one day had been found and adopted by an old merchant. This fair maiden could never play without sighing, because long ago she had been loved by a noble lord, who, however, banished her to the forest after she offended him. Beramo, listening to this tale, instantly realized that this was the true story of his love for Diliramma. Knowing now that she was still alive, he dispatched messengers to bring her back. Reunited with his long-lost love, he completely recovered his health.

Beramo then sent for the three princes of Serendip, asking them how it was that, despite all the physicians he had seen, they alone were discerning enough to advise him so wisely.

The first prince answered, "I believed your major problem was lack of sleep, and so I prescribed a change of dwelling every week knowing that the contrast would help you recover your ability to sleep." The second prince said, "I thought that your losing Diliramma was the major problem, and I believed that if you could divert yourself with other maidens, you would gradually forget her. For this reason I prescribed a different beautiful maiden in each of your seven palaces."

The third prince concluded, "I could not believe that Diliramma had been killed by animals because no trace of her was ever found in the forest. I believed that once it became widely known you would reward them with rich gifts, one of the seven storytellers might bring news about Diliramma."

Beramo was again most impressed by the intelligence of the three princes and sent them back to Serendip bearing precious gifts. There, King Giaffer greeted his long-departed sons with much joy and saw how they had truly reached perfection in absorbing so wisely the different manners and customs of the various lands. Content with this knowledge, he blessed them all and then died.

The eldest prince became the successor to the kingdom of Serendip and went on to rule his country well. The second prince returned to marry the virgin queen of India and became the ruler of that kingdom. The youngest prince married Beramo's daughter, and on his death succeeded to the throne of Persia. And so ends the story.

Appendix B

EXAMPLES OF CHANCE III AND IV IN BIOLOGY AND MEDICINE [1]

A good watercolor is a happy accident—if you qualify the statement by
saying that the greater the artist, the oftener the accident happens.
                                                          Charles Hawthorne

CHANCE III   (The prepared mind)

The principle of the ophthalmoscope, 1851

Hermann von Helmholtz was preparing a demonstration of an optical
system for his students one day when a sudden realization struck him.
He could modify the system to *visualize* the retina and not just to illu-
minate it.

Muscular contraction could be stimulated by an electric current, 1778

Luigi Galvani observed that frogs legs, suspended on an iron railing,
contracted when an electric current was generated nearby. Electricity
had been conducted to the muscle. Volta later went on to clarify the
basis for the phenomenon.

Vaccination against smallpox, 1798

A dairymaid told Edward Jenner that she couldn't get smallpox because she previously had contracted cowpox. Jenner realized that cowpox might deliberately be used to prevent smallpox.

Chemical synthesis of urea, 1828

Friedrich Wohler was trying to create ammonium cyanate by combining cyanic acid and ammonia. The chemical product of this reaction
turned out to be a four-sided prismatic crystal. He could recognize that
he had synthesized urea because he remembered what urea crystals
looked like—earlier, as a medical student, he had separated urea crystals from urine.

The principle of immunization with weakened organisms, 1879

Louis Pasteur was studying chicken cholera when his work was interrupted for several weeks. During the delay, the infectious organisms in one of his cultures weakened. When injected, these organisms no longer caused the disease. However, this same group of fowls survived when he later reinoculated them with a new batch of virulent organisms. Pasteur made a crucial distinction when he recognized that the first inoculation was not a "bad experiment" but that the weakened organisms had exerted a protective effect.

CHANCE IV   *(The individualized action)*

Principles of inheritance, 1866

Something of a failure in his church, the farmer-monk, Gregor Mendel, turned to his favorite hobby of raising, then hybridizing peas, beans, and bees. When he extended his hobby into his experiments, he could see that colors and shapes change through many generations in accordance with certain basic principles. These form the scientific basis of the laws of inheritance.

Evolution by natural selection, 1859

As a lonely child, Charles Darwin was a passionate collector of all flora and fauna. At age twenty-three, prompted by his uncle, he finally turned his hobby into a job (without pay) as a naturalist aboard the *H.M.S. Beagle.* On the Galapagos Islands, he observed how rich was the variety within a single species, and in Brazil he noted how only those insects protected by camouflage could manage to survive. The fittest survived; the others perished. Growing out of his hobby came Darwin's momentous theory: evolution occurred as natural selection acted on the range of normal variation.

Glossary

The nonspecialist will find here a simplified description of some less familiar terms.

altamirage: the quality of prompting good luck as a result of personally distinctive actions.

centrifuge: an instrument, which, as it spins forces more dense particles down to the bottom of a test tube, separating them from the lighter particles that are layered above.

cerebroside: a fatty (lipid) molecule made up of three smaller molecules linked together: a fatty acid, a base (sphingosine), and a sugar such as galactose or glucose (figure 6).

cerebroside galactosidase: the enzyme that split galactose from cerebroside. This is the salient enzyme deficient in human and canine globoid leukodystrophy (GLD) (figure 6).

chance: something fortuitous and unforeseen but open to human influence.

chromatography: a technique for identifying chemical compounds. The method is based on the fact that each molecule in a given solution moves at a characteristic rate on a strip of filter paper (paper chromatography) or on a thin layer of silica (thin layer chromatography).

corpora amylacea: round structures that accumulate inside certain supportive cells in the human brain. These "amyloid bodies" increase with age and are made up of molecules of glucose linked together in long chains.

creative process: currently, the term is chiefly used in the behavioral and descriptive sense to convey imperfectly in words the series of mental events culminating in a novel idea or other new product. The basic internal neurophysiological and neurochemical events going on during creative activity are still unknown.

creativity: the long and complex series of interrelationships between an individual and his environment culminating in something *new.*

creativity in science: that creative ability associated with something new, significant, and reproducible in a scientific field.

cytoplasm: the portion of a cell that lies outside the nucleus.

deposition disorders: diseases in which certain molecules accumulate because of a metabolic error. Deposits of these molecules pile up in the tissues. For example, metachromatic leukodystrophy is a deposition disease in which sulfatides are deposited. Also known as "storage" diseases.

ecology: the study of all the interrelationships between an organism and its environment.

formalin: a chemical used to preserve tissues. It also hardens tissues so that thin sections can be cut for microscopic examination.

galactosidase: an enzyme that splits galactose (a sugar) from another molecule.

globoid bodies: rounded phagocytic cells with multiple nuclei that contain an excess of cerebroside; the hallmark of globoid (Krabbe) leukodystrophy (GLD) (figures 6, 7).

globoid leukodystrophy (GLD; Krabbe's Disease): an inherited disease that causes a fatal progressive paralysis, blindness, and loss of mental abilities. The illness usually begins in children around four months of age. Certain dog strains (West Highland and Cairn terriers) also can have the disease. GLD has two major microscopic features. One is a degeneration of the myelin sheaths in the central and peripheral nervous system. The other is large numbers of rounded cells with multiple nuclei, called globoid bodies. GLD is caused by a deficiency of the enzyme that splits galactose from cerebroside (cerebroside galactosidase) (figures 6, 7).

histochemical method: a technique in which thin sections of tissue are treated with special chemical reagents before the section is examined under the microscope. Because certain chemical groups have characteristic chemical reactions, it is thus possible to tell if they exist in the cell.

hyaluronic acid sulfate: a negatively charged mucopolysaccharide of high molecular weight. It is obtained by attaching sulfate groups onto a molecule called hyaluronic acid, itself a constituent of normal connective tissue.

hypertrophic neuritis: an inherited disorder involving multiple peripheral nerves. The nerves become larger and firmer than normal and their individual nerve fibers degenerate (figure 1). Arms and legs become progressively weak.

infrared spectrophotometry: a technique for identifying and measuring chemical compounds. It is based on the fact that certain chemical groups absorb invisible rays (beyond the red end of the spectrum) in a distinctive manner. The sulfate group, for example, absorbs at a wave length of 8.02 microns.

Lafora bodies: round structures inside nerve cell cytoplasm seen in Lafora's myoclonus epilepsy. They contain long chains of glucose molecules (glucose polymers) (figures 10, 11).

Lafora's myoclonus epilepsy: an inherited fatal disease that usually starts during the second decade of life. Clinically, it causes a progressive seizure disorder, mental deterioration, and poor coordination. Microscopically, it is characterized by the presence of Lafora bodies and by degeneration of nerve cells in the cerebrum and cerebellum (figure 10).

leukodystrophy: a disease in which the myelin sheath slowly degenerates. "Leuco" refers to the white color these sheaths normally have. Dystrophy refers to the gradual wasting away of the sheaths. Leukodystrophies are caused by a metabolic error of the cells that normally construct and maintain the myelin sheaths surrounding the nerve fiber (figures 2, 4, 7).

limbic lobe: the phylogenetically old cortex that surrounds the upper brain stem, literally forming a border around it.

lipid: a fatty molecule.

lipidosis: a disease in which lipids (fats) are deposited inside the cells of several organs of the body. Many of these diseases are now known to be caused by an inherited deficiency of the specific enzyme inside lysosomes that normally break down the lipid.

lysosomes: small digestive bodies inside cell cytoplasm. Collectively, they function as a kind of internal disposal system in the cell. Lysosomes serve this digestive function because they are rich in such digestive enzymes as sulfatase A, sulfatase B, and cerebroside galactosidase.

metachromasia: a staining reaction in which certain blue dye molecules change color when they contact other molecules that have an opposite charge. For example, the *blue* dye, toluidine blue, will stain sulfated lipids a *reddish-golden brown* color. This new color indicates that negatively charged sulfated lipids are present.

metachromatic leukodystrophy (MLD; metachromatic leukoencephalopathy): an inherited disease that causes a fatal progressive paralysis, blindness, and loss of mental abilities. It begins anywhere from eighteen months of age up into late adult life. It has two major microscopic features. One is a degeneration of the myelin sheaths (which normally "insulate" nerve fibers in the central and peripheral nervous system). The other is an accumulation of metachromatically staining lipids both in nervous tissues and in the kidney. MLD is caused by deficient activity of the enzyme, sulfatase A (cerebroside sulfatase). This, in turn, causes an accumulation of sulfated lipids (called sulfatides or cerebroside sulfates). The abnormally high sulfatide levels are associated with a wasting away of the white myelin sheath (figures 2, 4).

mucopolysaccharide: a molecule of high molecular weight typically found in connective and other tissues. It is made up of many sugars with amino groups and other smaller acid molecules. Frequently sulfate groups are attached.

molecule: a chemical compound made up of atoms linked together in a specific way. Diagrams of the structure of various molecules are given in figures 3, 6, and 11.

multiple sclerosis: a disease of still unknown cause that attacks the myelin sheath in the central nervous system. The disease chiefly affects adults and its multiple patchy lesions of white matter form a sharp contrast with the more diffuse involvement in the leukodystrophies.

multiple sulfatase deficiency: a rare form of metachromatic leukodystrophy in which the enzymes sulfatase A, sulfatase B, and sulfatase C all show deficient activity. The condition resembles MLD. Sulfatides are increased. In addition, there is an increase of sulfated mucopolysaccharides (due to decreased sulfatase B) and of various sulfated steroids (due to decreased sulfatase C).

myelin sheath: the coating around the nerve fiber (axon) that serves as a kind of insulation. The sheath is made up of lipids, including cerebrosides and sulfatides. If the fatty sheath breaks down due to disease the nerve fiber stops conducting impulses.

negatively charged molecule: a molecule with a net negative charge conferred by its content of ionized sulfate groups, phosphate groups, or carboxylic acid groups.

neurologist: a physician specializing in diseases of the nervous system and muscles.

neuropathologist: one who studies the mechanisms of diseases of the nervous system, chiefly by the techniques of light and electron microscopy.

neuropathology: the study of the mechanisms of diseases of the nervous system.

phagocytic cells: cells that engulf or digest outside material.

polyglucosan: a glucose polymer (figure 11). Examples include: the materials deposited in Lafora bodies and corpora amylacea; starch; and glycogen.

polyneuropathy: a disease in which the peripheral nerves stop conducting nerve impulses. This causes weakness of the legs and arms and frequently numbness of the hands and feet, as well.

preconscious: a term used by Kubie to describe the subliminal mental processes of scanning and sorting that serve creative ends. Preconscious activities lie nearer consciousness than do unconscious activities. The term subconscious includes both.

recessive disease: an inherited disorder clinically expressed in a child both of whose parents contribute the abnormal gene. Although the mother and father appear clinically normal, one out of four of their children will develop the disease on an average.

resident physician: one who has completed internship and who receives specialized training on the junior staff of a teaching hospital. A residency training period in neurology is currently three years long.

serendipity: finding valuable things without actively seeking them as a result of accidents, general exploratory behavior, or sagacity.

sheath cells: cells responsible for the formation and maintenance of the myelin sheath. In the peripheral nerves these cells are termed Schwann cells (figure 1). In the central nervous system (brain and spinal cord) they are called oligodendroglia.

substrate: a reagent molecule acted on by an enzyme. For example, cerebroside sulfate is the substrate for the enzyme sulfatase A.

sulfatase: an enzyme that splits a sulfate group from a sulfated compound. Sulfatase A splits the sulfate group from cerebroside sulfate (sulfatide) as shown in figure 3.

sulfatide: a sulfated lipid (fat), specifically a sulfated cerebroside molecule (figure 3). Sulfatides are normally concentrated in the myelin sheath that surrounds the nerve fiber and reach abnormally high levels in metachromatic leukodystrophy (figure 2).

toluidine blue: a special blue dye that is charged positively. It is used to test for the presence of negatively charged molecules. When the two come together they form a complex. The complex has a new color which is not blue but rather shades of red to golden-brown. The phenomenon is termed metachromasia.

urine sediment: the heavier portion of urine that settles out after standing or centrifugation. It contains cells, casts, debris, and the granular bodies of MLD.

white matter: the inner portion of the nervous system that contains many myelin sheaths packed together. It appears white because the lipids in myelin are white.

Cast of Characters

Experimental thinking . . . is fundamentally co-operative, social, and cannot proceed far without the stimulus of outside contacts.

Frederick Bartlett

Each cherishes in his memory the remembrance of those who have fanned his flame.

Charles Nicolle

This was not my story alone. As in a good-sized Russian novel, there were many other people involved. There could have been many more. Everyone mentioned in the narrative is cited for a specific reason: each made some pivotal contribution that shaped the course of events at one or more points. Without the vital input of all these men and women the story might not have happened at all. It was no effort for me to summon up a flood of images about the facial expression and form of the person involved, of the exact spot in the hall or laboratory where an incident occurred, and of the texture of the moment itself. In fact, years ago I began to find these encounters so fascinating that I seem to have laid down the original mental traces of every episode in rich detail. Since then, my memory has been reinforced by automatically playing itself back every now and then. Warm memories linger in the mind not only because they were noteworthy earlier, but also because they are fanned repeatedly and replayed.

The vividness of these recollections made it relatively easy to write the first part of the book quite accurately. Some of the characters may have long ago forgotten their own role in this story, but I could not. Only rarely was it necessary to consult laboratory work books for dates, sequences, or other details.

This book was concerned not only with people but also with process. If I were to have attempted a full character delineation of each of the fifty-eight people, one rabbit, and one dog—all deserving characters in this story—there would have been no room left to consider the ecological processes that brought them together. This needed to be a smaller volume, and so I have given a thumbnail description of the essential contribution made by each person. The list of characters* given below should emphasize how complex is the web of human interactions involved in any creative endeavor.

James H. Austin: a curious, various persistent child, and neurologist to be.
James Austin, Jr.: liberal judge, active puzzle-solver, my paternal grandfather.
Henry Holtkamp: teacher, organ builder, grandfather on my mother's side.
Gus Weber: outdoor enthusiast and dog owner, my paternal great uncle. I never saw him, but I know Uncle Gus in my bones.
Sophia Holtkamp: model gardener and grandmother who stimulated my interest in Indian artifacts.
Frank ("Gibby") Gibson, M.D.: gracious uncle; inspiring model physician.
Raymond Adams, M.D.: outstanding teacher at Harvard Medical School; neurologist and Chief of Neuropathology at Boston City Hospital.
Paul Weber Austin: my father and model of the creative artist, pianist, and composer.
Derek Denny-Brown, M.D.: stimulating professor; my Chief of the Neurology service at the Boston City Hospital.
Joseph Foley, M.D.: genial Boston Irishman and attending neurologist, Boston City Hospital.
Naval Seaman Knox: a patient whose illness prompted the studies on hypertrophic neuritis.
H. Houston Merritt, M.D.: eminent Chief of the Neurology Department at The New York Neurological Institute.
Abner Wolf, M.D.: Chief of Neuropathology at Columbia-Presbyterian Medical Center.
Lord Russell Brain, M.D.: eminent English neurologist who wrote a key article on metachromatic leukodystrophy.
J. Godwin Greenfield, M.D.: noted neuropathologist and co-author of the above article.
The Clausen children: two young children afflicted with metachromatic leukodystrophy whose admission to the hospital in New York prompted my research on this disease.
Charles Poser, M.D.: a fellow neurological resident who directed my attention to the Clausen children.
Robert Katzman, M.D.: a fellow neurological resident who called my attention to an important series of articles about lipids.
Jordi Folch-pi, M.D.: pioneering lipid neurochemist at Harvard.
Judith Austin: supportive wife, mother of our three, and indescribably more.
Roy Swank, M.D., Ph.D.: generous head of Neurology at the University of Oregon Medical School and stimulating investigator.
Jack Fellman, Ph.D.: lively organic chemist and neurochemist at the University of Oregon Medical School.

* In order of appearance, and in the role they were in at the time the events occurred.

Warren Thompson: an older child afflicted with metachromatic leukodystrophy in Oregon.

Gerald Phillips, M.D.: medical school classmate and lipid biochemist who directed my attention to an important article about sulfated lipids.

Marjorie Lees, Ph.D.: lipid neurochemist who worked out an original method for isolating sulfated lipids (sulfatides) from the brain.

Lowell Lapham, M.D.: medical school classmate; neuropathologist, who gave me the first kidney tissue to study from metachromatic leukodystrophy.

Frank Witmer, Sc.D.: helpful chemist (and raconteur) whose interpretations of infrared spectroscopic data made possible the measurement of sulfated lipids in metachromatic leukodystrophy.

Sigfried Thannhauser, M.D.: pioneer in lipid storage diseases who provided the authentic reference standard of sulfated lipids.

Mrs. Erma Thompson: mother of the sick Thompson child whose consent to the autopsy of her son made it possible to define the chemical basis of metachromatic leukodystrophy.

Monte Greer, M.D.: head of Endocrinology at Oregon whose sensitive microbalance made it possible to measure small amounts of isolated sulfatides.

George Jervis, M.D.: pioneering investigator who first showed that an inherited neurological disease (phenylketonuria; PKU) was caused by a deficiency of the enzyme, phenylalanine hydroxylase.

Lahut Uzman, M.D.: neurological researcher whose article alerted me to the fact that white blood cells in a kindred neurological disease might contain abnormal deposits.

The McLean children: young brother and sister with a rare form of metachromatic leukodystrophy in which three sulfatases are deficient.

Margaret De Merritt: sparkling technician, later medical student and colleague, who helped originate new methods and kept things lively in the laboratory.

John Harris, M.D.: ophthalmologist at Oregon who told me about hyaluronic acid sulfate, a model sulfated molecule.

Darwin Lehfeldt: medical student whose laboratory work contributed to the experimental studies of sulfatides and cerebrosides.

Patient D.W.: child with globoid leukodystrophy whose illness drew my attention to the existence of this disease.

Saul Korey, M.D.: Professor and Chairman of Neurology at Albert Einstein Medical College whose prodding stimulated me to isolate globoid bodies.

Kunihiko Suzuki, M.D.: neurochemist and associate professor at the University of Pennsylvania who proved that the galactosidase which splits cerebroside was deficient in globoid leukodystrophy.

Roscoe Brady, M.D.: Chief, Section of Neurochemistry, at the National Institute of Health, Bethesda, who collaborated in the enzymic studies in globoid leukodystrophy.

George Dana, M.D., and Elizabeth Dana: close friends, who by stimulating an interest in World Federalism created the setting for a sabbatical in India.

Philip and Rhita Feingold: close friends and fellow World Federalists whose beliefs contributed to the decision to go to India.

Norman Cousins: President, World Association of World Federalists, whose personal magnetism, international orientation, and editorials in the *Saturday Review* have been a constant source of inspiration.

Bimal Bachhawat, Ph.D.: benevolent Indian biochemist whose collaboration made possible the discovery that an enzymic deficiency of sulfatase A was the cause of metachromatic leukodystrophy.

Peter Rabbit: He led me, repeatedly, on a merry chase.

Tom Austin: our dog, a Brittany spaniel, who prompted the sequence of events leading to the identification of glucose polymers in Lafora bodies.

Susumu Yokoi, M.D.: Associate Professor of Neuropsychiatry at Yokohama Medical School; collaborator in the isolation and characterization of Lafora bodies.

Richard Berry, M.D.: Professor of Neuropathology at Jefferson College of Medicine who contributed rare pathological material containing Lafora bodies.

Donald Armstrong, M.S.: friend, co-worker, and former graduate student, who discovered that soluble peroxidase activity is reduced in a model disease of aging (Batten-Spielmeyer-Vogt disease).

David Stumpf, M.D.: medical student working toward his Ph.D. in our laboratory at Colorado who helped characterize the abnormalities of sulfatase A in MLD and of sulfatase B in the Maroteaux-Lamy syndrome.

Edward Neuwelt, M.D.: medical student at the University of Colorado who, with David Stumpf, showed that the enzyme protein was present in MLD but was deficient in sulfatase A activity.

Norman Radin, Ph.D.: lipid neurochemist and Director of the Mental Health Research Institute at the University of Michigan who originated a system for measuring cerebroside galactosidase and discovered a way to increase its activity.

Drs. Christian de Duve, H.G. Hers, and F. Van Hoof: investigators at the University of Louvain in Belgium whose work helped establish the existence of lysosomes in cells and the lysosomal theory of disease.

Bertha Holtkamp Austin: my mother, a former laboratory technician, who stimulated my interest in people and in the biological sciences.

Horst Jatzkewitz, M.D.: biochemist at the Max-Planck Institute in Munich who also found increased sulfatides in MLD, and who showed with Ehrenpreisle Mehl, that sulfate is split from these lipids by the enzyme sulfatase A, acting as a cerebroside sulfatase.

The international nature of the contributors to research in MLD is shown in figure 12.

Permissions

I wish to express my appreciation to the following authors, their copyright owners, and their publishers for permission to reprint excerpts from their copyrighted works as indicated here and specified further in the notes:

George Allen & Unwin, Ltd., for two selections from *Thinking, An Experimental and Social Study*, by Frederick Bartlett; and for two adaptations from *Creative Malady*, by Dr. George Pickering.

Atheneum Publishers for one quotation and several adaptations from *The Dynamics of Creation*, by Anthony Storr.

J. B. Baillière, for four selections from *Introduction à l'Etude de la Médecine Expérimentale*, by Claude Bernard.

Bradford Cannon, M.D., for selections from *The Way of An Investigator*, by Walter Cannon, published by MacMillan Publishing Co., Inc. (Hafner subsidiary).

J. M. Dent & Sons, Ltd., for a quotation from *The Scottish Himalayan Expedition*, by W. H. Murray.

Dover Publications, Inc., for a quotation from *Hawthorne on Painting*, by Charles Hawthorne.

Harper & Row, Publishers, Inc., for quotations by Carl Rogers and by H. Anderson in *Creativity And Its Cultivation*, edited by H. Anderson; for quotations by Benjamin Disraeli and George Bernard Shaw found in *The New Book of Unusual Quotations*, by R. Flesch; and for a quotation by H. Gutman, from *Explorations In Creativity*, edited by R. Mooney, and T. Razik.

W. Heffer & Sons, Ltd., for quotations by Lewis Carroll, Francis Darwin, and Piotr Tchaikovsky, found in *An Anatomy of Inspiration*, by R. Harding.

King Features Syndicate for the quotation by Charles Kettering, appearing in the Reader's Digest, October 1961.

J. B. Lippincott Company for an excerpt from *Principles of Research In Biology and Medicine*, by Dwight Ingle.

Little, Brown, and Company, for short quotations by Louis Pasteur, Henry Sigerist, and Wilder Penfield, from *Familiar Medical Quotations*, by M. Strauss; for an adaptation of a story by Henry Forbes, cited in *The Difficult Art of Giving: The Epic of Alan Gregg*, by Wilder Penfield; for the adaptation of the chapter by James Austin in *Modern Neurology*, edited by Simeon Locke; and for the quotation from *As I Remember Him: The Biography of R.S.*, by Hans Zinsser.

Macmillan Publishing Co., for two selections from *The Wanderer of Liverpool*, by John Masefield, and for a quotation from *The Act of Creation*, by A. Koestler.

McGraw-Hill Book Company, for a selection from *Aequanimitas,* by Sir William Osler, and for a quotation from *Present Tense: An American Editor's Odyssey,* by Norman Cousins.

Methuen & Co., Ltd., for two quotations from *The Art of The Soluble,* by Peter Medawar.

The New Yorker Magazine for a quotation by Franklin P. Adams, originally appearing in *Diary of Our Own Samuel Pepys,* by Simon and Schuster.

New York University Press for two passages by H. Herbert Fox and H. Hughes from *Essays on Creativity in the Sciences,* edited by Myron A. Coler.

The *News* for their article on the rabbit, here entitled "Flashback; The Chase, 1942".

W. W. Norton & Company, Inc., for a quote by Joseph Conrad from *Heart of Darkness,* edited by R. Kimbrough, and for a quote from *The Courage to Create,* by Rollo May.

Pantheon Books for a quotation from *The Way of Zen,* by Alan Watts.

Random House, Inc., for an extract from *Chance and Necessity,* by Jacques Monod, translated by Austryn Wainhouse; for the words "future shock," from *Future Shock,* by Alvin Toffler; and for an excerpt by Albert Einstein from *Einstein: His Life and Times,* by Phillipp Frank.

The Reader's Digest, for the quotation by Bruce Barton from *The Dictionary of Quotations.*

The Regents Press of Kansas, for a quotation from *Neurotic Distortion of The Creative Process,* by Lawrence Kubie.

Simon & Schuster, Inc., for a quotation from *Pogo,* by Walt Kelly; for two selections from *Science and Sensibility,* by James Newman, one by James Newman, the other by Lord Rutherford; and for a quotation from *Science and Human Values,* by Jacob Bronowski.

Tavistock Publications for a quotation by Lancelot Whyte from *The Unconscious Before Freud.*

The University of Oklahoma Press for the condensation from *Serendipity and The Three Princes,* by Theodore Remer.

Teachers College Press for an extract and abridgement of pp. 21–22 from P. Witty, J. B. Conant, and R. Strang, *Creativity of Gifted and Talented Children.*

Van Nostrand Reinhold, for quotations and abridgements by F. Barron from *Creativity and Psychological Health.*

John Wiley & Sons, Inc., for two excerpts from *Scientific Creativity: Its Recognition and Development,* by Brewster Ghiselin; for a statement by R. Burman, R. Hanes, R. and C. Bartleson, *Color: A Guide for Basic Facts and Concepts;* for an extract and abridgment from M. Wallach in *Manual of Child Psychology,* edited by P. Mussen; for extracts and abridgments from M. Stein, C. Taylor and F. Barron, and for quotations from B. Ghiselin in *Scientific Creativity: Its Recognition and Development,* edited by C. Taylor and F. Barron.

Wilmarth Lewis for quotations of passages from letters by Horace Walpole in the *Yale Edition of Horace Walpole's Correspondence.*

Yale University Press for a quotation from *The Furtherance of Medical Research,* by Alan Gregg.

Notes

Preface

1. C. Jung, "Psychology and Literature," in *The Creative Process,* ed. B. Ghiselin (New York: Mentor, New American Library, 1952), p. 219.
2. J. Nurnberger, "In Memorium. Saul Korey, M.D., 1918–1963," *Journal of Neuropathology and Experimental Neurology* 24 (April 1965): 183–86. I. London, "Saul Roy Korey, 1918–1963," *Transactions of the American Neurological Association* 89 (1964): 278–80; L. Scheinberg, "Saul R. Korey, M.D., 1918–1963," *Neurology* 14 (January 1964): 158–60.

By Way of Introduction

1. A. Roe, "Psychological approaches to creativity in science," in *Essays on Creativity in the Sciences,* ed. M. Coler (New York: New York University Press, 1963), pp. 161–62.

1. Of Nerves and Neurologists; Boston, 1950

1. J. Austin, "Prologue," in *Modern Neurology,* ed. S. Locke (Boston: Little, Brown, 1969), pp. xix–xxi.

2. Enlarged Nerves; Oakland, 1951

1. J. Austin, "Observations on the Syndrome of Hypertrophic Neuritis (The Hypertrophic Interstitial Radiculo-Neuropathies)," *Medicine* 35 no. 3 (September 1956): 187–236.

3. Metachromasia; New York City, 1953

1. W. Brain and J. Greenfield, "Late infantile metachromatic leukoencephalopathy with primary degeneration of the interfascicular oligodendroglia," *Brain* 73 (1950): 291.

4. Microscopic Studies; New York City, 1953

1. J. Austin, "Metachromatic Form of Diffuse Cerebral Sclerosis. I. Diagnosis During Life by Urine Sediment Examination," *Neurology* 7 (1957): 415.
2. References to subsequent articles in the series on metachromatic leukodystrophy (leukoencephalopathy) from the author's laboratory are included in a recent review article: J. Austin, "Metachromatic Leukodystrophy (Sulfatide

Lipidosis), in *Lysosomes and Storage Diseases,* ed. H. Hers and F. Van Hoof (New York: Academic Press, 1973), pp. 411–37.

5. Sulfated Lipids; Portland, Oregon, 1955

1. M. Lees, "Simple Procedure for the Isolation of Brain Sulfatides," *Federation Proceedings* 15 (1956): 973.

6. Molecules and Meanderings, 1957

1. L. Uzman, "Chemical Nature of the Storage Substances in Gargoylism," *A.M.A. Archives of Pathology* 60 (1955): 308.

7. Controls and the Experimental Globoid Response, 1960

1. J. Austin and D. Lehfeldt, "Significance of Experimentally Produced Globoid-like Elements in Rat White Matter and Spleen," *Journal of Neuropathology and Experimental Neurology* 24 (1965): 265.
2. References to various articles by others, and to the author's series of articles on globoid leukodystrophy are included in a review chapter, J. Austin, "Globoid (Krabbe) Leukodystrophy," in *Pathology of the Nervous System,* ed. J. Minckler (New York: McGraw-Hill, 1968), 1: 843–58.
3. K. Suzuki and Y. Suzuki, "Globoid Cell Leukodystrophy (Krabbe's Disease): Deficiency of Galactocerebroside β-Galactosidase," *Proceedings of the National Academy of Science, U.S.A.* 66 (1970): 302–9.
4. J. Austin, K. Suzuki, D. Armstrong, R. Brady, B. Bachhawat, J. Schlenker and D. Stumpf, "Studies in Globoid (Krabbe) Leukodystrophy (GLD). V. Controlled Enzymic Studies in Ten Human Cases," *A.M.A. Archives of Neurology* 23 (1970): 502–12.
5. Y. Suzuki, J. Austin, D. Armstrong, K. Suzuki, J. Schlenker and T. Fletcher, "Studies in Globoid Leukodystrophy: Enzymatic and Lipid Findings in the Canine Form," *Experimental Neurology* 29 (1970): 65–75.

8. Enzymes and India, 1961, 1962–1963

1. J. Newman, *Science and Sensibility* (New York: Simon & Schuster, 1961), p. 464.

10. Tom and Lafora Bodies, 1965

1. F. White, *The Brittany In America,* 2d ed. (Chillicothe, Ill.: privately printed, 1965), p. 7.
2. M. Bischell, J. Austin and M. Kemeny, "Metachromatic Leukodystrophy (MLD). VII. Elevated Sulfated Acid Polysaccharide Levels in Urine and Postmortem Tissues," *A.M.A. Archives of Neurology* 15 (1966): 13–28.
3. S. Yokoi, J. Austin, F. Witmer and M. Sakai, "Studies in Myoclonus Epilepsy (Lafora Body Form). I. Isolation and Preliminary Characterization of

Lafora Bodies in Two Cases," *A.M.A. Archives of Neurology* 19 (1968): 15–33; M. Sakai, J. Austin, F. Witmer and L. Trueb, "Studies in Myoclonus Epilepsy (Lafora Body Form). II. Polyglucosans in the Systemic Deposits of Myoclonus Epilepsy and in Corpora Amylacea," *Neurology* 20 (1970): 160–76; T. Nikaido, J. Austin and H. Stukenbrok, "Studies of Myoclonus Epilepsy. III. The Effects of Amylolytic Enzymes on the Ultrastructure of Lafora Bodies," *Journal of Histochemistry and Cytochemistry* 19 (1971): 382–85.

4. M. Sakai, J. Austin, F. Witmer and L. Trueb, "Studies of Corpora Amylacea. I. Isolation and Preliminary Characterization by Chemical and His- tochemical Techniques, *A.M.A. Archives of Neurology.* 21 (1969): 526–44; J. Austin, T. Nikaido and H. Stukenbrok, "Studies of Corpora Amylacea. II. Histochemical and Electron Microscopic Observations," *Proceedings of the 6th International Congress of Neuropathology* (1970): 1029–30.

5. T. Nikaido, J. Austin, R. Rinehart, L. Trueb, J. Hutchinson, H. Stukenbrok and B. Miles, "Studies in Ageing of the Brain. I. Isolation and Preliminary Characterization of Alzheimer Plaques and Cores, *A.M.A. Archives of Neu- rology* 25 (1971): 198–211; T. Nikaido, J. Austin, L. Trueb and R. Rinehart, "Studies in Ageing of the Brain. II. Microchemical Analyses of the Nervous System in Alzheimer Patients," *A.M.A. Archives of Neurology* 27 (1972): 549.

6. M. Sakai, J. Austin, T. Nikaido and R. Rinehart, "Lewy Bodies." In prepara- tion.

7. D. Armstrong, S. Dimmitt and D. Van Wormer, "Studies in Batten Disease. I. Peroxidase Deficiency in Granulocytes." *A.M.A. Archives of Neurology* 30 (1974): 144–52.

11. *Fingerprints on the Window; Filling in the Hole*

1. *Profiles of US Medical School Faculty, 1971,* US Department of Health, Ed- ucation, and Welfare, report #20, Resources for Biomedical Research (Dec. 1974), p. 36.

2. *Doctoral Scientists and Engineers in the United States.* 1975 Profile, Na- tional Academy of Sciences, Washington, D.C.

3. R. Scheffler, *The Economic Rate of Return to post-M.D. Training in the Biosciences,* NIH Publication Contract Number NO 1-OD-4-2512 (Feb. 28, 1975), p. 41.

4. W. Penfield, *The Difficult Art of Giving: The Epic of Alan Gregg* (Boston: Little, Brown, 1967), p. 83.

12. *Overview: What Next? So What?*

1. J. Austin, "Recurrent Polyneuropathies and Their Corticosteroid Treat- ment," *Brain* 81, no. 2 (1958): 157–192.

2. H. Nadler and A. Gerbie, "Role of Amniocentesis in the Intrauterine Detec- tion of Genetic Disorders," *New England Journal of Medicine* 282 (1970): 596–99.

3. N. Bass, E. Witmer and F. Dreifuss, "A Pedigree Study of Metachromatic Leukodystrophy: Biochemical Identification of the Carrier State," *Neurology* 20 (1970): 52–62; D. Stumpf and J. Austin, "Metachromatic Leukodystrophy (MLD). IX. Qualitative and Quantative Differences in Urinary Arylsulfatase A in Different Forms of MLD," *A.M.A. Archives of Neurology* 24 (1971): 117–24.

4. D. Stumpf, E. Neuwelt, J. Austin and P. Kohler, "Metachromatic Leukodystrophy (MLD). X. Immunological Studies of the Abnormal Sulfatase A., *A.M.A. Archives of Neurology* 25 (1971): 427–31.

5. E. Neuwelt, D. Stumpf, J. Austin and P. Kohler, "A Monospecific Antibody to Human Sulfatase A; Preparation, Characterization and Significance," *Biochimica et Biophysica Acta* 236 (1971): 333–46.

6. N. Radin and R. Arora, "The Effects of Synthetic Ceramide Analogs on Cerebrosidase Activity," *Transactions of the American Society of Neurochemistry* 2 (1971): 100.

7. N. Radin, R. Arora, A. Brenkert and J. Austin, "A Possible Therapeutic Approach to Krabbe's Globoid Leukodystrophy and the Status of Cerebroside Synthesis in the Disorder," *Research Communications in Chemical Pathology and Pharmacology,* 3 (1972): 637–44.

8. J. Austin, D. Armstrong, K. Suzuki, J. Schlenker and T. Fletcher, "Studies in Globoid Leukodystrophy: Enzymatic and Lipid Findings in the Canine Form," *Experimental Neurology* 29 (1970): 65–75.

9. D. Stumpf and J. Austin, "Sulfatase B Deficiency in the Maroteaux-Lamy Syndrome (Mucopolysaccharidosis VI)," *Transactions of The American Neurological Association* 97 (1972):29–32.

10. A. Allison, "Lysosomes and Disease," *Scientific American* (Nov. 1960): 62–72.

11. J. Monod, *Chance and Necessity* (London: Collins, 1972), p. 110.

13. *Chance and The Creative Adventure*

1. M. Austin, "Dream Recall and the Bias of Intellectual Ability," *Nature* 231 (1971): 59.

2. L. Goodrich, *Albert P. Ryder* (New York: Braziller, 1959), p. 22.

14. *On The Trail of Serendipity*

1. Literary scholars have differed in the past in their interpretations of the origins of the three princes, and will presumably do so in the future. Cammann's view is summarized here because he has presented an authoritative recent review of the subject documented with 113 references and notes (S. Cammann, "Christopher the Armenian and the Three Princes of Serendip," *Comparative Literature Studies* 4 (1967): 229–58).

According to Cammann, the emperor Beramo (Behramo in the Peregrinaggio) of the three princes may well have been Bahrām Gūr (the Persian King Varkan V) who ruled pre-Islamic Iran from 420–440. A lengthy account of his life, entitled *Shaname,* was written by the poet, Firdausī, in

1010. Over a century later, between 1171 and 1200, Nizāmī collected five book-length poems into one volume, entitled *Khamse*. One of these poems celebrated the life of Bahrām Gūr, and was called "Haft Paikar" ("Seven Beauties").

The next version of the tales came from Amir Khusrau of Delhi (1253–1325), the greatest Persian poet India ever produced. Khusrau was the son of a Turkish father and a Muslim Indian mother, and was court poet to the kings and princes of his day. His own version of *Khamse* and of the "Haft Paikar" contained a poem entitled "Hasht Bihisht ("Eight Paradises"). It introduced some new tales of Indian origin reflecting his own background in Delhi. Khusrau also included in his version the legendary story of the three brothers and the camel driver. It is plausible to think that Christopher the Armenian's later adaptation, the Peregrinaggio, originated in Khusrau's tale. A native of Tabriz (in what is now Iran) before he emigrated to Venice, Christopher would have been able to translate Khusrau easily because Persian would have been his primary language.

2. T. Remer, ed., *Serendipity and The Three Princes; From The "Peregrinaggio" of 1557* (Norman, Okla.: University of Oklahoma Press, 1965).
3. W. Lewis, ed., *The Yale Edition of Horace Walpole's Correspondence* 26 (1971): 34–35, hereinafter cited as *The Yale Edition*.
4. Thomas Gray would later be known for his poem, "Elegy Written In A Country Churchyard."
5. The correspondence can be found in *The Yale Edition*.
6. Mann to Walpole, November 9, 1753, *The Yale Edition* 20 (1960): 399.
7. Walpole to Mann, January 28, 1754, *The Yale Edition* 20 (1960): 407–8. This Horace Mann is not to be confused with the American educator of the next century (1796–1859).
8. Walpole to Mann, January 28, 1754, *The Yale Edition* 20 (1960): 407–8.
9. Walpole to Hannah Moore, September 10, 1789, *The Yale Edition,* 31 (1961), 335.

15. *The Kettering, Pasteur, and Disraeli Principles*

1. My thanks to a correspondent who preferred to remain anonymous, and to Philip Archer, Ph.D. for this number.
2. A. Maurois, *The Life of Sir Alexander Fleming* (New York: Dutton, 1959), p. 109. The sequences by which nasal drippings entered into this experiment are not entirely clear.
3. R. Taton, *Reason and Chance in Scientific Discovery* (New York: Philosophical Library, 1957), p. 113.
4. In *Biologie de l'Invention* (Paris: Alcan, 1932), p. 30, Charles Nicolle says in effect that, "Chance serves only those who know how to win her." ("Le hasard ne sert que ceux qui savent le capter.") To those who would translate *capter* as "court," Nicolle might seem to be implying a courting action (of an underhanded kind). But if the statement is viewed in the context of the whole paragraph, it seems evident that Nicolle is still talking about receptivity and discernment, for in the following sentence, he concludes,

"To grasp the significance of a fact, to unravel it, is only within the capacity of well-endowed minds."

16. Personal Encounters With Chance I–IV

1. Interestingly, most everyone likes reds and blues. The most preferred colors in first order of preference are: blue, red, green, violet, orange, yellow. See R. Burnam, R. Hanes and C. Bartleson, *Color: A Guide to Basic Facts and Concepts* (New York: John Wiley and Sons, 1963), p. 209; there is more to color than meets the eye. Farther back, in the brain itself, color tends to evoke an image of form. Red is perceived as being moderately "large," as being spread out horizontally, and as possessing a well-defined boundary line. Blue is the "largest" and it, too, takes on a strong horizontal extension with well-defined edges. Blue, moreover, has the special quality of evoking shapes that are "curvey" rather than straight. See M. Lindauer, "Form Imagery to Colors," *Perceptual and Motor Skills* 36 (1973): 165–66.
2. It is interesting to note that the red-purple follows in sequence a field of its complementary opposite color: green-yellow. The correct response to such epiphenomena of meditation (termed *makyo* in Japanese) is simply to pay no attention to them. They go away with time.

17. The Spanish Connection

1. The story of the cave is a composite drawn both from a personal visit to Altamira, and from accounts in the following books: H. Wendt, *In Search of Adam* (Boston: Houghton Mifflin, 1956); G. Bibby, *The Testimony of The Spade* (New York: Alfred Knopf, 1956); D. and J. Samachson, *The First Artists* (Garden City, N.Y.: Doubleday, 1970); and P. MacKendrick, *The Iberian Stones Speak* (New York: Funk and Wagnalls, 1969).

20. Never On Monday; The Unhappy Accidents

1. The author would welcome any information about the original Murphy and his laws so that complete acknowledgment can be made for this section.
2. *The Reader's Digest Dictionary of Quotations* (The Reader's Digest Association, Inc., 1966), p. 137.
3. Quote from Pogo, by Walt Kelly.

21. Some Dimensions of Creativity

1. H. Hughes, "Individual and Group Creativity in Science," in *Essays on Creativity in the Sciences,* ed. M. Coler, (New York: New York University Press, 1963), pp. 93–101.
2. H. Fox, "A Critique on Creativity in Science," in *Essays on Creativity in the Sciences,* ed. M. Coler (New York: New York University Press, 1963), pp. 123–52.
3. The experiment cited is not novel. The idea that some new surge of "elec-

trical activity" occurs during a moment of inspired thought is an old one. One has only to recall that the early cartoonists (perhaps reminded of Thomas Edison's invention) drew a light blub glowing above the head of a character whenever he was seized by a new idea.

22. The Creative Personality; Pro

1. P. Witty, J. Conant and R. Strang, *Creativity of Gifted and Talented Children* (New York: Bureau of Publications, Teachers College, Columbia University, 1959), pp. 21–22.
2. M. Wallach, "Creativity," in *Manual of Child Psychology,* ed. P. Mussen (New York: John Wiley and Sons, 1969), 1: 1211–72.
3. Ibid.
4. *The Creative Process in Science and Medicine,* H. Krebs and J. Shelley, eds. (New York: American Elsevier, 1975), p. 19.
5. M. Wallach and N. Kogan, "A New Look at the Creativity-Intelligence Distinction," *Journal of Personality* 33 (1965): 348–69.
6. B. Eiduson, *Scientists: Their Psychological World* (New York: Basic Books, 1962).
7. A. Roe, "Psychological Approaches to Creativity in Science," in *Essays on Creativity in the Sciences,* ed. M. Coler (New York: New York University Press, 1963), pp. 153–82.
8. H. Zuckerman, *Scientific Elite* (New York: Free Press, 1977), p. 165.
9. C. Tuska, *Inventors and Inventions* (New York: McGraw-Hill, 1957).
10. *Scientific Creativity: Its Recognition and Development,* ed. C. Taylor and F. Barron (New York: John Wiley and Sons, 1964), pp. 385–86.
11. A. Roe, *The Making of a Scientist* (New York: Dodd, Mead, 1953); Eiduson, *Scientists.*
12. S. Hetrick, R. Lilly and P. Merrifield, "Figural Creativity, Intelligence, and Personality in Children," *Multivariate Behavioral Research* 3 (1968): 173–87.
13. R. Harding, *An Anatomy of Inspiration* (Cambridge, England: Heffer and Sons, 1942), p. 89.
14. W. Cannon, *The Way of An Investigator* (New York: Hafner, 1965), p. 28.
15. Roe, *The Making of a Scientist.*
16. A. Koestler, *The Act of Creation* (New York: Macmillan, 1967).
17. Creativity and intelligence are not synonymous, even though existing psychological tests do not always separate them. As one example, in the following reference creativity tests correlated as high with intelligence tests as they did with each other. R. Cave, "A Combined Factor Analysis of Creativity and Intelligence," *Multivariate Behavioral Research* 5 (1970): 177–91. Wallach ("Creativity") gives a good critical discussion of this point.
18. See Cave and Wallach.
19. F. Barron, *Creativity and Psychological Health* (Princeton: Van Nostrand, 1963), p. 242.
20. H. Gough, "Identifying the Creative Man," *Journal of Value Engineering* 2 (1964): 4, 5–12. For a differing viewpoint, see K. Dewing and G. Battye,

"Attention Deployment and Nonverbal Fluency," *Journal of Personality and Social Psychology* 17, No. 2 (1971): 214–18.

23. *The Creative Personality; Pro and Con*

1. J. Getzels and P. Jackson, "The Highly Intelligent and the Highly Creative Adolescent," in *Scientific Creativity: Its Recognition and Development*, ed. C. Taylor and F. Barron, (New York: John Wiley and Sons, 1964), p. 161.
2. F. Barron, *Creativity and Psychological Health* (Princeton: Van Nostrand, 1963), p. 212.
3. H. Selye, *From Dream to Discovery: On Being a Scientist* (New York: McGraw-Hill, 1964), pp. 21–28.
4. F. Barron, in *Scientific Creativity: Its Recognition and Development*, p. 223.
5. Ibid., p. 224.
6. T. Kuhn, "The Essential Tension: Tradition and Innovation in Scientific Research," in *Scientific Creativity: Its Recognition and Development*, p. 342.
7. A. Gregg, *The Furtherance of Medical Research* (New Haven: Yale University Press, 1941), p. 93. Pasteur might not always have qualified. So powerful was his intuition that he could almost write the conclusion without first having done the experiment. It was his faithful colleague, Roux, who exerted a critical brake on this situation (C. Nicolle, in *Biologie de l'Invention* [Paris: Alcan, 1932]), p. 62.
8. M. Dellas and E. Gaier, "Identification of Creativity; the Individual," *Psychological Bulletin* 73 (1970): 55–73.
9. M. Stein, "A Transactional Approach to Creativity," in *Scientific Creativity: Its Recognition and Development*, p. 224.
10. R. Brimblecombe and R. Pinder, *Hallucinogenic Agents* (Dorchester: Bristol, Wright-Scientifechnica, Dorset Press, 1975); B. Wells, *Psychedelic Drugs* (New York: Aronson Press, 1974); D. Sankar, *LSD, A Total Study* (Westbury, N.Y.: PJD Publications, 1975).
11. W. Harman, R. McKim, R. Mogar, J. Fadiman, and M. Stolaroff, "Psychedelic Agents in Creative Problem-solving: a Pilot Study," *Psychological Reports* 19 (1966): 211–27.
12. L. Zegans, J. Pollard and D. Brown, "The Effects of LSD-25 on Creativity and Tolerance to Regression," *Archives of General Psychiatry* 16 (1967): 740–49.
13. R. Fischer and J. Scheib, "Creative Performance and the Hallucinogenic Drug-induced Creative Experience, or One Man's Brain-damage is Another's Creativity," *Confinia Psychiatrica* 14 (1971): 174–202.
14. See note 10 *supra*.

24. *Motivations Underlying Creativity*

1. A. Storr, *The Dynamics of Creation* (New York: Atheneum, 1972), p. 178.
2. Ibid.

3. Ibid.
4. Ibid.
5. B. Eiduson, *Scientists: Their Psychological World* (New York: Basic Books, 1962), p. 126.
6. J. Conrad, in *Heart of Darkness,* quoted in *Essays in Criticism,* ed. R. Kimbrough (New York: Norton, 1963), p. 29.
7. Storr, *Dynamics of Creation,* p. 178.
8. G. Pickering, *Creative Malady* (London: George Allen and Unwin, 1974), p. 309.
9. Ibid., p. 282.
10. R. May, *The Courage to Create* (New York: Norton, 1975), p. 31.
11. May, *The Courage to Create.*
12. J. Masefield, *The Wanderer of Liverpool* (New York: Macmillan, 1930), p. 94.
13. G. McCain and E. Segal, in *The Game of Science* (Belmont, Cal.: Brooks/Cole, 1969), p. 106.
14. G. Hardy, *A Mathematician's Apology* (London: Cambridge University Press, 1967).

26. *The Search For Novel Stimuli*

1. H. Harlow, M. Harlow and D. Meyer, "Learning Motivated by a Manipulation Drive," in *Explorations in Exploration, Stimulation Seeking,* ed. D. Lester (New York: Van Nostrand Reinhold, 1969), pp. 83–95.
2. E. Berlyne, "The Influence of Albeds and Complexity of Stimuli on Visual Fixation in the Human Infant," in *Explorations in Exploration,* pp. 115–20.
3. A. Gottfried, S. Rose, and W. Bridger, "Cross-Modal Transfer in Human Infants," *Child Development,* 48 (1977): 118–123.
4. R. Spitz and K. Wolf, "Anaclitic Depression; an Inquiry into the Genesis of Psychiatric Conditions in Early Childhood, II," in, *The Psychoanalytic Study of the Child,* A. Freud, et al., eds., (New York: Int. Univer. Press, 1946), 2: 312–42.
5. W. Bexton, W. Heron and T. Scott, "Effects of Decreased Variation in the Sensory Environment," *Canadian Journal of Psychology* 8 (1954): 70–76.
6. D. Schultz, "Evidence Suggesting a Sensory Variation Drive in Humans," in *Explorations in Exploration,* pp. 181–97.
7. W. Greenough and F. Volkmar, "Pattern of Dendritic Branching in Occipital Cortex of Rats Reared in Complex Environments," *Experimental Neurology* 40 (1973): 491–504.
8. M. Rosenzweig, E. Bennet and M. Diamond, "Cerebral Effects of Differential Experience in Hypophysectomized Rats," *Journal of Comparative and Physiological Psychology* 79 (1972): 55–66.
9. *Advertising Age,* July 23, 1973, p. 68.
10. A. Burg, "How Much Caffeine in the Cup," *Tea and Coffee Trade Journal* (Jan. 1975).
11. The Coca-Cola Company, Consumer Services Department, 1973.

12. Tea Council of the U.S.A., Inc., 1973.
13. N. O'Donohue and W. Hagamen, "A Map of the Cat Brain for Regions Producing Self-stimulation and Unilateral Inattention," *Brain Research* 5 (1967): 289–305.
14. T. Crow, P. Spear and G. Arbuthnott, "Intracranial Self-stimulation with Electrodes in the Region of the Locus Coeruleus," *Brain Research* 36 (1972): 275–87.
15. C. Sem-Jacobsen and A. Torkildsen, "Depth Recording and Electrical Stimulation in the Human Brain," in *Electrical Studies on the Unanaesthetized Brain,* E. Ramey and D. O'Doherty, eds., (New York: Hoeber, 1960), ch. 14.
16. M. Olds and A. Yuwiler, "Effect of Brain Stimulation in Positive and Negative Reinforcing Regions in the Rat on Content of Catecholamines in Hypothalamus and Brain," *Brain Research* 36 (1972): 385–98.
17. B. Eiduson, *Scientists: Their Psychological World* (New York, Basic Books) 1962.
18. K. Dewing and G. Battye, "Attention Deployment and Nonverbal Fluency," *Journal of Personality and Social Psychology* 17 (1971): 214–18.
19. J. P. Houston and S. A. Mednick, "Creativity and the Need for Novelty," *Journal of Abnormal and Social Psychology* 66 (1963): 137–41. The Remote Associates Test used in this study is not a "pure" test for creativity; it also depends on intelligence.
20. H. Haywood, "Novelty-seeking as a Function of Manifest Anxiety and Physiological Arousal," *Journal of Personality* 30 (1962): 63–74.
21. D. Berlyne, "Arousal, Reward, and Learning," *Annals of the New York Academy of Science.* 159 (1969): 1059–70.

27. Eyes Left! Eyes Right!

1. D. Galin and R. Ornstein, "Lateral Specialization of Cognitive Mode: an EEG Study," *Psychophysiology* 9 (1972): 412–18.
2. M. Durnford and D. Kimura, "Right Hemisphere Specialization for Depth Perception Reflected in Visual Field Differences," *Nature* 231 (1971): 394–95. A. Luria and E. Simernitskaya, "Interhemispheric Relations and the Functions of the Minor Hemisphere." *Neuropsychologia* 15 (1977), 175–178.
3. R. Harding, *An Anatomy of Inspiration* (Cambridge: Heffer and Sons, 1942), p. 72.
4. M. Gazzaniga, "The Split-brain in Man," *Scientific American* 217 (1967): 24–29; J. Levy, "Lateral Specialization of the Human Brain: Behavioral Manifestations and Possible Evolutionary Basis," in *The Biology of Behavior,* ed. J. Kiger (Corvallis, Ore.: Oregon State University Press, 1972).
5. G. McKee, B. Humphrey and D. W. McAdam, "Scaled Lateralization of Alpha Activity During Linguistic and Musical Tasks," *Psychophysiology* 10 (1973): 441–43; see also Galin and Ornstein, "Lateral Specialization of Cognitive Mode."
6. A. Sugerman, L. Goldstein, G. Margerrison and N. Stoltzfus, "Recent Re-

search in EEG Amplitude Analysis," *Diseases of the Nervous System* 34 (1973): 162–66.

7. L. Goldstein, N. Stoltzfus, and J. Gardocki, "Changes in Inter-hemispheric Amplitude Relationships in the EEG During Sleep," *Physiology and Behavior* 8 (1972): 811–15.

8. E. Beck, R. Dustman and T. Schenkenberg, "Life Span Changes in the Electrical Activity of the Human Brain as Reflected in the Cerebral Evoked Response," in *Neurobiology of Ageing,* ed. J. Ordy and K. Brizzee (New York: Plenum Press, (1975), 16: 187.

9. J. Risberg, J. Halsey, E. Wills and E. Wilson, "Hemispheric Specialization in Normal Man Studied by Bilateral Measurements of the Regional Blood Flow," *Brain* 98 (1975): 511–24.

10. P. Bakan, "Hypnotizability, Laterality of Eye Movements and Functional Brain Asymmetry," *Perceptual and Motor Skills* 28 (1969): 927–32. In this study, "right movers" were less readily hypnotizable and were more often found in natural science majors (as opposed to the humanities and social sciences) at Michigan State University. See also K. Kocel, D. Galen, R. Ornstein and E. Merrin, "Lateral Eye Movement and Cognitive Mode," *Psychonomic Science* 27 (1972): 223–24; W. Weiten and C. Etaugh, "Lateral Eye Movement as Related to Verbal and Perceptual-motor Skills and Values," *Perceptual and Motor Skills* 36 (1973): 423–28; P. Bakan and F. Strayer, "On Reliability of Conjugate Lateral Eye Movements," *Perceptual and Motor Skills* 36 (1973): 429–30; and M. Kinsbourne, "Direction of Gaze and Distribution of Cerebral Thought Process," *Neuropsychologia* 12 (1974): 279–81.

11. R. Gur, R. Gur and L. Harris, "Cerebral Activation, as Measured by Subjects' Eye Movements, is Influenced by Experimenter Location," *Neuropsychologia* 13 (1975): 35–44; D. Galin and R. Ornstein, "Individual Differences in Cognitive Style—I. Reflective Eye Movements," *Neuropsychologia* 12 (1974): 367–76; D. Hines and C. Martindale, "Induced Lateral Eye-movements and Creative and Intellectual Performance," *Perceptual and Motor Skills* 39 (1974): 153–54.

12. C. Pribram and A. Luria, eds., *Psychophysiology of the Frontal Lobes* (New York: Academic Press, 1973).

13. J. Bogen and G. Bogen, "The Other Side of the Brain, III: The Corpus Callosum and Creativity," *Bulletin of the Los Angeles Neurological Society* 34 (1969): 191–217.

14. D. Galin, "Implications for Psychiatry of Left and Right Cerebral Specialization," *Archives of General Psychiatry* 31 (1974): 572–83.

15. J. Austin and S. Takaori, "Studies of Connections Between Locus Coeruleus and Cerebral Cortex," *Japanese Journal of Pharmacology* 26 (1976): 145–60.

28. *The Quest*

1. A. Maslow, "The Creative Attitude," in *Explorations in Creativity,* ed. R. Mooney and T. Razik (New York: Harper and Row, 1967), pp. 43–54.

2. V. Frankl, *Man's Search for Meaning* (New York: Washington Square Press, 1965).
3. R. Dubos, *A God Within* (New York: Scribner, 1972).
4. H. Gutman, "The Biological Roots of Creativity," in *Explorations in Creativity*, p. 30.

29. *The Creative Setting*

1. Throughout the literature on creativity, one sees emphasized the fact that creativity is cultivated rather than that it is genetically determined. Still, in animals, it is simple to breed strains that are "bright" at solving maze problems, and surely many of the same principles apply to humans, as Francis Galton has argued in *Hereditary Genius*. But for sound ethical reasons, one does not remove identical twins at birth from creative or noncreative parents, then rear one twin in an impoverished environment, the other in an enriched environment, and retest them at intervals thereafter. For these reasons, it is next to impossible to prove with scientific certainty that heredity plays an obvious role in creativity in man while sharply separating genetic influences from all the cumulative effects of environmental (including parental) influences.

   If we content ourselves with the facts, and don't bother trying to untangle the nature/nurture contribution, it is of interest that five families have a Nobelist parent-child combination. These families include the Braggs, the Thomsons, the Curies, the Bohrs, and the von Eulers. The two Tinbergen brothers also were separately awarded the Nobel prize, one in Economics and one in Medicine (H. Zuckerman, personal communication, 1977).

2. G. Domino, "Maternal Personality Correlates of Son's Creativity," *Journal of Consulting and Clinical Psychology* 33 (1969): 180–83.
3. L. Datta and M. Parloff, "On the Relevance of Autonomy: Parent-Child Relationships and Early Scientific Creativity," *Proceedings of the American Psychological Association,* 75th Convention (1967): 149–50.
4. B. Eiduson, *Scientists: Their Psychological World* (New York: Basic Books, 1962).
5. A. Ziv, "Facilitating Effects of Humor on Creativity," *Journal of Educational Psychology* 68 (1976): 318–22.
6. R. Crutchfield, "Instructing the Individual in Creative Thinking," in *Explorations in Creativity,* ed. R. Mooney and T. Razik (New York: Harper and Row, 1967), pp. 196–205. The study has the advantage of numbers, because 267 children were the test subjects and 214 of their classmates served as controls.
7. S. Parnes, "Can Creativity be Increased?" in *A Source Book for Creative Thinking,* S. Parnes and H. Harding, eds. (New York: Scribner, 1962), pp. 185–91.
8. F. Barron, "The Disposition Toward Originality," in *Scientific Creativity: Its Recognition and Development,* C. Taylor and F. Barron, eds. (New York: John Wiley and Sons, 1963), ch. 11.
9. H. Anderson, "Creativity in Perspective," in *Creativity and Its Cultivation,* ed. H. Anderson (New York: Harper Brothers, 1959).

10. M. Wallach and N. Kogan, "A New Look at the Creativity-Intelligence Distinction," *Journal of Personality* 33 (1965): 384–96.
11. D. Pelz, "Creative Tensions in the Research and Development Climate," *Science* 157 (1967): 160–65.
12. W. Cannon, *The Way of An Investigator* (New York: Hafner, 1965).
13. H. Jatzkewitz, "Zwei typen von cerebrosid-schwefelsauerestern als sog. 'pralipiode' and speichersubstanzen bei der leukodystrophie, typ Scholz," *Hoppe-Seyler's Zeitschrift für Physiologische Chemie* 311 (1958): 279.
14. I subscribe to this hypothesis (the "Ortega hypothesis"). However, in physics at least, arguments have been presented to the contrary. For a discussion of this issue, see J. Cole and S. Cole, "The Ortega Hypothesis," *Science* 178 (1972): 368–75.
15. S. Arieti, *Creativity: The Magic Synthesis* (New York: Basic Books, 1976), p. 329.
16. H. Zuckerman, *Scientific Elite* (New York: Free Press, 1977), p. 81.
17. Ibid. Could information about the role of Jewish mothers in these families clarify the basis for this interesting difference?
18. Ibid., p. 74.
19. H. Lehman and P. Witty, "Scientific Eminence and Church Membership," *Scientific Monographs* 33 (1931): 544–49.
20. Zuckerman, *Scientific Elite*, p. 251.
21. D. Hoops, *The American Impressionists* (New York: Watson-Guptill, 1972).
22. F. Ingelfinger, " 'Obfuscation' in Medical Writing," *New England Journal of Medicine* 294 (1976): 546–47.
23. R. Strub and F. Black, "Multiple Authorship," *The Lancet,* Nov. 13, 1976, pp. 1090–91.
24. S. Parnes, "Effects of Extended Effort in Creative Problem-Solving," *Journal of Educational Psychology* 52 (1961): 117–22.
25. P. Abelson, "Conditions for Discovery," *Journal of the American Medical Association* 194 (1965): 1363–68.
26. C. Dragstedt, "Who Killed Cock Robin?," *Perspectives in Biology and Medicine* 5 (1962): 364–76.
27. D. Ingle, *Principles of Research in Biology and Medicine* (Philadelphia: J. B. Lippincott, 1969), pp. 114–15.
28. A. Toffler, *Future Shock* (New York: Bantam, 1970).

30. *The Creative Prelude*

1. B. Ghiselin, "The Creative Process and Its Relation to the Identification of Creative Talent," in *Scientific Creativity: Its Recognition and Development,* ed. C. Taylor and F. Barron (New York: John Wiley and Sons, 1963): pp. 355–64.
2. L. Kubie, *Neurotic Distortion of the Creative Process,* Porter Lectures, series 22 (Lawrence, Kan.: University of Kansas Press, 1958).
3. C. Nicolle, *Biologie de l'Invention* (Paris: Alcan, 1932), p. 69.
4. H. Poincaré, "Mathematical Creation," in *The Creative Process,* ed. B. Ghiselin (New York: Mentor, New American Library, 1952), pp. 39–40.

31. Moments of Creative Inspiration

1. One wonders whether the possibility that a louse might get on his own clothing occurred to Nicolle just as he stepped over the patient.
2. R. May, *The Courage to Create* (New York: Norton, 1975), p. 62.
3. Ibid.
4. A. Maslow, "New Introduction: Religions, Values, and Peak Experiences" (new edition), *Journal of Transpersonal Psychology* 2 (1970): 83–90.
5. J. Perkins, "Regulation of Adenylate Cyclase Activity by Neurotransmitters and Its Relation to Neural Function," in *The Nervous System,* ed. R. Brady, (New York: Raven Press, 1975), 1: 381–94.
6. R. Harding, *An Anatomy of Inspiration* (Cambridge, England: Heffer and Sons, 1942), p. 59.
7. S. Rosner and L. Abt, *The Creative Experience* (New York: Grossman, 1970).
8. A. Koestler *The Act of Creation* (New York: Macmillan, 1967), pp. 120, 706.
9. Harding, *An Anatomy of Inspiration,* p. 40.
10. B. Kaltsounis, "Effect of Sound on Creative Performance," *Psychological Reports* 33 (1973): 737–38.
11. H. Hughes, "Individual and Group Creativity in Science," in *Essays On Creativity In The Sciences,* ed. M. Coler (New York: New York University Press, 1963), pp. 93–101.
12. Hughes identifies seven other variations on the creative theme, based on what kind of creative product ensues. The variations include: *replacement*—this involves providing a new alternative solution to a previous problem; *deliberate invention*—in this instance one consciously introduces a number of associations and then tries to find some logical connections among them. The technique called "brain storming" is an example of deliberate invention. *Recognition of errors*—here, one looks at existing solutions to find out what is wrong with them, and on this basis then goes on to define new solutions; *routinizing*—means reducing a complex recurring problem to a simple routine; *generalizing*—means recognizing whole classes of problems that are solvable by known means. *Stimulation and release*—refers to the ability some people have to stimulate others and release creative energies in them, although they may not be especially creative themselves. Through *collaboration* one extends with ingenuity the ideas of another person.

32. Follow Through, A More Personal View

1. T. Maugh, "Creativity: Can It Be Dissected? Can It Be Taught?," *Science* (June 21, 1974): 1273.

33. All Quiet On The Eastern Front?

1. M. MacCallum, "Transcendental Meditation and Creativity," in *Scientific Research on the Transcendental Meditation Program,* Collected papers, ed. D. Orme-Johnson and J. Farrow (New York: M.I.U. Press, 1975), vol. 1.

Box 370, Livingston Manor, New York. It is difficult to separate the effect of meditation per se from the total program of expectation in which it is enclosed.

2. G. Schwartz, cited by C. Martindale and O. Hines, "Creativity and Cortical Activation During Creative, Intellectual and EEG Feedback Tasks," *Biological Psychology* 3 (1975): 91–100.

3. A. Watts, *The Way of Zen* (New York: Vintage, 1957).

4. C. Peirce, in C. Frankel, *The Pleasures of Philosophy* (New York: Norton, 1972), p. 176.

5. T. Hirai, *Psychophysiology of Zen* (Tokyo: Igaku Shoin, 1974).

6. R. Wallace, H. Benson and A. Wilson, "A wakeful hypometabolic physiologic state," *American Journal of Physiology* 221 (1971): 795–99.

Is meditation really any more than sleep or drowsiness? Experienced meditators who have been studied while meditating have momentary bursts of theta activity in their EEG. They describe an accompanying pleasant sensation, insisting that they are awake and aware of the reality of their surroundings (R. Herbert and D. Lehman, "Theta Bursts: an EEG Pattern in Normal Subjects Practising the Transcendental Meditation Technique," *EEG and Clinical Neurophysiology* 42 [1977]: 397–405). Still, the issue is currently being debated (*Science* 193 [1976]: 718–20). It suffices to note here that meditation, like creativity or sleep, is not a uniform phenomenon. There are multiple gradations of experience within meditation, and even within the same person these stages of meditation vary observably from one day or month to the next. Despite this complexity, it is evident from a subjective point of view that special states of clear awareness sometimes do occur in meditation that are obviously different from what we usually think of as sleep or drowsiness. The psychophysiological correlates of such states remain to be fully defined.

7. J. Banquet, "Spectral Analysis of the EEG in Meditation," *EEG and Clinical Neurophysiology* 35 (1973): 143–51.

8. R. May, *The Courage to Create* (New York: Norton, 1975), p. 100.

9. P. Groves and R. Thompson, "Habituation: A Dual Process Theory," *Psychological Review* 77, no. 5 (1970): 419–50.

10. M. Sheard and G. Aghajanian, "Stimulation of Midbrain Raphé Neurons: Behavioral Effects of Serotonin Release," *Life Sciences* 7 (1968): 19–25. The stimulation parameters used require further study.

11. M. Brunelli, V. Castellucci and E. Kandel. "Synaptic facilitation and Behavioral Sensitization in Aplysia: Possible Role of Serotonin and Cyclic AMP," *Science* 194 (1976), 1178–81.

12. Moreover, there are probably several models even within the serotonin system, extending (as it does from the brain stem) both upward and downward. For example, if a different experimental design is used to evaluate increased activity within the serotonin system, the sensitization of the startle reflex is reduced (M. Davis and M. Sheard," p-Chloroamphetamine [PCA]: Acute and Chronic Effects on Habituation and Sensitization of the Acoustic Startle Response in Rats." *European Journal of Pharmacology* 35 (1976): 261–73.

13. C. Brown, "Two Types of Habituation in Chicks: Differential Dependence

on Cholinergic Activity," *Pharmacology, Biochemistry and Behavior* 4 (1976): 235–38.

14. When a given transmitter is released from the end of one nerve, its effect on the firing rate of the next nerve cell depends on what kind of receptor it encounters on the next cell. Some receptors cause slowing, others cause acceleration. At most of the connections studied so far in the central nervous system, biogenic amines reach inhibitory receptors, and therefore slow the next cell. However, in some instances, the transmitter may reach stimulatory receptors and *directly* increase the cell's firing rate. Stimulating connections add one more layer of interesting options to the complexity of the nervous system.

15. R. Watson, K. Heilman, B. Miller and F. King, "Neglect after Mesencephalic Reticular Formation Lesions," *Neurology* 25 (1975): 294–98.

16. M. Capps and C. Stockwell, "Lesions in the Midbrain Reticular Formation and the Startle Response in Rats," *Physiology and Behavior* 3 (1968): 661–65.

17. C. Martindale and J. Greenough, "The Differential Effect of Increased Arousal on Creative and Intellectual Performance," *Journal of Genetic Psychology* 123 (1973): 329–35.

18. C. Martindale and J. Armstrong, "The Relationship of Creativity to Cortical Activation and Its Operant Control," *Journal of Genetic Psychology* 124 (1974): 311–20.

19. K. Bowers and L. Keeling, "Heart-Rate Variability in Creative Functioning," *Psychological Reports* 29 (1971): 160–62.

20. R. Gur, R. Gur and L. Harris, "Cerebral Activation, As Measured by Subjects' Lateral Eye Movements, is Influenced by Experimenter Location," *Neuropsychologia* 13 (1975): 35–44.

21. Martindale and Armstrong, note 18 *supra*.

22. C. Martindale and D. Hines, "Creativity and Cortical Activation During Creative, Intellectual, and EEG Feedback Tasks," *Biological Psychology* 3 (1976): 91–100.

23. E. Green, A. Green and E. Walters, "Voluntary Control of Internal States: Psychological and Physiological," *Journal of Transpersonal Psychology* 2 (1970): 1–26.

24. A. Green, E. Green and E. Walters, "Brainwave Training, Imagery, Creativity, and Integrative Experiences," paper presented by A. Green at the Biofeedback Research Society Conference, Feb., 1974. Reprint kindly furnished by the authors.

25. E. Maupin, "Individual Differences in Response to A Zen Meditation Exercise," *Journal of Consulting Psychology* 29 (1965) 139–45.

36. In Closing

1. R. Gerard, "The Biological Basis of Imagination," in *The Creative Process*, ed. B. Ghiselin (New York: Mentor, New American Library, 1952), pp. 226–51.

Suggested Further Reading

1. W. Cannon, *The Way of An Investigator* (New York: Hafner, 1965); W. Beveridge, *The Art of Scientific Investigation* (New York: Norton, 1957); H. Selye, *From Dream to Discovery: On Being a Scientist* (New York: McGraw-Hill, 1964); A. Koestler, *The Act of Creation* (New York: Macmillan, 1967); B. Noltingk, *The Art of Research, A Guide for the Graduate* (Amsterdam: Elsevier, 1965); D. Ingle, *Principles of Research in Biology and Medicine* (Philadelphia: J. B. Lippincott, 1969); J. Watson, *The Double Helix* (New York: Atheneum, 1968); *The Creative Process in Science and Medicine*, ed. H. Krebs and J. Shelley, (Amsterdam: Excerpta Medica; New York: American Elsevier Inc., 1975).
2. F. Bartlett, *Thinking, An Experimental and Social Study* (London: Allen and Unwin, 1958). A. Szent-Györgyi, "Looking Back," *Perspectives in Biology and Medicine* 15 (1971): 1–5.
3. *Scientific Creativity, Its Recognition and Development*, ed. C. Taylor and F. Barron (New York: John Wiley and Sons, 1963).
4. A. Roe, "Psychological Approaches to Creativity in Science," in *Essays on Creativity in the Sciences* ed. M. Coler (New York: New York University Press, 1963), pp. 153–82.
5. J. Guilford, *The Nature of Human Intelligence* (New York: McGraw-Hill, 1967), pp. 312–45, M. Stein, *Survey of the Psychological Literature in the Area of Creativity with a View Toward Needed Research* (New York: Research Center for Human Relations, New York University, 1962); M. Wallach, "Creativity," in, *Manual of Child Psychology* (New York: Wiley, 1969), pp. 1211–72.
6. M. Coler, "The Two Creativities," *Chemical and Engineering News* 44 (1966): 72–84.
7. C. Bernard, *An Introduction to the Study of Experimental Medicine* (New York: Macmillan, 1927).
8. W. Cannon, "The Role of Chance in Discovery," *The Scientific Monthly*, 50 (1940): 204–9; R. Taton, *Reason and Chance in Scientific Discovery* (New York: Philosophical Library, 1957).

Appendix A: Condensed Plot of "The Three Princes of Serendip"

1. T. Remer, ed., *Serendipity and the Three Princes, from the "Peregrinaggio" of 1557*, tr. from the Italian by Augusto and Theresa Borselli (Norman, Okla.: University of Oklahoma Press, 1965).
2. S. Cammann, "Christopher the Armenian and the Three Princes of Serendip," *Comparative Literature Studies* 4 (1967): 256.
3. Echoes of the original *Hasht bihisht* (eight paradises) of Amir Khusrau, ibid.
4. Echoes of the earlier *Haft paikar* (seven beauties) of Nizami, ibid.

Appendix B: Examples of Chance III and IV in Biology and Medicine

1. For references to this appendix, see the following works: R. Taton, *Reason and Chance in Scientific Discovery* (New York: Philosophical Library, 1957); W. Beveridge, The Art of Scientific Investigation (New York: Norton, 1957); A. Moorehead, *Darwin and The Beagle* (New York: Harper and Row, 1969); M. Marquardt, *Paul Ehrlich* (New York: Schuman, 1951). (Marquardt implies that Ehrlich knew 606 would work. If so, one wonders why he did not try it earlier.); and A. Maurois, *The Life of Sir Alexander Fleming* (New York: Dutton, 1959).

Index